WRITING
PROPOSALS
&
SYNOPSES
THAT SELL

André Jute

WRITERS' NEWS

First published in Great Britain in 1994 by
Thomas & Lochar, PO Box 4, Nairn IV12 4HU

Reprinted 2000

British Library Cataloguing in Publication Data
Jute, André
   Writing Proposals & Synopses That Sell -
   (Writers' News library of Writing Series; Vol 7)
   I. Title II. Series
   808

ISBN 0-946537-95-X (hbk)

Printed in Great Britain by Bell & Bain for
Writers' News PO Box 168, Wellington Street, Leeds LS1 1RF

For
Librarians
and the
Proponents
and
Administrators
of
Public Lending Right
everywhere

Introduction

During my publishing career it has been my privilege and responsibility to consider and publish the first books of thousands of new
authors. How I wish that they had been able to take advantage of
the advice given here by André Jute and indeed routinely included in
the pages of Writers' News. For though fascinated by it, so few new
writers really understand how publishers work and what will go
down well or frighten them off. I well remember authors who told
me their book would mean nothing unless they could come and
read it aloud, that I had to accept a work before being allowed to
study it in detail, that they had written at three times the agreed
length and would not allow a word to be changed... but even many
of the far more sensible majority committed at least on blunder -
such as failing to put their name and address on the manuscript,
sending it as a pile of loose unnumbered pages, putting it so tightly
in a binder that it was hard to open to read, including precious original photographs or slides, having a curious number of chapters,
(with some too short or long), failing to adopt a standard house style
or spelling regime throughout, insisting on time-wasting fuss.

One simple fact has to be grasped. Especially when editors work
harder and have a poorer support system than ever before, anything
that prevents a rapid assessment of the work in its own right will
militate against it. While even those publishers who deny they want
unsolicited manuscripts will usually give them a glance, others who
are theoretically more writer-friendly rapidly lose their patience if
their task is made unnecessarily hard. Few manuscripts are so outstanding as to demand publication if all the rules are broken and it is
obvious that a great deal of time is going to be wasted. A good editor
works more rapidly than most writers can imagine. Thirty seconds to
a minute sees many works safely rejected.

Publishers may learn that returning a work too rapidly invites the
criticism it has not been properly read, but writers need to assist and
not hinder productivity. Wine tasters know instantly if a bottle is off,
cooks if an egg is bad. Help rather than hinder editors make their
quick initial judgements by studying and accepting Andre's advice.
Above all, accept his spirit that books have to be sold. The publisher
is not privileged to have a chance to examine yours; you are the one
offering your services as a supplier, and suppliers usually have to
make their products saleable and work with rather than against their

customers. Thus a book proposal must do its job fully. Your synopsis needs to be more than just a summary. your sample chapter must faithfully represent the total book; Andre's chapter on the same is headed: An Only Slightly Crooked Guide! Your manuscript presentation should look businesslike. You need to know how publishers and their contracts work. And so on.

The purpose of course is to ensure you produce material likely to sell, and the process of being published usually starts with the editor putting aside your manuscript (while the bulk of lesser fry are rejected) for more detailed later examination. Yes, it is a hard business, but is not made easier by doing it badly. the upside is that each year thousands share the joy of seeing their work published. Moreover many of today's bestselling writers, fiction and nonfiction, were first discovered surprisingly recently.

First you need to enjoy André's racy book, and then keep it for reference, (which means always having it handy and not lending it). Naturally each writer of such a title has slightly different ideas, but the great central core of advice is always the same, and you neglect it at your peril. Treat it as your passport to publication success.

David St John Thomas, President Writers' News February 2000

CONTENTS

1 WHO, WHAT AND WHY:
THIS IS A TARGETED BOOK   **9**

2 WHO COUNTS IN BABEL
POSITION & POWER IN PUBLISHING   **15**

3 MAKE OR BREAK
WHAT YOUR PROPOSAL MUST DO   **32**

4 MORE THAN A SUMMARY
WHAT YOUR SYNOPSIS MUST DO   **61**

5 THE LITERARY MECHANIC
PRESENTING PROPOSALS & SYNOPSES   **80**

6 SAMPLE CHAPTERS
AN ONLY SLIGHTLY CROOKED GUIDE   **93**

7 UTMOST GOOD FAITH
WHAT TO LOOK OUT FOR IN CONTRACTS   **104**

8 HOW TO DO IT
EXAMPLES FOR ALL PURPOSES   **123**

INDEX   **189**

1
WHO, WHAT AND WHY
THIS IS A TARGETED BOOK

WELCOME. You will benefit from these pages if you already write and sell, or would like to write and sell:

- Fiction of any length or class or genre
- Non-fiction for popular, academic or technical readerships
- Any book about your hobby or passion

Even if you are a new writer You may be offered a contract for a book you haven't written yet if you can put up a good proposal for a book on:

- Any professional subject which you know very well
- Any popular subject of which you have wide-ranging knowledge or experience—many hobbyists fall into this category
- An interesting special subject for which you are the unique source of information, such as tragic or inspirational experiences in your family
- Any reasonably commercial subject whose source material you control, such as the love-letters of a famous couple or sole access to the papers of a good biographical subject
- Any subject at all to which you can bring special, usually new, knowledge or insights or even a fresh angle

Aspirants can sometimes also obtain a contract for an as yet unwritten book from a proposal for:

- A novel in some of the genres, particularly romance and crime

New writers with television aspirations can also sell:

- A teleseries or teleserial from a well-developed concept; this can be anything from a games show to a soap
- A teleseries or teleserial of which you have written only one episode plus a proposal and outline for the rest

In all these cases you will be asked for an outline or synopsis and almost always a sample chapter or chapters or at least one episode.

Many publishers now ask to see a synopsis and sample chapter or chapters even when a complete manuscript is available. All the yearbooks and the best how-to books for writers advise the inclusion of a synopsis even when the full manuscript is also sent. Professional writers have always sent some kind of a summary for the use of executives other than their immediate editors though, as we shall see, these could be no more than a paragraph sometimes contained in the covering letter; my own preference is to send a sample blurb as if for dust-jacket front flap or the paperback (pocketbook) rear cover.

This book is about the writing of proposals, outlines, synopses and samples that sell whole books, television concepts and films, written or to be written.

Books you *have* to write first If you're a new writer, you can forget having a high-level literary novel commissioned until you are well established. 'Commissioned' is publisher-speak for 'contracted before it is written'.

Unless you are an established public figure, such as a politician or a journalist, the same goes for books on politics or religion or any other subject that does not have an established popular or academic market.

If you are a published writer, you can have any of the above commissioned. You should also be offered contracts from proposals for, in order of ease of selling:

- Any book on a subject for which you can offer a fresh insight, or merely a different angle of approach and presentation, especially in the perennially popular subjects
- Any book on a subject in which you are more than mildly interested and which you are able to research either on the ground or in the library
- A series of books on any subject of which you have special or deep knowledge, with you as writer and/or consulting editor or packager
- A television series (jargon: 'concept') for which you create characters and situations
- Political or religious observations, preferably disguised as something else
- A novel to any standard, including the highest literary levels, but only if you have published successful novels before

In all cases you will be asked for a proposal/outline/synopsis and, depending on whether the publisher is British or American, and on your track record with that publisher or your standing in the profession, for a sample chapter or chapters or episode as well.

Articles and Short Stories In relation to the expected return, short pieces are more troublesome to have commissioned than longer pieces and books.

Those writers who can have a short story commissioned can be pointed out by name: they know who they are. Everyone else has to write the short story first and offer it.

Anyone can have an article commissioned, including the rawest novice if he* can put up a persuasive proposal. The differences between the novice and the established writer is that the professional can find an agent who will handle short pieces for him, and that the pro will be paid a 'kill fee' if the article, once written, is not used.

Films and plays Novices need the complete script in their hand to sell a feature film. Those with a track record in films, not neces-

* Throughout 'he' includes 'she'

11

sarily as writers, may have a script commissioned from a proposal. Playwrights can transfer from the theatre as can novelists, especially if adapting their own work, without necessarily having more in hand than an outline in master scene synopses (described later); the most successful need nothing more than the reputation bestowed by their original property. Film producers look on successful playwrights with awe and writing for the theatre is still a good way into films.

In Britain there is an industry development body which tries very hard to give new writers a chance, often by putting them together with producers. Its main function is to fund producers with 'script development money'. The writer first has to persuade his producer that he can write a producable script, and for this a complete script is the best option. The writer then receives the BFCC cash while he works with the producer on 'developing' the script. In Britain, Australia and Canada, as well as in the States, there are film schools with close connections to the industry; stars from these schools are likely to be taken up by the profession with their academic and practical work as their recommendation.

Even novices can have themselves commissioned to write documentaries, especially on subjects in which they can in their proposal prove expertise or new insights. Television in particular is a voracious consumer of documentary material. There is also a huge market in informational or promotional material for government and commercial institutions.

No one who is not already a successful playwright is likely to have a play commissioned from an idea; the skill of telling a story almost entirely in dialogue is too rarefied for a producer ever to trust the untried writer with the money paid up front. The same applies to radio in those countries where it is a force in drama; the newcomer needs the entire script or at least one complete episode of a series.

Why even well-published professionals need this book At first it amazed me that professional writers should write such poor proposals and synopses. But a moment's thought provided the reason.

Most writers write to entertain or inform, not to persuade. That is the right way, to present the facts and let the reader make his own conclusion. It is one of the mysteries of the craft of writing that the harder the writer tries overtly to sell his ideas, the less likely he is to convert readers.

But a proposal and a synopsis are designed specifically to sell. They have no other purpose. And, to be cynical, the best samples are created to sell the project (book, film, whatever) rather than form part of it; we shall see that I recommend junking specially-written samples before you start work on the project proper.

As selling documents, the proposal and synopsis are ill-suited to the writer's best skills of laying the facts before a reader and letting him make his own decision. Instead the writer is trying to force a favourable decision from whoever has the power to commission his work.

Writing a selling proposal and synopsis, and a persuasive sample, are skills the professional writer has to learn just as he learned and refined his expository or narrative skills. You might think that in many ways writing to sell is a harder task, because 'if we were born with a copywriter's skills we'd be working in advertising' instead of in fiction and non-fiction. That is not true. I have been an advertising copywriter and know that that too is a learned skill. If I can learn it, so can you. After a lifetime spent earning a living in the 'human communications' trades, I honestly doubt that any real communicator is born: we all have to learn the hard way.

Introducing myself Besides having been an advertising copywriter, what qualifies me to write this book?

This. In twenty years as a writer, with around thirty books written, all but the first two or three were commissioned from proposals. My commissioned books include novels, the kind reviewed by *The Times Literary Supplement* and the *New York Times* and entered for the Booker Prize, popular fiction under a pseudonym, and non-fiction on subjects from automobiles via literature to typography and writing. As I write this, I have nine books commissioned and in various stages of progress, including novels, how-to books and other non-fiction books. I am the originator and general editor of a major series of books for graphic designers. All these books were commissioned by leading publishers from proposals/outlines/synopses and in some cases samples ranging from none through a double-page spread to several chapters.

How to use this book View my remarks as guides rather than rules carved in stone. Adapt the hints and tips to yoᵁ ᐧ own circumstances and material and—above all—to what you can discover about the publisher, editor or producer your proposal is aimed at.

Keep at it. A writer writes. Practice makes perfect.

2
WHO COUNTS IN BABEL
POSITION AND POWER IN PUBLISHING

BEFORE you can offer a manuscript to a publisher, you must know which publishing house to send it to. Within each publishing house, you must know which individual to approach. A proposal, an outline, a synopsis and a sample chapter are all usually addressed to the same person. But they should be *aimed* at several others. In your presentation you should try to target each of these people. To do this effectively, you must grasp their various responsibilities within the publishing firm, how their performance is assessed and how they are rewarded.

Confusingly for those who write for periodicals as well as for book publication, many of the job titles in the two types of publishing are similar; but their bearers have vastly different responsibilities.

IN BOOK PUBLISHING

For the moment let us list the job titles and their functions in roughly increasing order of salary:

- Publishers' readers, both outsiders and salaried staff
- Editors, some of whom may be outside consultants
- Commissioning editors
- Editorial directors

- Subsidiary rights sales managers
- Sales directors
- Marketing directors
- Publishers

The publisher's reader There was a time when those on the fringes of literature could earn a pittance as publisher's readers. Their function was to sift the 'slush pile' of unsolicited manuscripts and reserve the gems for the editor's attention. Such people were usually well educated and widely read. Often they supplemented their income by writing book reviews for a variety of journals. The conglomerate multinational publisher with its big-business operating methods has done for this whole underclass of impoverished but cultured accolytes to the arts.

Personally, I don't mourn their passing. They tended to form a coterie which was inimical to outsiders, however talented.

Nevertheless, for the new writer trying to break in, their replacement by inside 'readers' has been a disaster. The main function of many of these 'readers' is to discourage hopeful writers from sending in their unsolicited manuscripts.

Even those readers who start out with the good intention of finding publishable manuscripts are soon discouraged when they discover that roughly one in every four hundred of the manuscripts they read will be considered for publication by their superiors.

Nor do such people have much skill in judging what is publishable. Often they are given the job as training for an editorial position. The good ones don't stay in such drudgery for long enough to discover many new authors; they are likely to use the first publishable author they discover to promote themselves into a better job.

Nonetheless, there are houses where every manuscript presented in the proper form is given as much attention as it deserves. Mills & Boon is one such. Harlequin routinely discovers new queens of the rip-roaring romance in their slush pile. But at these places publisher's readers are highly esteemed, intelligent people either on their way to somewhere important, or already arrived there.

The problem is that you cannot know in advance whether the reader who will see your proposal is a time-server or an editor with clout or, rarely, an outsider who has earned respect for his opinion. This makes it all the more important to seize their attention

- on the first page of your proposal,
- on the first page of your sample chapter,
- in the first line of your introductory letter.

Those are all the chances you get.

Your proposal or synopsis must be so good that the time-servers can send it upstairs to show they are still doing the job, reading the slush pile and picking out the few gems it contains.

And it must be good enough to prove to those on their way to better things that this is the project that will carry them onwards and upwards in their chosen career.

A special class of reader Unless the editor has special knowledge in the field, and often even then, text books and other academic works are sent to one or more specialists in the field, normally an appropriate teacher, for an independent opinion. Since the motto of academe is publish or perish, and the number of available slots for books in a field are limited, reports can be quite as bitchy, if less witty, than in the days when the fringe literati were employed as readers. One textbook writer who earns over £500,000 (near enough a million dollars) *every year* told me, 'I treasure three reports on my first book as dire warnings of how wrong so-called experts can be. They condemned the book as incompetent. It has sold almost two million copies and is in its eleventh edition in twenty-five years.' But editors soon learn to spot the three salient facts such a report should contain: does the sample or book follow the syllabus set for courses in which it could be prescribed as a text, does it cover the ground comprehensively (include all the facts), does it present its material comprehensibly to its intended audience ('is it pitched at the right level').

Such academic readers are often called 'consulting editors'. If they do more than just report, if for instance they edit books in a series, they are called 'general editors'.

17

Personally, I see the expert called in to comment on any of my factual books as a research assistant I don't have to pay; I always ask the publisher when I deliver the manuscript

- to let me have a copy of any readers' reports
- to let the reader know I will see the reports
- to be certain to tell the reader that the most detailed and ruthless criticisms will be welcomed and followed up in every particular so that together we can make a better book.

Unfortunately you have to be well established and know the publisher well—and, more to the point, to have established with him that you will not argue about the reports but use them to improve your work—before you can ask for readers' reports even after the event, never mind in advance, when it might appear as an attempt to warn off hyper-critical readers.

In the much rarer case where a novel will be reported on by a reader who is himself a good novelist, the book can be much improved by open-minded use of the other writer's contribution; here the problem is usually to overcome the diffidence of the other writer which flows from his respect for the integrity of your work. In addition you have to know in advance that the book will go to a writer whose opinion you respect so that you can ask for a much more detailed report than is normally prepared for the publisher alone.

The editor An editor can be anyone from a lowly assistant to a key man in the firm without whom it collapses. There is a vast New York firm where the publisher takes all the decisions himself and men, who at other firms would be very senior executive editors, meekly bring him even routine decisions for adjudication.

The title *editor* is given to almost anyone who works on an editorial floor. What it actually means can vary from a glorified reader whose main function is to keep the real editors from ever having to read an unsolicited manuscript—all the way up to a member of the board who on his or her own initiative can commission or buy your book or a whole series of books. It really depends on the firm. One large children's book list in London, for instance, is run by a lady called the 'editor', abetted by a group of persons called 'editorial assistants' who have real power in that they can all put up books and ideas to her and are encouraged to do so. These editorial assistants have quite as much clout as people elsewhere called 'senior editors' or even 'commissioning editors'. Their boss, a member of the main board of her large publishing house, simply does not believe in scattering impressive titles wholesale, and herself aspires to no higher honour than 'editor'.

Unless you know the head of the publishing house, or some very senior staff member, well enough to put your manuscript in his own hand, you will deal with an editor of some kind. The purpose of this whole book is to help you persuade that editor to 'sponsor' your work within the publishing house, to fight in every committee to have your book published or your idea commissioned.

An editor promotes his status, position, income and reputation by the quality, critical reception and sales of the authors and books he discovers and sponsors. Think of your potential editor's own ambition when you create your proposal and synopsis, and demonstrate to him on the first page of each that you have done so. In later chapters I will show you how. Meanwhile remember this: very few publishing institutions are loyal to authors, but more likely than not your editor when he is promoted or leaves will invite all his good authors to go with him to his new eminence or to his new publishing house. Such invitations usually lead to bigger advances.

The commissioning editor This is normally but not necessarily a very senior editor. A commissioning editor commissions books, usually to some plan agreed by the editorial board; often he or she is made responsible for a series. The maintenance of an established series, where only a book or two is added every year, might be entrusted to inexperienced editors, but new series and major ventures are almost always in the hands of battle-scarred veterans.

If you know the name of the commissioning editor of the series you want to write for, you should address your manuscript or proposal straight to him or her.

The stock-in-trade of most commissioning editors is that they know enough authors in their field to get a respectable list going quite quickly. But they are always on the lookout for new talent and new angles. If you can point out to a commissioning editor that some aspect of his subject is not covered in his list, you are halfway there. That is already an impressive display of market awareness.

If you can take a commissioning editor by the hand and lead him to a new series of books that will add $x\%$ to his firm's turnover, you have made an ally for life. You may be able to have yourself appointed General Editor or Consulting Editor of the series and you may receive a fraction of the advance and an override royalty for each book in the series even when someone else writes it.

There are also some firms where the title 'commissioning editor' denotes a supervisor slotted in above, say, a group of 'senior editors'. In this case it would be the senior editors who commission books, but in any event you can do no harm by finding out the name of the commissioning editor and addressing him; he can pass the proposal to the most likely senior editor.

The editorial director Another vague title, as it can mean either any editor with a seat on the board or the most senior editorial staffer, the one whose aesthetic opinion takes precedence over all others. In the large conglomerate publishers that now predominate, there is usually only one editorial director, sometimes called a 'publishing director' but at medium-sized and small firms, where everyone is likely to hold literary opinions and where the head of the firm may well be an editor himself, decisions are usually taken in consultation with the head of the firm. For the majority of books, the editorial director is the man who decides how much to pay for each book.

But he doesn't do so alone. Usually he will ask for opinions from other sources, such as the sales and marketing departments, before making an offer.

The subsidiary – rights sales manager Many books do not recover the money invested in them in the so-called 'home market'.

The home market for an American publisher is the Continental United States and for most the lower forty-eight; the Philippines and Alaska are so far that freight charges eat up additional profits and consequently most publishers' accountants would like to think of these integral parts of the American 'home' market as export markets. Conversely, most American publishers would like Canada, which theoretically belongs to something called the Traditional British Market, as part of their home market.

The 'home market' for a British publisher is the United Kingdom and the Republic of Ireland. British publishers are also used to picking up substantial extra gravy in other parts of the world. This convenient arrangement, a legacy of Empire, is known as the Traditional British Market, or TBM. It is not confined to commonwealth countries – it includes, for instance, Israel and South Africa. The TBM is, roughly speaking, any part of the world where English is an official language and which is not part of the American market. It is such a vague concept that the territories included in it are usually specifically listed in an addendum to British publishers' contracts. All TBM sales except those to the 'home' market are known in British contracts as 'export sales' and attract a lower royalty; it is quite common for books to have higher export than home sales.

The 'rest of the world' is normally, in contractual jargon, 'open' to either the American or the British publisher for the sale of the English-language edition. In practice the 'rest of the world' consists of territories where languages other than English are spoken; below we shall see that substantial sales of English-language editions are possible in these territories.

These definitions are coming to mean less and less as publishing firms grow to cover the globe by buying indigenous houses in 'foreign' countries or setting up large branches there. Simultaneously, the markets fragment as in, to give only one example, the rise of the Australasian complex as an important marketing centre for English language books. Another factor is the large multi-national trade grouping, of which the European Community (the 'Common Market') is just one example; the EC's policies aimed at preferential treatment of members is one reason why American companies have been so keen to buy

British publishers.

Often books are sold to a single publisher 'with world rights'. An American publisher might sell on the British rights, or a British publisher might sell on the American rights, and more often than not to the highest bidder regardless of whether that is their own associate company.

Foreign language editions ('translations' in the vernacular) are always reserved and usually licensed by the publisher on behalf of the author.

This is where the subsidiary-rights manager or director comes in. If he thinks that your book will have substantial appeal in the 'other' English market, or in translation markets, it can tip the balance for the editorial director, who may already have an idea of how many copies the book will sell in his 'home market' (plus the 'export market' if he is British and expects to obtain rights to the TBM). Or, if the decision is already made because 'home market' sales will obviously be strong, enthusiasm from the rights director may add a big chunk to your advance.

Other subsidiary rights handled by this executive include book clubs, condensation (as in *Readers' Digest Condensed Books*), serialization in a magazine or a newspaper, one-shot publication in a magazine or newspaper for major topical books, and a film or television sale (though most professional writers prefer to keep the film and television rights for an expert literary agent to sell).

Your proposal should therefore highlight your book's possible appeal, if any, in the other English language markets, in foreign languages and for other subsidiary rights.

If your book covers a subject in which English is the international professional language, as it is for pilots, graphic designers, geneticists, musicians, and countless others, be certain to point this out. Very often it means that in addition to the translation there is a big sale of the English edition in non-English speaking countries.

This may also apply to novels: one of my novels had a big Swedish language public-sale edition plus a Swedish language book club sale, and still the English language edition sold steadily in Sweden. The difficulty is that for novels, unlike for non-fiction with a guaranteed professional market, this effect is impossible to predict, though the novelist making a proposal for a new novel should at least point out that he has a pre-existing following in Sweden or Czechoslovakia or wherever. (Sales to former Communist countries are worth having. One day all these places will have exportable hard currencies and meanwhile you might earn enough in bits and bobs to pay for a luxurious holiday on the Black Sea.)

Book clubs, mail-order sales and institutional sales could be so important to a publisher that there may be a special executive in charge of 'direct sales' as well as a subsidiary-rights manager. Institutional sales are those made to schools and colleges or to large institutions like the armed services or big corporations or to government. If your book will have potential for institutional sales or book clubs or is especially likely to attract mail-order sales, your proposal and synopsis should say so prominently.

The sales director The editorial director will have received his first calculation of the possible sale of the book from the sponsoring editor. This is normally an optimistic figure. If so, the sales director will soon deflate it.

If the sales director says he cannot sell a book, it dies the death right there. In some of the few surviving old-fashioned publishing houses, it is theoretically possible that the publisher may feel so strongly about a book that he publishes it despite opposition from the sales force—but the number of cases of this actually happening can be counted on the fingers of one hand.

The sales director will want to know that the book fits an easily sold niche or genre or format. He likes selling what he has sold successfully before. Essentially he fills table and shelf space in book shops. He would like to think this space 'belongs' to him; if he does not fill it, another sales director will grab it for good. Each square foot of table and running foot of shelf is allocated to some kind of book: gardening, crime, romance. That is why the genre of your work must be on the cover of your proposal.

Next, he wants to know if there are any regional or local links that can be exploited in the promotion and that should be followed up by a special limited sales effort. This is because many books benefit more from a concentrated effort in quite a limited area or time span than from a diffuse push that makes no mark anywhere.

One sales director describes selling books as 'a log-rolling exercise. You sell a few here and a few there and eventually it builds up, just about the time you have to start concentrating on the next lot of newly launched books. But if you can start with just one big order somewhere, that boosts the morale of the entire sales force—and the competitive instinct takes over.'

Unless there is a specialist direct-sales manager, the sales director will be in charge of mail-order and institutional sales, and will want to be told of the potential in the proposal and synopsis. Large educational sales in particular can build up the numbers very suddenly, even if the profit margin is pitiful.

The marketing director In the smallest houses you will find some kind of a publicity person, who may also be consulted on whether a book can be effectively promoted and publicised. At the biggest houses, and especially if you are to be offered a lot of money for your book, there will be a marketing director or equivalent in charge of advertising, promotion and publicity, and sometimes of the sales force as well. He will want to know whether your book has a 'hook' big enough to get air time and public interest.

The big blockbusters are not just delivered to the shelves, they are promoted there. It happens before any critic or member of the public reads the book. The big bookshop chains want to know how much money the publisher will spend on promoting the book, and on that basis make their decision of how much shelf and floor space they will give it. If a publisher pays big bucks for a book, it follows that he must spend big bucks to promote it in order to ensure big orders from the bookshops. If the book or the author has no hook into the public psyche of the media, especially television, the promotion will fall flat and the book won't sell. That is the point of consulting an expert promoter.

The publisher The head of the house, in both the creative and the business senses, is the publisher. Sometimes he is called the 'managing director' or 'president'. He can come from an editorial or sales background; less frequently he comes from an administrative or financial background. He is the boss of all the others.

His job is part-editorial, part-marketing. Very expensive books will be sanctioned by him personally but others might come out of budgets he sets to be administered by the lesser editors. The top books in any month or season are often introduced to the sales force by him in person, while lesser books are introduced by their sponsoring editors. Every salesman receives the message loud and clear.

If you can catch this man's attention—and you normally have seconds to do it rather than minutes—you could be on your way to great things. That is the point of spending so much time in this book on the first pages of proposals, synopses and sample chapters, and of the mnemonic links and short summaries and blurbs to be discussed later.

We have now come the full circle, from where your proposal enters the publishing house to where the finished book is introduced to the sales force.

There is another important point many authors overlook: between sending in your proposal (or manuscript with synopsis) and eventual publication stretches a period of probably not less than thirty months. Your proposal and/or synopsis must enthuse your sponsoring editor for all this time. It is not enough just to get in, you must do your part of the job well enough to be certain your sponsoring editor finishes it.

There are other people who may be asked for their opinion of your proposal or synopsis. My series for graphic designers was not commissioned, you may be certain, before the production manager and house designers had been consulted on the feasibility of producing books with so much colour inside the price band I envisaged, and on the general desirability of such books to the profession of graphic design.

The production manager is also interested in the potential for book club and institutional sales because these large numbers can help, by increasing the print run, to bring the production cost per unit – and therefore the price of the book – down most dramatically; in some cases a book club or educational sale can make an economic proposition of a book that without it is unpublishable at any reasonable price.

And don't forget that secretaries, personal assistants and other general skivvies are often asked for an opinion, and in a few years might turn out to be subsidiary-rights directors or something equally important. Do be pleasant to them.

Libel Let's first of all deal with the one I didn't list. Most big publishers today employ a lawyer either on the premises or on a retainer. He probably reads most proposals for which the firm intends to offer, and at least those manuscripts or parts of manuscripts referred to him for an opinion by the editorial director.

As far as the author is concerned, the lawyer's responsibility is that the firm's authors should not lead it into liability for libel damages or break the laws on obscenity and blasphemy where such laws are still on the statute books. This is a negative function.

If there is likely to be a problem of libel with your material, you should be the first to point it out. That removes the possibility of an instant rejection on the grounds that you should have noticed such an obvious danger yourself. Pointing out the potential problem not only makes you look professional: it also gives those on the publisher's team who may like your idea an opportunity to argue, 'Well, he knows the libel problem but still thinks it worthwhile to put in his time and do the job thoroughly. The least we can do is get a legal opinion and see if there isn't some way of working around it.'

Walking close to the line can lead to controversy, which is good for sales. Publishers love it. They even love to libel those who cannot hit back. It's just business, nothing personal.

What publishers hate is the unannounced, unforeseen libel that hits them with a lawsuit out of the blue because the author was careless or ignorant. The small print in any publishing contract gives them the right to collect their legal defence costs and any damages they have to pay—from you. But they know they won't collect. You'll just be finished in publishing, forever.

NEWSPAPER AND MAGAZINE EDITORIAL HIERARCHIES

There are three classes of newspaper and magazine editors of concern to the writer:

- *The* editor
- The managing editor
- Functional editors, such as the features editor, the news editor, the colour magazine insert editor, the woman's page editor, the literary editor, the reviews editor, the technical editor, the financial editor and so on

British writers offering proposals to American newspapers should note that, unlike in British newspapers, in the States there is a strict separation between news, opinion and features staffs and that you should be careful to send only tailored proposals to the right address.

The editor He is in charge of the paper's policy. It does no harm to send your proposals addressed to the editor and let his secretary sort out where they belong and reroute them. But it looks more professional and saves time to send them to the right place in the first instance.

The managing editor Another of those means-whatever-you-want-it-to-mean titles, though in most newspapers and magazines it indicates either the man who links the editorial staff with the financial/administrative people, or the man who links the editorial staff with the design staff, or both. In any event, the managing editor is usually a person with a foot in both the managerial and editorial camps. Whether he is superior or subordinate to *the* editor depends on where in the hierarchy he is placed.

On many magazines and newspapers the managing editor is responsible for seeing that regular columns come in, that commissioned articles arrive on time, and so on. It follows that the job includes seeing that the writer is paid. What does not necessarily follow is that the managing editor decides how much to pay for each individual contribution, though in my experience more often than not he does. He may also decide the placement, prominence and so forth of each contribution.

Only rarely does the managing editor decide by himself which pieces are commissioned or bought, and which declined. All the same, the managing editor is a good contact at any magazine or newspaper because he is in an excellent position to distribute your proposal promptly to the right functional editor and to follow it through to a decision.

Functional editors The decision to commission or buy your piece is usually made by the editor of the section in which it will appear. Thus the news editor will buy a report of a fire, while the woman's page editor will buy photographs of new fashions (but note that many periodicals have 'picture editors' whose main business is commissioning professional photographers), and reviews of hardware will be assigned by the reviews editor of a computer or camera magazine.

Note that the colour magazines of the British Sunday newspapers—which are notably good payers—in most cases have their own fiercely independent editors who commission their own articles. A motoring piece in the paper itself may, depending on its slant, be commissioned by the travel editor or the motoring editor or the financial editor or even the fashion editor while a very similar piece in the colour magazine will be commissioned by the magazine editor.

Since at least some of the editors will return the piece to you without showing it to the other possible purchasers, your motoring article could have five bites at the cherry by offering it in turn to each of these editors. But sending your offer to the managing editor or the chief editor gives you only one bite.

The key words for newspapermen are 'new' and 'exhaustive'. Their ambition is to cover every subject exhaustively while it is still news. The same ethos informs the features pages of newspapers, though less blatantly. Your proposal or synopsis must show that you understand this and can help them achieve their elusive ambition. That is why the easiest pieces to sell are 'tomorrow's news'.

Magazine editors too like 'new' and 'exhaustive'; in addition they love 'informative' and 'entertaining'. Since magazines are much more closely targeted on their particular audiences than newspapers, you must demonstrate in your proposal or synopsis that you are reaching out directly to that particular audience to tell them something they want to know. That's what sells the advertising, which in turn keeps the magazine solvent.

Magazines and to a lesser extent newspapers that publish fiction *demand* that the stories be closely targeted on their audience. Your proposal and synopsis should be very clear that your story speaks to precisely that audience and in their language. This information should be in the first paragraph—if you can't manage to make the point in the head or subhead. That is what the editor wants to know before the content and quality of story. Before submitting anything, it is vital to study the short stories already published in the magazine to discover precisely what the individual editor is looking for.

Magazine and newspaper people are paid and promoted by their results as revealed in readership surveys and advertising placements. The relationship between the editor and writer is not in this sense either as direct or as close as in book publishing, but it becomes closer with the length and regularity of the writer's contribution to a newspaper or magazine, to the point where the relationship between a regular columnist and his editor bears a faint resemblance to the relationship between a book-writer and his sponsoring editor. The smaller or more specialist the magazine, the more likely that the editor will be rated on his ability to attract and retain high-quality columnists and contributors.

TELEVISION AND FILM

In television and film there are, as far as the writer is concerned, five key persons: his literary agent, his lawyer, the script editor, the producer; and the distributor/financier.

Except for those writers who deal exclusively with the publicly-funded broadcast organisations in Britain, Canada and Australia or with small independent television or film producers outside the United States, a competent agent is virtually essential for channeling scripts to the right hands. In many production companies you cannot get your script read unless it is offered by a recognised agent.

An agent has to be persuaded by the script, synopsis and proposal, just like any other party. I always hope that my agent scrutinises my material with a critical eye, because any small improvement may give one an edge over the competition.

Nuisance suits alleging breach of copyright are now so prevalent that most film and television producers won't read your script unless it is accompanied by a signed release. A lawyer is essential for agentless writers because most writers lack the expertise to know which of the releases used by film and television companies they should sign; an agent learns by experience which releases are harmless and which a licence to steal.

Once you have passed these barriers, where does your script go? Almost always to a script-reading unit or person. There are a few script editors who make a profession of this honourable craft, but the majority are serving an apprenticeship on their way to being producers, directors or writers. Those with the biggest dreams are looking out for the script or proposal that will bankroll their ambition. In the largest units there are invariably script editors who are on the lookout for particular types of scripts for pet producers and directors. It is a good idea for you as a writer to build up a relationship with a script editor if you can.

If you know the name of an individual producer, whether part of a large organisation or an independent, you can send your script directly to him in the hope that he will be so taken with it that he will fight tooth and nail to finance its production. Chances are high that he will return your script unread, lose it or at best give it straight to the script editors. If you want to go this route, remember that a producer's reading time is very limited—you *must* have an outstanding synopsis.

Most writers cannot place their script directly with the distributor/financier but remember that when your script is presented to him by the producer, the most stringent time limit of all will apply. If you leave the one-page encapsulation of your idea (discussed later) to the producer, it may not contain what you yourself would have chosen to emphasise. Only you can decide whether you or the producer is best qualified to identify the aspect of your concept most likely to attract a financier.

The good news is that film and television producers are frantic for good scripts. If you don't believe me, check the reruns on your television screen and the amount of trash produced every year. This doesn't happen because film and television producers are schlock merchants or suffer from an excess of greed. It happens because there aren't enough good scripts to go around. The great Zanuck told us a long time ago that there are three ingredients of a successful film: story, story and story. It is still true—and everyone in the business knows it. You may be certain that any script which clears the legal hurdles will be read at least far enough to discover if it will further the script editor's or producer's dream. You can give yourself a better chance if your proposal makes it quite clear that you understand what script editors and producers are about and that you sincerely want to promote their dream of a quality production that speaks to an audience.

3
MAKE OR BREAK
WHAT YOUR PROPOSAL
MUST DO

A publisher who has seen thousands of proposals in his career gives one important piece of advice: 'Tell them to put their name and address on the proposal.' Not just in the covering letter, on the proposal itself. And not just on the cover of the proposal but on its last page as well, and on every part of it that is not securely fastened to the main body of the proposal, in particular on illustrative material like photographs.

Proposal and synopses defined For convenience, we sometimes talk in this book of the proposal and synopsis as if they were two separate documents. In many cases, however, they are combined into a single document, and the parts may not be easy to separate. But we can distinguish the two concepts without any difficulty as long as we stick to theory:

- The *proposal* contains all the information the publisher requires to make a decision except the detailed description of the contents of the proposed book.
- The *synopsis* contains a detailed description of the contents of the book and the order of its presentation.

Thus, what the one is not, the other is. But you will see that in practice it can often be quite difficult to keep the two apart and then, unless it will cause confusion, I suggest you don't bother. You will see from the examples in the last chapter of this book that most of my proposals and synopses are combined documents. This is chiefly to avoid wasting publishers' time with unnecessary repetition.

In consequence, this chapter is mainly but not solely about the proposal and the next chapter is mainly but not solely about the synopsis.

THE PURPOSE OF THE PROPOSAL AND SYNOPSIS

We have classroom definitions of the proposal and the synopsis. Now let us ask what they are good for, what they will do *for* you.

- A *proposal* should be precisely what it says, an offer to write a book on a specified topic for a specified market if a publisher is insufficiently interested to commission it; in the case of an already written manuscript it is an advertisement and a logical place to put information relating to the book's commercial potential.
- A *synopsis* should be a summary of what will be in the book offered for commissioning, or is in the manuscript offered for publication.

Even unwritten books require synopses, and even written manuscripts require proposals; the theoretical distinction is useful for separating marketing information from content information.

The proposal and synopsis, whether separate or combined into one document, are normally accompanied by a *sample chapter*

- intended to be typical of the book to be written, or
- selected to be representative of the standing manuscript.

We'll return to the sample chapter in a chapter of its own, and we will deal with the style and presentation of the synopsis in the next two chapters.

ANCILLARY DOCUMENTS

There are, depending on the stage you have reached in your writing career, up to three further items that normally accompany a proposal and synopsis, which you should consider essential for your dealings with publishers. They are the covering letter and, for established writers, a publications list and a sheet quoting extracts from reviews which can be used to promote the new book.

The covering letter The covering letter should be as short as possible but it must include a summary of the synopsis, putting the single most important high point of the proposed book in a single sentence. Here a single-page letter sells both a book and a series:

Dear Ms Soandso
The Brief Guides (series)
The Brief Guide to Political Economy

This is to offer you a book either on its own or as part of a series. I'm the author of about thirty books and the general editor of two other series to be launched next year; a partial publications list overleaf will give you some idea.

The **book** is a brisk introduction to the ideas underlying modern economics, and therefore modern policy-making in virtually all fields, presented in historical order. It is intended as a quick crib for the busy executive or scholar from another field, and therefore I have made the reading as enjoyable as possible. The book can stand by itself or as part of the series described in the stapled pages accompanying the manuscript.

The **series** will fill an obvious gap in English publishing that in France is serviced by that great *Que Sais-je?* series, and in the States partially by *Facts on File* though the latter is mainly fancier in presentation and at a higher price level than I have in mind.

I enclose IRCs for reply and look forward to hearing from you soon.

Yours sincerely

If you have relevant experience, that too should be mentioned in the covering letter as well as in the proposal, again in a single sentence if you can or, failing that, a single short paragraph.

If you have a track record of published books, it is worth referring to it when you're writing to any editor with whom your name will not necessarily ring an instant bell. Unless you are Jeffrey Archer, don't assume your name will be known. Even well-established authors often have to introduce themselves. It's galling, but it is a fact of life when dealing with any large publisher.

All these matters may be expanded elsewhere; they must not make the covering letter longer than a single sheet for the novice and the writer new to that publisher, or longer than two pages for well-established writers known to the publisher addressed. 'Any letter longer than two pages reveals a lack of thought and consideration for the time of others,' says Peter Grose, sometime literary agent and book publisher, now publisher of *Best Sellers* magazine. Relevant experience and published books (or articles, performed plays, television scripts, etc) will ensure that your proposal gets priority.

In the sample letter the words 'fill an obvious gap' are intended to arouse instant greed, and the reference to two successful series that every reference publisher will know is another button pressed to the same purpose. All in all this letter ensures at least an immediate flip-through of the thin proposal (the 'stapled sheets') and perhaps even a dip into the thinnish manuscript of the complete book accompanying the proposal.

Publications list If you have written more books than can be mentioned in a short paragraph, attach a list. Including an abbreviated publication history works like a recommendation because the names of your other publishers are references for the quality of your work and your professionalism. In addition it does no harm to include an extract from a key review if there is space. Here is a sample from my own publications list:

REVERSE NEGATIVE: W W Norton, New York 1979; Hyland House, Melbourne 1979; Secker & Warburg, London 1980, reprinted 1982; Sphere, London 1981.

Swedish: Lasabra 1983; book club Bra Spanning 1983. Portuguese: Europa-Amerika, Portugal and Brazil 1982. Australian Literature Board Publishing Grant. "Wild but exciting" — NY *Times*.

Many publishers will give you brownie points for continuing to work, so either in your letter or your publications list you must convey the information that you have a book or two in your bottom drawer awaiting cutting and rewriting. The novice just says, 'Besides the book I am offering you, I have XYZ on exciting this-or-that awaiting rewriting and am halfway through the first draft of ABC on the other fascinating matter.' The leathery old pro can be slightly more subtle. Here is how I do it in the publications list:

DZERZHINSKY SQUARE & LANGLEY, VIRGINIA & 100 BROADWAY: Trilogy commissioned by Grafton Division of HarperCollins, London. Two novels in editorial, one in progress.

The professional writer who is too lazy or too modest to include such a list must not blame his publishers and editors when they exhibit ignorance. For myself, I include the list every time I offer work even to editors I work with regularly. At the very least it offers an editor an opportunity to say, 'Gee, we should reprint that,' or, 'Hey, I'd forgotten he's interested in Lesser Mongolian Sloths—just the expert I've been tearing my hair out for.' In one memorable year I was offered three automobile books by publishers I would never have thought of offering a car book to, all because of the single car book on the publications list I enclosed with proposals totally unrelated to any mechanical contrivance.

The newcomer can head his list 'Work in Progress' and use up the space with a brief description of the manuscript in the bottom drawer awaiting cutting and rewriting, and the one on his typewriter in first draft. Such a tactic gives an impressively professional air to your material.

As a matter of personal preference, I like to keep information to a single sheet where possible. To keep my publications sheet to a single page, printed one side only, some information has been left off and the rest printed in a tiny, eye-straining typeface; the heading, 'Some Books in Print', implies that those out of print have been left off and that others are not included for lack of space. All of that makes its own impression.

Extracts from reviews That your book or books are reviewed at all is an achievement in itself. Don't waste the advantage. Make a set of extracts and include them with proposals and synopses. Your editor can have his designer put some of them on the jacket of your book to commend you to your public. The reason for sending the list even to your own publishers with every proposal and synopsis and manuscript is that not everyone at the publisher's will know of these plugs; many executives will be too busy to send for the cuttings-books. Make it easy for them to buy from you!

If you have had only one book published, make extracts from all the reviews, or as many as will fit on one page. If you have had many books extensively reviewed, you must follow your own mind but my preference is to select only enough quotes from the major media around the world to fill a single page because that is usually as many as can be used on a dust jacket. My selection (which I change according to the sort of book I'm proposing) usually includes the major papers both in English and foreign languages, the main woman's magazines and the broadcast services; the point is to show that my work is well regarded in any market the publisher might wish to consider.

On the other hand, books by Jeffrey Archer and Wilbur Smith, to name only two authors, are always published with page upon page of extracts from reviews, often to the extent where obviously more than just remaining blank space is filled and the publisher must add and pay for another sixteen pages. Of course in this case the extracts are designed to impress the book-buyer, not the publisher, but the difference of opinion indicates that it is a subject worth giving serious consideration.

WHAT PROPOSALS AND SYNOPSES MUST DO

Every other piece of necessary information must go into the proposal and synopsis. It is not accidental that we start this chapter with the soft sell of the cover letter and, where available, the publications and review extracts lists. They are clearly selling documents. And so are the proposal and synopsis.

Caution! It is worth warning you that anything in this book about creating the synopsis is intended primarily to help you sell the project rather than to help you plot or create it. If you want to know about synopses that will be of use to you in your writing as distinct from your selling capacity, try one of my other books for writers: for thriller writers there are several relevant chapters in *Writing a Thriller,* and creative writers of all types can turn to the two-book set *Start Writing Today!* for the basics and *Keep on Writing!* for a more advanced discussion.

Your name and address These must be on the cover and last page of every self-contained document, and on the back of every photograph, illustration or other loose sheet. There are hundreds of thousands of pieces of paper floating around any publisher's office at any one time and yours could simply be lost. It is symptomatic of the care that publishers take that so few go missing, but don't tempt fate. In addition, if an editor or other executive likes a proposal, don't make him search for your name so long that he loses interest; above all don't give him any reason to suppose you are an amateur who doesn't take care of the basics.

With modern word-processors it is a simple matter to put your name on every page in the running head or footer, together with the name of your proposal and the page number.

It is a good idea, if you have an agent, to link his name with yours on the front and rear pages of all documents, so that publishers don't have to hunt for the information in your letter or somewhere else. Agents have their own stick-on address labels, of course, but professional writers quite often send material directly to an editor who has asked for it or who they know will be interested; the editor will probably know the name of your agent but you cannot assume his colleagues will. There are some questions publishing executives prefer asking agents rather than writers: 'Is s/he likely to be any good on television?' 'Does s/he really know about GBH or is s/he just bluffing?' Often such questions are chiefly aimed at determining whether you're a stayer the publisher should invest in for the long-term.

The date The first version of a proposal is rarely the one commissioned. Even when the first version is commissioned, it is more often than not because all succeeding versions have been found wanting in more ways than the original. It is necessary to date versions of proposals so you may know which is the latest one, and so that in discussion with editors you may be certain you are all talking about the same piece of paper. Also, there is a regrettable but definite trend towards incorporating the proposal in the contract, which makes it very important to be able to identify the precise version.

A useful form of dating is year and month, as in 9508 for August 1995, which is unambiguous and yet not too obviously a date (it can be mistaken for a numbering system). This last point means that you won't offend the sixth or seventh publisher you offer the idea to because he instantly notices that a fair period elapsed before the proposal reached him.

Genre What sort of a book is it? This is an extremely important piece of information because it determines to which department or editor your proposal will be directed if it is not addressed to some executive by name, or to whom he will redirect it if, as often happens, it hasn't yet arrived at precisely the right desk. Even if it has arrived at the right desk, the fact that you have advertised the proposal fairly, honestly and decently is a mark of your professionalism.

Unless the genre is perfectly clear from the title (*How to Rebuild Your Wooden House with Hand Tools*), put the genre under the title either as a genre-description:

- a novel
- a novel of suspense
- a family saga
- an historical romance set against the Civil War
- a how-to book
- a critical study
- an unauthorised biography

or as a subtitle, which you need not necessarily use on the book:

- How to (do something)
- The influence of Eisenhower's Abilene childhood on his statesmanship
- A true story based on psychiatric case notes
- True-life chilling tales from beyond the grave
- Heroic myths recounted for children

The purpose is to link the book to the shelfspace available in bookshops which is invariably allocated to a certain kind of book, as we have discussed earlier. Most editors concentrate on certain genres of books—and sigh with relief when they see one which will grab them a fat chunk of that shelfspace. The genre is also as far as many other publishing executives read. It is all they want to know, being so confident in their own skill (selling, promoting) that they will accept the editor's judgement about whether your proposal will make a good book.

New subjects You should assume that the publisher knows less about the subject than you do and could overlook the fact that some of the material that you will cover is novel or even unique. If you will cover new ground, always say so under a separate heading, and highlight the information or section in the synopsis. Publishers love the new (excepting only experimental novels).

Level of sophistication of the proposed book Now that we know what sort of a book it is, at what level do you intend pitching it? Of course, some books are automatically pitched by their genre or their author's name at a certain level and market. For example 'A Western' has only two possible pitches, pulp and high literature.

In general, however, few authors can afford not to say at which level their book is pitched. In many educational texts, the level is determined by the syllabus-section covered: First-year Physics, Leaving Certificate Flower Arranging; or the words Basic, Intermediate and Advanced have useful distinguishing features. Many editors think 'Introduction to' a better label than 'Basic'. In popular instructional non-fiction books, the word 'Basic' may have a negative effect. 'Beginner's' is even less appealing. Richard Reynolds of B. T. Batsford in London says plainly, 'Put "Beginner's" in the title and you cut your sales in half. Nobody wants to be a beginner.' A word all editors understand is 'popular', which implies that a lowest-common-denominator reader can understand everything in the book.

It is arguable that the most effective popular non-fiction titles respond to the reader's dreams. Dr D. G. Hessayon has made a fortune out of *The Flower Expert* and many other books for gardeners that in fact start from basics and stop well short of the expertise that the author himself commands. But in the proposal you should distinguish between the selling-point of the title and the informational point of the intended pitch. Don't lie to your editor either intentionally or by oversight: if the title promises more than you will deliver, explain why readers will nevertheless be satisfied.

To avoid confusing your pitching level with the title in the editor's mind, put the level in all lower case letters in parenthesis somewhere under the title and genre:

COIN COLLECTING
a hobby book

(to take the coin collector as far as an achievable but fulfilling minimum collection and provide him/her with the appropriate expertise)

The format makes it absolutely clear to the editor that you do not intend using these words on the actual book. Alternatively, you can make the point in the text of your proposal where you discuss the aims of the book:

...in which we will help the novice collector to put together a collection that is fulfilling in its own terms. The book will also arm him with the experience and expertise to discuss coins knowledgably with his peers. A second book can then be considered to conduct satisfied customers of the first book to the heights of the hobby...

It is however essential that this information be on the first page of the proposal.

The level is tricky when you get to novels. The best advice is to see how publishers have billed popular paperbacks of the same class as your manuscript or intended book, and to use the same shorthand on your proposal and synopsis. If books are called 'fantasy sagas' on the shelf where you would like to see your own book, call yours a fantasy saga; and so on. But be aware that some of these words have precise meanings, even in the mouths of the advertising folk. A 'saga', for instance, is at the very least a novel of 150,000 words; it probably covers a substantial period of time in the lives of the characters, who are likely to belong to one or more extended families; and the word is increasingly used to describe a multi-part epic. To make matters worse, the meanings of these words are as changeable as quicksilver—you should take your cue from the most up-to-date lexicon available: the shelves of your bookshop.

THE AUTHOR AS FIRST SALESMAN OF THE BOOK

Every publishing executive will want to know the primary market at which the book is aimed. And *you* must tell him not only where the book is aimed, but where to find that market, how big it is, and how to tickle it just so in order for it to buy the book he will commission from you. In general, editors and other publishing executives not only know less about the market for your particular book than you do, *but they are not expected, and cannot be expected, to know more.* Few authors know this when they enter the profession; many hardened professionals have not yet learned it and suffer for their ignorance.

Yet it is a logical condition, as a modest amount of thought will persuade any writer who cares enough to apply his mind. Most editors are responsible for a wide variety of books in a large number of fields; editors move around at an increasingly alarming rate.

Let us, to make the discussion easy to understand, take a best-case example, the senior or even chief editor at a specialist art and architecture house. In the States it is at least possible that he has studied art somewhere; in London he is far more likely to be a general humanities graduate. All of that might still be good enough if you want to do a general picture book of a whole museum or a basic how-to-paint-landscapes book—and if the editor isn't an absolute beginner in that particular job. But the chances are that even the bosses came only last week from a house specialising in craft books or architectural books.

So even for what you might consider a very general low-level book you will have to make a marketing input. And when it comes to doing a specialist book, say a discussion of Kokoschka, your contribution is even more vital. You may still be able to count on the editor's ability to help you with the content, but you will be expected to provide the marketing facts for the publishers to check.

Now let's take an additional step: let us say the house decides to start a small graphic design list. The decision has been triggered by your proposal for a book on graphic design, which instinctively they like. But they wouldn't have liked it half as much if you hadn't included the convincing information that there is a huge unserviced demand for such a book. They are likely to have known nothing about the market for graphic design books until you told them. And yet isn't graphic design a logical extension for a list specialising in art and architecture?

This isn't an example taken at random. I recently conceived a series of graphic design books. In dealing with several publishers who already had graphic design books on their lists, it soon became quite clear that they were utterly ignorant about the requirements of potential buyers of their books. Their marketing was, in short, a joke. I ended up closing with a craft publisher I already knew from my interest in automobiles; at least I knew they were competent at marketing, that they would take the trouble to find out what they didn't know. They had in fact, even before my proposal came in, been dipping a cautious toe in the graphic design market because it is an obvious adjunct to their art and architectural lists. They were already far more knowledgeable than the so-called specialists, yet the eventual business plan devised by their commissioning editor and approved by the board quite clearly used my proposal as a springboard. Without my marketing information to add to theirs it is doubtful that I would have placed the series with them because they would never have made such a huge investment on the basis of incomplete knowledge.

Even if the publisher is an expert in a particular market, it warms his heart to see that you have taken the trouble to ascertain that he can actually sell the book you are proposing to him.

Never forget: the shorthand we use, 'sell a book to publisher', is dangerously misleading—it is a licensing operation which turns the writer into the publisher's partner, a special sort of partner who shares only in profits and pays out nothing towards losses. Publishers never forget it.

Despite the prizes that ride on the presence or absence of marketing information, there is nothing esoteric or difficult about acquiring it. Most is common sense and easily gathered in agreeable surroundings like bookshops and libraries; in fact, if you stick to writing what you know about, you probably already know the market for such books inside out.

For whom is the book? We might write books because we burn to get something on paper, but publishers publish books to sell for a profit. For the publisher to make a profit, someone has to buy the book. Who will buy your book?

If you have a sponsored book or a yearbook, the answer is easy: the sponsors, the members of the association or the aficionados of the sport or interest that the yearbook services. About ten years ago I was at a huge gathering of literati from all over the world. You can imagine how self-important we felt. The man who deflated us was a journalist on the local newspaper's sports page. He did it by telling us, when someone was foolish enough to ask, how many copies his fishing yearbook had sold: more than the combined sales of the ten biggest sellers by authors at the conference. He had conceived the idea for the book after discovering how many angling licenses were issued in his state; without his realising it, he had given away a major trade secret.

If you are writing to a syllabus you can determine with a minimum of effort—which you should make, rather than depending on the publisher—how many students will have that syllabus prescribed.

If you are writing for a particular profession, for instance general practitioners with an interest in the growing field of geriatrics, the relevant professional body can tell you how many there are.

If there are other books in the field, mention the fact; they wouldn't be there, with more appearing, if there were not a demand for them. If the books available form a definite range covering aspects of the field but with a hole your book will fill, mention that. If the book was suggested to you by a newspaper article bemoaning the lack of information on the subject, include this information. If the book was suggested to you because you needed it for your work or hobby and couldn't find anything useful, you should mention the total number of practitioners of your profession or craft or hobby, for that is the potential market.

A great many practical books are bought by dreamers; I have many more woodwork books than I shall ever have time to use. This helps me to understand the members of the Bentley Drivers Club in whose homes my *Designing and Building Special Cars,* definitely a grubby-bits book, can be found standing on the shelf next to the pretty-cars picture books. These people are far too busy to take their expensive cars apart to the last nut and bolt, but they still want to know how it is done in case they ever find the time. And don't forget that many illustrated books are things of beauty in themselves and are bought for coffee tables by people who don't belong to the professional bodies or hobbyist clubs.

If your book will be beautiful enough for coffee tables, don't be embarrassed to say so. If it will, in addition to appealing to the expert and the core aficionado, have something to attract the casual student and the dreamer, tell the publisher. He really wants to know.

It is impossible to tell you precisely what you must say, because the market for every kind of book is different, and each book within a market appeals to a slightly different part of that market. All the major examples in this book include the marketing sections for you to study as examples.

Primary market for novels A novelist has to enjoy very substantial general hardcover sales through bookshops and book clubs to ignore sales to libraries. However, the days have passed when libraries bought new or low-selling established novelists as a sort of cultural duty. Publishers can no longer launch a novelist only on his hardcover library sales.

All the same, the library is an important baseline in publishing calculations. First of all, the genre you name on your proposal is important because in certain genres the libraries can still be counted on. Crime fiction is one, romance another, quality thrillers yet another. Check the sort of books in your library and, if you can do so without stretching the truth too far, label your proposal with one of the popular genres.

Established authors should, if they have a proven library readership base, mention it. Public lending right administrators, even in countries where you are not entitled to the payment, may be able to give you their estimate of how often your book has been borrowed. Impressive readership figures will not only enhance your standing with your publishers but quite possibly increase the size of the advances they are prepared to offer you.

It seems possible that libraries will increasingly become a force in the paperback market as well.

Of course, most of what we have said so far about novels in libraries applies to certain classes of non-fiction books as well, especially those that are loosely categorised as 'creative writing', such as biography. But the library was never the mainstay of hobbyist and practical non-fiction.

The market for general hardcover novels outside libraries is far more problematic. There *is* a market but this is one of the few instances where your editor is often better qualified than his author to point to the market.

There is a small but definitely swelling trend to publish new authors first in paperback and then, if they make the grade by finding a public, to promote them to hard covers.

In addition there is a growing trend to publish even quality books by established authors as paperback originals. There is also the format, familiar on the Continent but until recently rare in the States and the British markets, of the large trade paperback, which has a card cover like a standard paperback but wider so that it can fold over itself to make pseudo-dust-flaps; this is priced between the traditional paperback and a hardcover. It is something else to watch, especially for new novelists, because these formats (quality original paperbacks and large trade paperbacks) may, especially at those houses where the books published in them are selected by a separate editorial team, provide an entry not previously available.

All of that said, what is the primary market for novels? Paperbacks, of course. The paperback market is, except for the esoteric technical matter of colour printing, just about the only part of the book publishing industry that has reached the twentieth century: stack 'em high and sell 'em low.

If you think your book will have paperback interest, say so. If an earlier book was paperbacked, put the information on your publications list. I take the paperback market so seriously that when I can I show my proposal to my paperback editor first and ask him how much he would pay to license the book from a hardcover publisher; then I take the deal to a hardcover publisher and ask him to commission the book; if the paperback man shakes his head, the hardcover publisher never even hears of the stillborn book. But newcomers are not in a position to do this and established authors who want to try it require nerves of steel because the literary hardcover houses dislike this sort of behaviour. Typically they dislike it for the wrong reason, that they think you are attempting to curb their editorial independence, rather than the right reason, that you're trying to make up for their marketing and commercial inadequacies.

In any event, with the rise of the publishing conglomerates, which increasingly place hardcover and paperback divisions under the same management, your proposal, synopsis and sample chapter are likely to be scrutinised with the emphasis on marketability rather than literary merit.

SECONDARY MARKETS AND SUBSIDIARY RIGHTS

In a sense, the title of this section is misleading. First, for the executives interested in these sales, secondary markets and subsidiary rights may well be their entire livelihood and therefore of all-consuming interest. Secondly, these rights may in many instances be the primary sale, with the number of units sold through bookshops trailing a long way behind. Thirdly, even if there are no unit book sales directly involved, as when selling a topical book for serialisation to a national newspaper or for syndication, the amounts of money involved may be very large. Fourthly, even if no book sales are directly involved, subsidiary rights, such as an extract sold to a paper, can generate large book sales.

Educational sales Even if your book is not intended directly for the educational market, it may well be suitable for educational use. If so, you should tell the publisher. It is useful if you point out at which level your book will be useful, and why.

Conversely, even if your educational textbook is written strictly to a syllabus, it may also interest members of a specific public (hobbyists or professionals) or even the general public (families, say, for a book on health); point this out to the publisher.

An editor at a major educational publisher says, 'It is incredible how careless otherwise sophisticated writers can be of what would amount to large sums earned for them and for us from these extra sales. But, except in the most obvious cases, how can the publisher know if the expert in the field doesn't tell us?'

Book clubs Next to educational sales the most important subsidiary market is book clubs—and many publishers would put the book clubs right at the top of the list.

The relevant executive at any publisher will of course know the major book club in any given field. But you cannot be certain that your proposal will reach the hand of that executive if you do not include the book club information, because it might not be thought relevant to pass it to him before it is rejected. If your book is one of those which would have been viable only with precisely targeted marketing, you will have missed an opportunity.

List all the book clubs you know that operate in the field, the obvious ones as well as the less likely ones; if necessary grade them for likelihood or liveliness. In addition, list all the peripheral book clubs: for instance, a book on mould-making for fibreglass reinforced plastics, let us say for use in technical schools in the first instance, would be of interest not only to a

DIY book club but to nuts-and-bolts automobile book clubs and boating book clubs as well, because cars and boats include many moulded reinforced plastic parts.

Special interest groups Related to book clubs, and often more profitable for the author in that he gets a larger royalty than from sales to book clubs, are special interest groups. Suppose you are a keen flower arranger and have written a book about your hobby. It is up to you to tell your publisher that there is a large, well organised group of flower arrangers which, under their national body NAFAS, puts out a magazine, in which an advertisement will reach only potential buyers of the book, with no wasted effort and no wasted money. And, of course, on the strength of it you will be invited to give demonstrations at many of their branches' regular monthly meetings, which will serve to promote your book still further.

Institutional sales Besides educational sales, there are other types of institutional sales, sometimes catered for by an executive distinct from the educational sales manager, for instance to government departments, the armed services or large corporations. If your book has scope for extra-educational volume sales, mention it under a separate heading so that the information stands out.

International sales of the English edition The most usual reason for the English language edition to sell in large numbers in non-English-speaking countries is that English is the common language of the profession the book addresses. Pilots of all nationalities speak at least some English, and most can read a navigational text in English with varying degrees of fluency.

Furthermore, there are large groups of people who, even if the literature of their profession is to some extent available in their own language, read and speak English fluently. It is irrelevant that there is a substantial literature on the theory of business management in Dutch, because every Dutchman likely to be interested speaks perfect English; your book on the selection of retail locations is never likely to be translated into Dutch, even though many of your examples might be chosen from the

Netherlands. All over Southeast Asia the preferred language of the professional, managerial, middle, student and other book-buying classes is English. If you are aware of a need for your book in these markets, point it out; if similar books sell in these 'foreign' markets in their English editions, say so.

Translations The established and professional author will of course ensure that any potential publisher knows that his books are translated and into which languages; this information can go into the publications list. If you have particular success in one market, don't forget to draw attention to the fact; it may just be the foreign market that publisher is trying to break into, or one in which he would for some reason like to develop further with the help of an established author.

The new writer, or the professional without translations, should, if they know, mention in which languages there may be call for a book such as they are offering.

If the book is set in foreign parts, and especially if the characters are foreign nationals, or the subject close to the heart of a foreign nation, this is important information and should feature prominently in your proposal or synopsis or both. There is a well-founded presumption that people like to read about themselves; a London publisher believes that at least one French publisher will want to translate any book by an Englishman about the perfidious French.

A tangential point often overlooked by anglocentric writers is that a little space must be left blank in the English edition to allow for the more expansive spread of some other languages like German. This is a question of layout. It is rarely a problem in heavily illustrated books, where white space is normally designed in, but even here it can do no harm to point out that the layout of captions should allow space for translation. A modern trend is towards books that carry captions or text in several languages, normally some combination of English, German, French, Italian and Spanish, with Arabic and Japanese rising fast. You don't have to provide the translations, merely to point out that space can be provided for them in case the publisher wishes to seek an international co-production. Especially when dealing with the book packagers, as distinct from publishers, such thoughtfulness is much appreciated.

A book packager performs all the functions of a publisher except that he does not publish books. He originates, commissions, edits, designs and prints books, or any combination of these functions, but the books are published under the imprint of another house, and sold by their salesmen. Book packaging is the fastest growing field in publishing.

If you are truly capable of providing your own translation into any language, under no circumstances neglect to mention it. Finding qualified translators, especially for literary work, is often a headache for foreign publishers, one which miraculously disappears when the author can do the job himself—at least he can't complain about his own translation. That the author can do his own translation is an inducement for the foreign publisher to take on the book, and the income from the translation sale is an added insurance for your 'home' publisher— plus something extra, perhaps even something substantial, in your own pocket. A byproduct is that after a while you may be offered opportunities to translate the work of other writers.

What opposition is there? 'A writer who proposes a book to which there is absolutely no competition is either a genius or a conman,' says one genial publisher. There are, of course, completely original books. I can offhand think of three: *The Joy of Sex, The Secret Diary of Adrian Mole, The Country Diary of an Edwardian Lady.* Each one was published in a year in which more than 55,000 books were published in the English language.

But the majority of books are published onto shelves carrying direct or, if their authors are lucky, indirect competition. Publishers appreciate your view of where in this spectrum of competition your intended book will fall, and you should also make it clear how yours will be an improvement on existing books. Though publishers may inadvertently publish 'me-too' books, they hardly ever do so deliberately: they like to believe *their* authors' books have something special to commend them. Make it easy for them to keep the faith by differentiating your book not only in the proposal and in the synopsis, but as far as possible in reality.

Suitability for various markets Don't just say, 'A lot of books on trachordial biosynthesis are sold east of Suez,' add, 'And just to be certain our book sells better, I shall include a chapter comparing trachordial BS in China with that in Japan and the somewhat similar Australian model.'

Even within the home market, stamp collectors aren't an undifferentiated mass. It helps the publisher to decide that you know your oats if you explain in your proposal or covering letter that while you will take the real novice by the hand and guide him to the true faith, you will have much to say which the relatively experienced collector will find astounding, and quite a bit that even the hardened expert will find either new or controversial. Mention that the synopsis or the sample chapters contain examples addressed to each class of reader. If there is a lot of material, provide page references to the examples because many publishers will make a beeline for your examples, which they believe is the truest indicator of both your expertise and your ability to bring the subject alive for readers.

Attraction to various markets Even if you're selling a novel, a publisher may be interested to know that the key event happens in his secondary territory, or in the very next country to that, from which bookbuyers exposed to his edition can receive television broadcasts. A publisher bought my novel *Iditarod* even though he acquired only the British and Canadian rights *because* the eponymous race on which the novel is based happens in Alaska and is widely covered on Stateside television which is, of course, also received in Canada.

In another case, a publisher commissioned a novel from me because my proposal contained the information that the story was set in Australia: it just so happened that his firm had built a $2 million warehouse in Australia and urgently required something to sell through it. Unique example or not, it put groceries on my table because the key information was there for the man to see and act upon. The point in this paragraph is that you cannot know what will motivate even a publisher you have worked with for a decade or two, never mind one you have never met, which today is very often the case even when an established author works with a publishing house he has been with for years.

It is also easier to do effective promotion for a book in a limited geographical area, a point we raised in our discussion of the specific interests of the individual publishing executives.

Presentation of material A matter related to the level at which you will pitch the book, but going beyond it, is the presentation and organisation of the material in the book you propose (or describe). Your synopsis will of course make the organisation clear, if only by offering the names of the numbered chapters. But the publisher will also want to know if you intend a mainly-illustrated book, a mainly-text book, or something in between, and how the parts will be separated—and why.

Let's take a tricky example, a book that you promise will appeal to complete novices and coffee-table dippers, to experts in the field, and to hardcore scholars, all within the same covers. This is a promise quite likely to make an editor sit up and put a cynical smile on his face. If you can show how it can be done, you've probably made a sale. Now, *can* it be done? Yes, it can, and on the same page. For instance, you can appeal to the coffee-table experts by telling their part of the tale mainly through captions to the illustrations, you can address the experts through the running text, and the hardcore scholars through the boxed-off tables and extensive factual appendices, which you will of course list so that the editor can find an expert somewhere and ask him for an opinion on their value. In fact, such a rigorous requirement can be used to give an otherwise visually dull book plenty of movement and interest on every double-page spread, a point also worth mentioning.

But you cannot expect the editor to think up these solutions for you. The editor is your devil's advocate: he raises questions and obstacles and you provide answers and perform high jumps. If you do not answer a question an editor is certain to raise, he will most likely assume you were not expecting the question— and are therefore an amateur. Consequently he will not investigate your proposal any further.

Unless a book is simply to be full of text, like a novel, it is always worth either showing or saying something about the presentation, if only to make clear that you have already planned the hierarchy of headings that will lead the reader in a logical manner through the material. Any point of presentation that is not clear from your sample should be mentioned in your proposal or synopsis, and even points that are illustrated in the sample may need emphasis by a statement of some kind in the proposal if they are of especial importance.

Colour and other costs Many elements of presentation will affect the costing of the book. Foldouts and inserts of material on a different kind or weight of paper are especially expensive.

Colour printing is however no longer quite as fearsomely expensive as once it used to be; modern electronics have brought the price down and moved control of the quality closer to the creator of the book—if he knows what he's doing! The number of colours is important because each colour requires a run through the press, with attendant costs. Generally speaking you can have black (which is almost always required for text) plus one or two colours, or you can have 'process colour' where black plus three colours (cyan, magenta and yellow) are used to create the full colour spectrum as required. You must specify whether you want black plus one or more particular colours, which are called spot colours, or full-colour process printing. You would use spot colour(s) on, for instance, a diagram to clarify the separation of parts. If you required many parts in a multitude of different colours, you would use full colour process printing to create all the colours on the diagram, because a large number of print runs for many separate spot colours would be prohibitively expensive. There is no way realistically to reproduce colour photographs, whether of life or art, except by full-colour process printing.

If only part of the book needs to be in colour, say so for the benefit of the production manager; his costings can make or break your book. Can you arrange that the pages in colour be grouped together in one or more sections, each of not more than eight or sixteen pages or multiples of eight and sixteen? If you can then further arrange the placement of the colour pages to suit the 'imposition' of the book, the cost can be substantially reduced.

Imposition is a technical word used by printers and bookbinders which refers to how the individual sections of a book are printed on large sheets of paper; these are then folded, the edges are guillotined off to separate the pages, and the pages are later sewn together in order to make the book.

The important point to remember is the multiples–of–eight–and–sixteen–pages rule. When you need to know on which pages you can have colour, ask your editor and he will get the details for you from the production manager. At the proposal stage merely say, 'The book will require x number of pages in n colours/full colour which can be grouped together in y sections of z pages each.'

Matters like the choice of paper are normally left to the production manager but if there is some reason for requiring special paper or binding, you should say so. For example, if you find that all the competition to your proposed book is printed on light card, laminated and ringbound, you should at least mention it. Usually there is a good reason for this, which should also be mentioned: the books perhaps remain open all day on the user's desk for constant reference and must therefore be durable and fold over to take up the least possible space.

Size and orientation of book You should specify the physical size of the book only if the contents require a particular size. If not, don't bother, or stick to general phrases such as 'pocket' or 'large format'. Most publishers have standard sizes they like working to, and the editor can generally see which format the book fits into. In specifying the size, try avoiding 'landscape books' unless absolutely essential. A landscape book is one that is bound along a short edge and so is wider than it is tall; bookshops hate them. (But don't force readers to turn the book to look at the pictures simply to avoid a landscape format.) The more usual orientation, bound along a long edge and taller than it is wide, is called portrait.

Do not specify what size you want a novel to be.

Wordage For a novel or a magazine article, the number of words is always mentioned.

In magazines, every word is individually counted.

In books the number of words per page is entirely nominal

and the total wordage is calculated on the assumption that every line of every page is full. Count the words in, say, fifty full lines and calculate the average number of words per full line; calculate the average number of lines per full page, making no allowance for chapter ends and section breaks; multiply the number of pages in the typescript by the number of lines per full page by the number of words per full line—and that number is the word count a book publisher wants to know.

If a book is to be illustrated, the total number of pages it is expected to run to is always mentioned; it should be a multiple of sixteen pages with multiples of eight acceptable only for thinnish books and if unavoidable.

It does no harm to state the length of a book as so many words or pages 'plus x pages of index, y pages of appendices and glossaries, z pages of bibliography'. There are certain classes of books in which substantial end matter is either expected or makes the book more instantly saleable—academic books are one example.

'End matter' is everything in quotes in the paragraph above plus notes and references if not placed as footnotes or grouped at the end of each chapter but gathered together at the end of the book.

Illustrations It should be clear from your proposal whether you will find or draw the necessary interior illustrations yourself or will expect the publisher to provide them. The cover illustration is always provided or selected by the publisher; in most instances it is none of the author's business, so don't even mention it in your proposal.

The glossy magazines invariably supply their own photographs and other illustrative matter but for the others you should mention how many illustrations you can supply. The rule is normally that the less a magazine pays, the keener it is to have you supply the illustrations.

In book proposals editors don't expect to be told the precise number of illustrations but are keen to know the balance of illustration and text you propose. Phrases like 'largely illustrated' or 'lightly illustrated but with strong captions' are perfectly adequate in proposals and synopses where a sample accompanies the proposal. Where there is no sample chapter, or where the sample does not clearly indicate the division between text and illustration or is for some reason not representative of the major part of the book, you must take care with your description of your intentions to be certain your editor and his production manager understand you clearly.

Price Don't mention the price you want your book to sell at unless it is part of some marketing point, for example that it is intended for students in a market where all the competition is priced out of their reach. I do however normally mention the price range of competitive non-fiction and especially of illustrated books because the editor will probably be asked that question at his editorial board.

Caution! The New York rights attorney and literary representative Laurens Schwartz considers all but the most exceptional pricing information a trespass on the publisher's prerogative; if you agree with him, leave pricing information out altogether until you are asked for information or an opinion.

Advertising and promotion Very few books are advertised on television or the other expensive media (posters, important newspapers and magazines). Authors always complain that publishers do not promote their work as it deserves. But publishers would love to promote your work well beyond its desserts, if only they could do so economically.

It is precisely at the key pressure point of economical advertising and promotion that the author can help. The author is the specialist in his own field. This is true even for novelists in quite popular genres: the author is likely to know the small magazines in his little patch of the science fiction/fantasy universe better than even an editor who publishes nothing but sf/fantasy. In non-fiction this case is even more likely, and gets likelier the more esoteric the subject.

We have already seen how an advertisement in the flower-arrangers' magazine is as effective as buying a finely targeted book-club membership list. The ad is likely to be a lot cheaper than one in the books section of *The Times*—and to return a great many more sales for every dollar or pound spent.

Tell the publisher about these special promotional outlets. If he doesn't know, the opportunity for targeted promotion may make the difference between returning your proposal or manuscript and commissioning or buying it. If he knows already, he will admire your professionalism and let that weigh in your favour.

Don't assume that a promotional opportunity is obvious to your publisher just because it is obvious to you. Recently I found a publisher quite ignorant of *The Late Show,* the BBC's key television arts programme—he insists on being in bed before eleven and this show is aired after that.

A bit about the author Yes, we'd all like our work to speak for us, but a publisher doesn't so much lay out his money on a single book as make an investment in the author and his lifetime output. Especially when it is the writer's first book, which is not likely to make any money, the publisher wants enough information to be able to judge if the writer is the kind of person who will overcome all the difficulties and create more books over which to average the losses with the profits.

Another reason the publisher wants to know something about the writer is that often the writer's experience and background affect both the content and the credibility of his work. It is generally believed that readers like the author to have had direct experience of what he writes about.

Finally, there is class and fad. Some publishers like to publish only PLU, people like us; at its most defensible, this means that they like to publish agreeable authors with whom they find it easy to communicate. Other publishers are politically inspired to believe that truth only arises from the working classes: they're still looking for the footsoldier or truck driver who will write the great American novel. As for fashions, during the height of the punk fad, one New York agent described the average publisher's dream writer: 'A girl with her ass hanging out of her jeans, a spiky two-tone haircut and a British cockney accent.' But, if you fit the bill, grab the help; times are so tough for writers that they are entitled to use every advantage they are offered.

Relevant personal circumstances If you have relevant experience, always say so. If you write a column for a paper, or have a TV or radio spot, tell the publisher because it can be used in the promotion of the book.

Bulleted marketing points By now your head is probably reeling from all the information you are asked to offer the publisher. You are wondering where to put it all. The best plan is to put all the most important points in a bulleted marketing list on the front page of your proposal or, if on the second page, with a note on the first page referring the publisher to it.

In most publishing houses the man who will make the final decision to buy or decline your book is at least partly a salesman, and in many he is wholly a salesman. He wants to know what your book has that all the others competing for the same limited funds do not have. He wants to know that he can sell your book, and will most definitely ask *how* he can sell it. Help him with a bulleted marketing list of points his salesmen can impress on bookshop buyers.

Don't try to cram everything into the bulleted list. Mention only the main points, which can then be expanded inside the proposal. This is my rule: ten points maximum, no more than two lines per point. Here is a bulleted marketing list for this book:

- by the bestselling author of *Writing a Thriller*, *Start Writing Today!* and *Keep on Writing!*
- plugs from Ruth Rendell in *The Times*: 'a private godsend'
- and *Writing Magazine*: 'a master's voice'
- an essential book for every writer because of radically changed circumstances in publishing
- indispensable for both novice and professional writers who want to survive
- contains many strikingly successful examples from the author's own experience
- the author himself has had over thirty books commissioned from proposals
- the author has experience of the publishing side, as

general editor of two major series running to over a hundred books

- **André's friendly 'me-to-you' style is well proven and much liked by readers as extremely supportive, yet he doesn't shirk the hard truths**

Notice that I wrote this part of the proposal in the third person. That makes it easier for the editor to do any necessary rewriting when the publisher tells her to turn my list into selling points to be printed on the dummy jacket the salesmen will use to 'pre-sell' the book. But if you find the third person impersonal strange when writing about yourself, or are irritated by the change in tone from the rest of the proposal, write the bulleted marketing list in the first person. If you are bothered by writing about an unwritten book as if it already exists, write the bulleted list as a promise rather than a fait accompli. Here is the final point recast in the first person promissory mode:

- **I shall write it in a friendly 'me-to-you' style which readers will find so supportive that I will not need to shirk the necessary hard truths**

Don't however let modesty lead you into the passive voice ('To be written in the...') which is a pain to read and doesn't sell anything. If you must, use a brutal shorthand instead.

- **proven friendly 'me-to-you' style, very supportive of readers, makes necessary hard truths easier**

Now we are in a position to put together a convincing synopsis which will highlight the suitability of your concept for a book that the readers described in the marketing sections of your proposal will want to buy.

4
MORE THAN A SUMMARY
WHAT YOUR SYNOPSIS MUST DO

As wartime prime minister, Winston Churchill requested that even the longest reports submitted should be reduced to a single page. In his Nobel Prize commendation there is specific mention of his speeches, of which the key parts of most occupy far less than a page. The famous parts of his speeches are worth studying for more than their striking turn of phrase: each of these key sentences or paragraphs is in fact a synopsis of the rest of the speech, phrased to elicit maximum emotive response.

The synopsis is a key component in the selling of a literary project for print, film or broadcast. It is the most concentrated document you will ever write, with more riding on every single word than anywhere else in a writer's career. We're not suggesting that you should reduce it to one page—though you may have to for specific purposes—but that you must make every word work very hard for its living, precisely as Churchill strove to do.

Notice that here we don't say, 'The synopsis is a key component in the creation of a book.' It is true that there are correspondences, in some cases large correspondences, between the synopsis or outline you create to help you plan and execute the book and the synopsis you offer a publisher, but the synopsis you offer the publisher is specifically a selling document rather than a creative one. If you include creative considerations that are irrelevant to selling the concept to an editorial board, your editor *may* be interested, but the majority of the other people on this key committee will merely be irritated. You will have wasted their time with matters they don't understand, don't care about, can't help you with, and possibly don't believe are important even to you. You won't make a sale.

It is possible to synthesize the synopsis from your own working outline but only if you are a very tidy, complete and disciplined worker. In real life it is often easier to start from scratch with your selling purpose in the forefront of your mind. Here we shall assume that you are creating a synopsis solely to sell your book.

In this chapter we shall discuss what the synopsis is intended to do, and some larger ways and means of achieving its ends. These are not abstracts. Think of the impression you wish to leave in the mind of a publishing executive, an impression conducive to him saying, 'Yes, let's buy this book!'

For the moment don't worry about the mechanics of getting your points over; it is far more important that you understand why you have to do certain things. You must understand it not from your viewpoint, but from the possibly alien viewpoint of a sales manager or other publishing executive who will have very little in common with the editors you may have met, and very likely even less with you. In the next chapter we shall return to the mechanics of getting everything on paper in the right order.

SELECTING THE KEYS THAT WILL OPEN DOORS

We know what we want to achieve: to have an as-yet unwritten book commissioned or a written manuscript read with keen anticipation. We have whetted the appetite with the proposal. We have advertised the content by genre and market as saleable. Now, in the synopsis, we want to concentrate on the impression made by the content.

A full circle of motivation is essential Let's start with the formats most difficult to précis before anything is written: booklength narrative prose (novels, biographies, histories, travel books and so on, the genres generally grouped as 'creative writing') and the feature-length film or miniseries for television. What is the single essential that every successful piece in these categories must have?

By definition a novel is a description of something exceptional that happens to a character the reader identifies with. By accepted usage the events of the novel occasion a change in at least the main character, for which the jargon is 'character development'. That is a complete description of *every* competent novel, biography and film (and most other narrative works) ever written.

An editor reading your synopsis does not look first for the fascinating situations you have thought up, or even the delightful characters, but to check and doublecheck that you understand that every action of every character must be motivated by the personality he starts the novel with as altered by interaction with the other characters or by events. The shorthand jargon for this is 'a complete circle of motivation' with the often unspoken additional requirement 'worked out in action rather than explication' implicitly understood by all editors and professional storytellers.

In films and narrative television, to which this entire section applies equally, the jargon is that 'all events and actions are fully established', meaning that nothing happens just because the writer says it happens but because some prior chain of actions has made it inevitable. In films, where two talking heads are living death, they don't even bother with the implied 'worked out in action etc'—films are *all* action.

The key thing your synopsis must therefore prove is a fully motivated and closed chain of action. 'Fully motivated' we have touched on above; 'closed' merely means it must have a beginning, a middle and a definite end at which the action is exhausted and the character is changed.

More on motivation, character and plot This is such an important breakpoint in the career of the new writer, or the writer having his books commissioned for the first time, that I want to emphasise it.

Established writers who routinely have books commissioned can skip to the next section; they wouldn't be successful without a good grasp of these principles.

Let's take the two concepts in reverse order.

'Closed' is in practice an easy concept to grasp because it clearly relates to the mechanical aspects of plotting that you can pick up through practice or from any moderately good book for writers.

Because what is true for the novel is also true for all forms of creative writing with literary aspirations, biography and history can give us an additional handle on these two concepts.

Suppose you are writing a biography, which is a history of one person. It is easy to demonstrate a closed chain of *events*: X was born, did such and such, and died, leaving a grieving better half, so many children and much joy for posterity. It shouldn't take more than a long paragraph to do this job thoroughly: *Who Was Who* does it several times on every page. Such a facts-only synopsis, even if about the most charismatic, telegenic and tabloid-prone public person, would be rejected straightaway. There's little interest in *what* happened unless it throws light on character.

Now add the reasons *why* X did all those astounding things, *why* X just once in a long life acted stupidly, *why* X liked chorus girls—and all of a sudden you are cooking. Things didn't just happen to X: *X made them happen* and *for a reason*. These reasons are the links in your chain of motivation, and they lie at the heart of your book. This is what readers want to see, and what the editor, on behalf of future readers, is looking out for. To close this chain of motivation all that is required is to consider each event in X's life and ask *why* X acted as history records; if the accepted reason for the action seems unlikely, you must find the real reason—that's your unique contribution and the key to your book.

'Fully motivated' is therefore tricky because it must be understood in terms of character, an intricate thing to the wisest of us. You must master this trick of characterisation, which can however be learned, before you can write a novel or a biography or a popular history or a film, and certainly before you propose that a publisher or producer commission any creative writing from you. Therefore I shall assume you have conquered the skill, even if my phraseology is new to you. If you want to study the chain of motivation further, the key chapters in my books *Start Writing Today!* and *Keep on Writing!* describe methods of seeing matters from the character's viewpoint.

Closed circles in non-fiction In non-fiction that aspires to be literature, the circle is always closed by the drives of historical or living people motivating their actions; that has been covered in the sections above and no more need be said.

Just below this level, where the purpose may not be literary but could be scholarly, instructional or popularising, your synopsis should at least demonstrate that your selection of events makes a comprehensive and coherent unit. Furthermore, you must show that you have covered the unit (timespan, place, person, etc) either exhaustively or to the depth your readers will require or are entitled to demand.

When is a popular book complete? In the popular market the answer to this question is almost always, 'When it reaches its maximum price.' Forgetting for the moment those popstar books where the pictures are very big to fatten a minimum life up to the maximum price the fans will pay, the amount of information in most non-fiction books is almost always limited by the price beyond which the publisher dare not go, which in turn determines (together with the number expected to be sold) how many pages the writer can have.

The upshot of this is that the smart non-fiction writer checks the opposition and—excluding breakthrough books, gimmick books and price busters for some perceived low-end hole in the market—proposes something with the same number of pages and colours as the more expensive, but not necessarily most expensive, books in the field. Within this scope he must then fit what he wishes to say and adapt his synopsis accordingly.

Accepting that limitation, or the similar one of a book for a series to a predetermined length, the writer must deal with the problem that most subjects are capable of almost infinite expansion. If you're writing about your hobby, this problem is particularly acute. Aspirants and novices fear publishers will think their proposal thin. Consequently they stuff in too much. In fact a common complaint from publishers is that writers, including those practiced hands who should know better, do not make a better book by packing in more subjects—but skimp on every one for lack of space: 'The synopsis was richly satisfying but the book reads thin.' Trying to cram in too much also causes fearful problems in book-design departments, where they are a lot more interested in a readable size of print and in balancing white space than in whatever subject fascinates the writer, plus expensive typesetting headaches in the production department.

For this, and other reasons, experienced editors like to know what you intend putting into the book. You can do this by chapters, which are the smallest acceptable units, but you should preferably do it section by section. In some highly illustrated books (tables as well as graphics are important space-hogs) you should show what you intend to do spread by spread or page by page.

That way the most experienced editors can help you decide what to leave out when they see the ship starting to sink under the extra barrels of tar you're loading. The organisation of your synopsis is also a fine indication to the editor and publisher of your organisation of the material and whether you have achieved coherence.

'A spread' is shorthand for 'double-page spread', which is two facing pages open.

Don't forget, the author can get more money for two books of reasonable length than for one fat one, not least because two inexpensive books will always sell better than one expensive book.

If your synopsis is truly light of the weight required to fill the pages, you can be certain an editor will point it out to you. But if you plan page by page, or section by section, this small humiliation will never happen to you. Personally, I'd rather have an editor tell me I was giving too little for the money—as a sometime designer myself I can without hypocrisy plead sympathy with the design department's wish for a decent amount of white space—than accuse me of skimping a necessary subject because I wanted to flash some esoteric knowledge. Any writer who has ever been accused by critics of being a 'high-tech exhibitionist' will agree with that sentiment.

Novices and aspirants, skip this paragraph! It is for pros only. Professional writers, who have been around the block a few times and *know* their synopsis contains all the material that can be thoroughly covered in the space, should beware of techno-freak editors who want the writer to cram in every nut and bolt. There is a difference between editors and readers: editors read so much they become blasé. What to a reader is brand new and interesting is often old hat to the editor, even if he learned about it only last week, and learned it from you, the writer. What is new and exciting to such an editor is often far too esoteric for real readers who pay for their own books. If in doubt on a popular book, fight to include the lowest level of information that will interest the greatest number of book buyers; if you can't win, agree and 'run out of space' just before the delivery deadline, when the editor will be far keener to have the book in hand than for a rematch – and with luck will have forgotten what the argument was about. A writer's business isn't to entertain jaded editors but to sell the maximum number of books to paying customers.

Apparent completeness in a tight space So far we have projected the synopsis onto the book, as a slide onto a screen. But the purpose of the synopsis is to convince several people, some of them extremely busy and, with the exception of your editor, not necessarily keen readers. Therefore you want to make the synopsis only as long as is absolutely necessary to perform its function, which is to sell your book or film or teleseries. Tricks of tight language can carry you only so far, then you discover that the art of the synopsis is not what you put in but what you leave out.

A salesman who sold more of my books than any other actually moved his lips while he read. He had learned that I made a one-page summary of the synopsis (next chapter), and he used to ask the publishing director for a copy. He 'knew' my books better, therefore sold them better.

You cannot leave out any point that (in its condensed form) demonstrates the essential motivation of important events (or, in non-literary non-fiction, arguments or information); this is what will sell it to the public and it is this that proves to the editor that you're offering a complete package with a wheel at each corner. But the in-between events, the boring links of every life, of every story, can be left out. The minor events can also be left out.

Nor need you explain the motivation in detail: it is enough to show in a sentence or a phrase that you know what inspired every major event. The editor isn't actually checking that you know the facts: he will assume until you prove otherwise that you are not only an expert, but *the* expert. (He has to: you're *his* expert.) He's not even checking that you chose the right motivation in every instance; he wouldn't be considering your book if he didn't have some general feeling that in the majority of cases you have it right. What he's checking is that *you have considered all the possibilities*, because that's how he knows you are an expert: you're the one who knows which questions to ask.

The key of memorability Don't cut so tight that you kill the book. Even a synopsis for a book of heavy scholarship starts looking dull if it is cut back so far that none of the enthusiasm of the writer shines through. No one can tell you what to leave in— it is your subject and your book—but my own test is that something memorable and striking must remain on each page of the synopsis, even if it isn't essential to proving that the book will form a coherent unit or that I know my subject. The easiest way of achieving this is to find a suitable subheading and add a short, striking example to the description, or if possible replace the description under that subheading with the short, striking example. If the book is to be illustrated, a sample illustration in the synopsis makes a radical change of pace.

In creative writing, don't cut so tight that you kill characters. If your character was witty, leave a sentence demonstrating his wit even if it isn't strictly essential to the chain of motivation. At the very least you must at least once show each major character in action, as distinct from merely describing authorially what he does. If the book is written, you can quote a short paragraph. If it is not fully written, pull a paragraph from the sample chapter, or create a special paragraph and put it in quotes or set it on the page to a narrower measure than the rest of the synopsis. Select or write the piece to give the readers of the synopsis a feeling for the characters so favoured. Unless you can contrive to give your judges at least a flavour of the characters, they will not identify with them. If they do not feel empathy with your characters, why should they want to publish your book?

It is this business of making readers identify with your characters that makes creative writing difficult, and in the confined space of the synopsis the difficulty is magnified many times. It is all too easy even for a professional to fail. But in this one respect success is vital – and every editor knows it.

Mnemonic hooks If you're a new writer, the principle of this section applies to the editor you first approach, because unless you startle or otherwise impress him, he won't remember your name. For those writers who can assume that their editor will remember their names, mnemonic hooks are aimed at those members of editorial boards to whom your proposal and synopsis might be circulated but who may never have met you and who will probably have only a vague idea of your achievements and/or expertise. These people often have little time for reading and may only glance at your various pieces of paper. In either the proposal or the synopsis you want to give each of them at least one item in their own field of professional interest and one outside it: these will remind them of your proposal when your name is mentioned in the meeting at which your editor will make his case that the firm should commission your book. In those houses where the proposal is not circulated but the sponsoring editor makes a verbal pitch to a committee, there is the additional and very onerous requirement that these mnemonic hooks must be so brief and so prominent that someone whose primary interest is focussed elsewhere cannot overlook them and will mention them to the relevant parties.

In most non-fiction whatever you select as examples will be striking enough to stay in the minds of most non-experts; the problem is to include in the synopsis only enough examples to be remembered while at the same time covering the ground thoroughly. Too many examples will flood the mind so that none will be remembered. Select your most striking example to go into the 'synopsis of the synopsis' on the cover of the synopsis—we'll discuss this in the next chapter.

In narrative writing, whether fiction or non-fiction, try to make these striking details do double duty by impressing the writer's authority and knowledge on the readers of the synopsis.

Literary latitude and geography When I am working with a publisher who has commissioned several books from me so that he is in no doubt about my ability to finish a book, I will sacrifice the completeness of the synopsis for memorability; I take great care not to waste the time of such executives with reams of paper because I know the others on their board will take their word that I am good for the book.

But be very careful to whom you offer proposals or synopses designed for publishers whose minds are in perfect tune with yours. A perfectly sound American publisher, shown one of these ultra-condensed proposal/synopses as a sample of 'Jute at the height of his form', wanted to know where the story was. According to my agent, the poor bewildered man complained, 'All he says is he wants to write a novel set in Russia and here's a couple of macabre jokes plus some sick expertise about green linoleum on the floor of an executioner's workshop, so why don't I give him all my money and let him get on with it.' But he complained ten weeks after my agent took back the two-page proposal/synopsis—still remembering the 'jokes' and the green linoleum! By contrast, the British publisher who had asked for the proposal/synopsis, specifying that he wanted it short, commissioned a trilogy on the basis of it but cannot remember the colour of the linoleum. I suspect he never read the two pages, presumably trusting me to write down faithfully the essence of whatever it was I told him on the phone or over lunch or whenever the idea first arose.

It is as easy to go too far the other way. Another American editor returned a longer synopsis specially prepared for American consumption six times before he would offer it to his editorial board, three times because he thought it 'still too short to be taken seriously' and thrice more because, he said, 'It's too funny. Make it more serious.' We weren't discussing Armageddon, only a trilogy of lightweight adventures. The thing ended up sixty turgid pages—a quarter the length of one of the proposed books!—and I wasn't surprised when it fell down in his editorial board, dead of its own weight.

The point is that when writing your synopsis you should bear in mind not only your standing in the profession, and the state of your personal relations with particular publishers, but certain geographic variations as well.

A particularly tiresome American trait has already been mentioned: the increasing insistence of contracts departments that the proposal and synopsis be made a formal part of the contract. This means that the editor wants the writer to make the synopsis as complete as possible, which perverts the purpose of selling the book by creating an impression. Significantly, New York agents (who are professionally inclined to give publishers the benefit of the doubt because that is how they make their living) have for several years been concerned with the deadening effect this has on the resulting books. But professional writers are in no financial condition to revolt and aspirants are in such a competitive bind that they are best advised to shut up and do as they are told.

It seems likely that publishers' legal departments, though not admitting it publicly, are not at all unhappy to grasp the opportunity offered by the ultra-detailed synopsis to put an advance damper on the possibly libellous content of many books. We live in increasingly litigious times, with jury awards skyrocketing. That the practice will cross the Atlantic sooner rather than later is signalled by steeply rising libel awards in London.

The synopsis as a learning experience There must be a happy medium, but it seems to me always to be discovered by trial and error, the most time-wasting method conceivable. It really helps if you know for whom you're writing the synopsis. The editor above who went six rounds with me has not, if one takes a long and hopeful view, wasted his time or mine. I have learned what he must have in order to persuade his editorial board to give me their firm's money, and he has learned to trust my instincts at least a little. The last I heard he was sitting at his desk in New York reading a long manuscript commissioned from me by another publisher. Sooner or later we may be in business together, each easier in his mind for knowing that the other is a stayer.

There are three lessons to be learned from these experiences. The first one is patience, the second that you must give buyers (editors, publishers) what they want if you want to make a sale, and the third that the important thing is not to sell one book but to build a relationship which sells many books. The second point is the subject of this book but the two other points I have dealt with extensively in my earlier books for writers.

Saying more than you need We have already seen how the over-long synopsis somehow loses the essential concept in a forest of verbiage. But a greater disaster than losing the commission after putting in so much work, as described above, would be to have such a monstrosity commissioned. An overdetailed synopsis steals the freshness of your ideas in the writing of the book, and readers notice that you're just going through the motions. Books by professionals which read as if they are resigned to finishing the bloody thing because they have already spent the advance are, on investigation, often found to have grown from excessively detailed synopses.

Indeed, the modern electronic word-processor makes it possible to create an outline (in an application called an 'outliner' which is sometimes included with the word-processor itself) and by making it ever more detailed arrive eventually at a complete book. Experienced editors can spot these pseudo-books at a mile; readers have an instinctive revulsion to the few that slip through the net and are published. In fact such books are full-length synopses and the reason they are so easily spotted is that their 'creative' process has killed all freshness and enthusiasm. You have been warned.

The Style of Your Proposal and Synopsis

Part of the impression your synopsis evokes will simply be the appearance created by its layout, the mechanics of which we will discuss in the next chapter. But besides the content of the proposal and synopsis, which is of course of the greatest importance, you can enhance your chances of making a sale by paying careful attention to the style of proposal and synopsis, and in particular to the language.

Business class and literary class In general, but only in general:

- your **proposal** should be businesslike
- your **synopsis** should achieve a fine balance between businesslike brevity and the literary quality or popular excitement you're trying to convey, and
- your **sample chapter** should faithfully reflect the quality and style of your manuscript.

As we have already discussed, it is to your benefit to consider these three items as selling documents and to create them accordingly. But there are several further reasons, related to the sort of business writing is, for crafting the proposal, synopsis and sample chapter with exceptional care.

Firstly even a how-to book is a relative of literature. 'Businesslike' in publishing does not mean the shortest line between two minds, but the shortest *agreeable* line between the mind of writer and publisher. There is always space for a striking phrase, an elegantly balanced sentence or a telling point. As we have seen above, if you deny your creative instincts too rigorously, you can detract from the appeal of the entire project.

Secondly, publishing executives have become accustomed to these small flourishes of the creative spirit in successful proposals. They miss them if they are absent, as businessmen in other spheres of endeavour would not.

Again, it is a matter of balance. If you're new to the game, rein yourself in; better not to gush. If you're a longtime practitioner, consider if your key mnemonic reference is instantly accessible to a forty-five year-old sales director—or if you haven't left it out altogether because over the years you've been writing these things tighter and tighter from the professional meanness with words that overcomes us all in time.

Present tense and active voice A synopsis for film is always written in the present tense. The present tense like no other adds immediacy and helps the visual imagination form a complete image from very few words.

By tradition, a synopsis for a book may also be written in the present tense, even if the intended book or standing manuscript is in the more common narrative past tense. I wholeheartedly recommend the present tense to you, not least for its hard-selling aura of immediacy. The present tense tells a publisher you mean business, and *now!*

At the literary end of the market, if your synopsis is in the present tense always include a note that the manuscript is or will be in the past tense for easier reading at length. Do this even if a sample chapter is supplied because the synopsis and sample may be split, and even if both are in the same folder some executives will read only one or the other.

The book itself you will of course write in the active rather than the passive voice wherever possible: that is a basic trick of our trade. But it is amazing how many professional writers forget this essential skill when writing a proposal or synopsis. Don't shackle yourself with the passive voice!

Will No, for once I'm not talking about the determination you require to succeed as a writer. The word 'will' is a useful promise for the writer who, once the book is commissioned, is essentially in charge of his own destiny. A writer, working alone, can promise to make a book such and such, or to include such and such, and then go away and do it as soon as the publisher says, 'Go!' It's that simple.

In the limited space of a proposal and synopsis, there is no room for messing around with tentatives. Recently a phrase caught my attention on the front page of a proposal lying on a publisher's desk. 'Will you commission this?' I asked. 'I'd love a book in this field,' he replied, putting his finger on the phrase 'tends to show' on the proposal, 'but this writer hasn't made up her mind what she really wants to say.'

The guidance in the paragraph above applies in general to all kinds of writing with the specific exception of high scholarship, where you should demonstrate the fine balance of your opinion even in the synopsis.

There is no need to flaunt spurious certainty where none is possible, but you must come down on one side of the case or the other. If you don't have an opinion on a subject, you shouldn't be writing about it. If a balance of facts is essential to show how you arrive at your opinion, that is the progression of your synopsis. But no one should be left in doubt at the end as to your own opinion.

However, delaying the expression of your judgement while you muster all the facts can be a fine tension-building device when you come to write the book.

This applies even to fiction. A very professional novelist says, 'I once lost a multi-book deal when the money was as good as in the bank because I carelessly let the publisher discover that I had not yet decided how to conclude the first book.' If you have any doubts, keep them to yourself until after the contract is signed.

'Show' As a novice writer you were no doubt advised that you should 'show in action, not merely describe'. If you're professional enough to be reading this book you have taken the lesson to heart so that we need not discuss that particular principle further. But the wide dissemination of this rule, coupled with the tendency for publishing executives to confine their reading to proposals, synopses and sample chapters, has made 'show' the most overused word in publishing.

Keep a typewritten list of synonyms for 'show' beside your keyboard when you write proposals and synopses. I know two writers who have theirs written in thick felt pen on large sheets permanently stuck on the wall before them, a visual reminder of the importance of the proposal and synopsis to today's writer. And several writers at a conference swore by 'action words' similarly stuck on the wall as a defence mechanism against passive writing. More, in my advertising agency we had a printed list of the 800 words every housewife understood turned into wallpaper and the walls of the creative offices papered with it. I keep my list of 'show'-synonyms and substitutes for all seasons and purposes on my computer and give part of it here in alphabetical order as a start for you to expand.

accuse	contend	evidence
acquaint	contrast	evince
add	convey	examine
adjudicate	correlate	exemplify
adjust	corroborate	exhibit
advise	decide	explain
allege	declare	explore
allude	deduce	expose
analyse	define	expound
announce	delineate	express
answer	delve	fathom
appraise	demonstrate	find out
apprise	denote	flag
argue	depict	flaunt
articulate	derive	focus
ascertain	describe	grasp
assert	detail	highlight
assume	determine	hypothesise
assure	develop	identify
attest	diagnose	illuminate
authenticate	dig	illustrate
bracket	digest	imagine
brief	discern	impart
bring up	disclose	imply
broach	discover	import
broadcast	discuss	impute
capture	display	indicate
chart	dissect	inform
circulate	disseminate	inquire
claim	divulge	interpolate
clarify	draw	interpret
clear up	elucidate	introduce
collate	embody	investigate
communicate	enlighten	itemise
compare	enunciate	judge
conclude	equate	justify
confirm	establish	learn
connote	estimate	list
contemplate	evaluate	log

maintain	recite	strip
manifest	recommend	study
mark	record	substantiate
mean	recount	suggest
mention	refer	summarise
narrate	reflect	support
note	register	suppose
offer	rehearse	surmise
open	relate	survey
outline	render	symbolise
parade	report	tally
penetrate	represent	target
personify	resolve	tell
plot	retrace	test
plumb	reveal	transmit
point out	review	uncover
polarise	rule	understand
ponder	sanction	unearth
portend	scrutinise	unfold
portray	settle	unravel
pose	share	unveil
present	signify	update
probe	sketch	urge
proclaim	solve	validate
proffer	speak of	ventilate
promulgate	specify	verify
pronounce	speculate	vindicate
propose	spell out	voice
prove	spotlight	vouch
purport	state	weigh
pursue	steer	
rank	stress	

The soberly extravagant promise A book is the result of an enthusiasm. The proposal and especially the synopsis must reflect this enthusiasm. But a proposal and a synopsis are also documents announcing and advertising your professionalism in our chosen trade.

Though you must of course tell no lies, either of fact or as promises you know you cannot make good, a certain amount of hyperbole is expected and allowed for. It is surprising how few books are bought and published as a matter of routine, even in the largest publishers. Every book has some excitement attached to it for at least one editor or, more often than you might think, at least one non-editorial executive who can see his own performance enhanced by that book. Without excitement, a proposal, and especially a synopsis, will be stillborn.

The question is how to strike the balance between the excitement generated by enthusiasm and the very necessary appearance and substance of professionalism. Let me hammer this crucial point home as hard as possible: without excitement they will not want to do your book, but if they are not convinced of your professionalism they won't do it either, because their jobs will be on the line if they pay out for too many books that fail to live up to expectations. This is one of the few places where the newcomer has the advantage over the fairly new professional. A publisher in doubt about a professional with a short track record simply declines the proposal because he is too embarrassed to explain to a professional that he doesn't trust him and therefore wants him to work on spec. On the other hand, if a newcomer has a complete manuscript it costs little to look it over and judge whether the apparent lack of professionalism in the proposal or synopsis arises from a cause no more harmful than an excess of enthusiasm. Note the phrase 'costs little'; it's a relative phrase, and applies at present. Every year it costs more to read a manuscript; every year publishers are less keen to ask for unsolicited mss and correspondingly keener to receive commissioned mss which do not need further editorial work. If your proposal and synopsis are professional, they inspire confidence that when it arrives your manuscript will be professional too.

Where to strike the balance? Most of all, it depends who you're trying to sell to. Obviously the editors of a university press publishing educational or scholarly texts will be attracted to a different balance from the one that will appeal to the publisher of a mass house operating in the popular market. Personally, when in doubt I remember the many, many times publishers who did not know me at all at the time when they commissioned that crucial first book told me later that what convinced them to take the chance was my enthusiasm spilling over the edges of the proposal and synopsis. I always give the balance of doubt to enthusiasm. But you should remember that I work in popular fiction and non-fiction, where enthusiasm is a prerequisite, and in a class of straight novels where both the risks and the possible rewards are very high. Consequently a high degree of enthusiasm on the part of both the writer and the publisher does much to ease the pain of high-rolling decisions made on always inadequate information. Consider your market and circumstances in deciding your pitch—then, on the principle that the publishers of even the most po-faced books are people too, add ten percent in the scales on the side of enthusiasm.

5

THE LITERARY MECHANIC
PRESENTING PROPOSALS AND SYNOPSES

THE synopsis usually settles its own order because it is a narrative with a beginning, a middle and an end. Alternatively, it summarises a non-fiction development of ideas or instructions or information which will make sense to readers only when a proper groundwork has been laid, which then determines the order of presentation and thereby the organisation of the entire project.

The proposal, excluding its hardest selling element of the bulleted marketing list which should be on the first or second page, should be ordered outwards from the general statement of the purpose of the book. However, since the 'general statement of the purpose of the book' is frequently subsumed into the brief, often one-word, description of its genre, that is not much help as a guiding rule. As a first approximation you can use the order applied to discussing the elements of the proposal in Chapter Three, and rearrange the heads of the resulting proposal to reflect the varying importance you attach to each item of information *for that particular book*. As the reproduced examples show, the most successful proposals balance importance of information with the need to place information relevant to those executives with the shortest attention span nearest the front of the proposal. Furthermore, they enhance this effect by careful use of layout. It is to achieve this crucial balance that we place so much stress on the bulleted marketing list and its prominent placing. The bulleted marketing list, considering how hard it works for you and how little space it consumes, is a bargain, however tough it may be for you to knock it into shape.

STRAIGHTFORWARD MECHANICS

The professional invariably asks, 'How short can I make the proposal and synopsis?' The novice says, 'How long can it be?' The answer in both cases is, 'As short as you can make it and still communicate all the necessary information.'

Proposal length A businesslike proposal can say a great deal in four or five pages. If a proposal accompanied by a separate synopsis runs over ten pages, it could probably be either cut to reduce superfluous information or tightened up to present it more efficiently.

Synopsis length A synopsis should be as long as is required to demonstrate a closed circle of motivation and action, or to outline an argument or course of instruction. The length will depend on the type of book. You will also need a minimum of space for memorable examples. It is impossible to name a number of pages even as an average; books are simply too different.

A quality bind It is a mistake to use too fine a paper, printing, or binding for your proposal, synopsis and sample. You should concentrate on content rather than flashy presentation. Of course everything should be cleanly typed or xeroxed, and bound or presented in a folder as required, but editors soon learn that material which looks as if the writer hired an advertising agency to help him sell his idea means that he skimped attention on the content.

Professionals print their proposals on the same printer and paper they will use to prepare the manuscript.

My own proposals/synopses are usually stapled at the top left-hand corner. They are always printed on the same cheap computer printer paper which I will use for the manuscript (and which I use for correspondence to even the grandest publishers). If a cover is required, pages which need to be loose are inserted in a cardboard pocket folder; the fanciest binding I use has a transparent foldaround plastic cover into which a good number of pages (up to feature film script thickness) can be stapled to make a booklet. All this simplicity makes its own statement: this author puts his maximum effort where it should be, on the content. Whenever I deviate from this rule, I lose time or money.

What to bind Sample chapters for books are normally not bound, perhaps because book manuscripts never are, but everything else should at least be stapled. Anything for film or television that runs to more than a dozen pages should be spiralbound or stapled along the spine into some kind of a folder, simply because that is what script editors and producers are used to.

Sample chapters in non-fiction should be separated and the pages of each chapter paperclipped (not stapled) together to make it easy for the publisher to skip from the middle of one chapter to the beginning of the next.

Magazine articles and stories are supplied paperclipped rather than stapled.

THE ART OF POURING A GALLON INTO A PINT POT

We have already discussed the purpose of the synopsis: to demonstrate that your book or script will leave no question unanswered, and to display a few highlights which are designed to fix your material in the editors mind. What remains to be discovered is the shortest practical way of achieving those two purposes.

The master-scene synopsis Though many of our examples show the synopsis combined with the proposal, there may be occasions when you want to write a separate synopsis. And, of course, you must have the complete circle clear in your mind even if you intend to interweave its elements with the more commercial matter of the proposal.

The master-scene synopsis is a planning and plotting tool

from the world of films. Its purpose is to reduce complicated and subtle constructs to the briefest form so that any gaps in motivation may be exposed. In theory it gives a sequential number to and describes the shortest unit of action in a film that takes place in one location; in practice it accepts as a unit the period of time and action until the camera's attention shifts elsewhere.

The format has universal application. You can use it for structuring a book. If you remove the scene numbers and join some of the sentences to make the flow less abrupt, you end up with the shortest possible description of the contents that proves there are no gaps.

Big conceptual jumps The numbered paragraphs of a structured textbook serve the same purpose: a logical, structured flow without gaps. If this is the kind of book you write, it is always useful for editors if you show the layered structure by the numbers you intend to use.

A problem in books to a syllabus arises where the syllabus leaves out a large chunk of the logical order of developing the subject; the reason is normally not that the powers that be are stupid but that they too are ruled by the inflexible number of teaching days in the school year. Fitting a syllabus over three, four, five or six years is often a matter more of jigsaw-cutting than of desirable continuity; in any event the author has no option but to fit in. The best way of handling these breaks is simply to ignore them. Break to a new chapter where the break in logical progression occurs. Unless the publisher suggests it first, do not add even a short paragraph drawing attention to the omission as this might raise question that teachers may not have time to answer. If the publisher asks for such links, then it is on his head if the book is rejected by those teachers who choose their own textbooks. I once sat on a faculty committee that almost without discussion rejected all the books on one publisher's list because it had these undesirable links; it was an unforgettable lesson.

The purpose of illustrative examples Though the sample chapter shows what you have in mind, or have already produced, we have seen that a synopsis without the humanising touch of the odd illustration fails to come alive. But the examples in the synopsis are there for other reasons as well.

First, even a sample paragraph or two from the actual book, or created to represent it, proves that you write acceptably. This is no joke: last year I was shown a thirty-page proposal and synopsis of appalling brittleness, and would have advised the publisher to decline the project if I hadn't known and admired the author's books. In this case there was no sample chapter, but your synopsis should include a sample paragraph or two of 'real writing' even if there is a sample chapter with the material. The publisher who asked for an opinion in the case cited above believes that a proposal which does not successfully convey the flavour of what the author intends is a common cause of stillborn projects. 'A bad book may come, and often will, from a good synopsis, but a good book almost never comes from a bad synopsis. So we tend to turn down ideas which are merely clumsily presented, which with a little more creative breathing space might have been very good indeed.'

Secondly, the illustrative examples serve, as we have seen, as a mnemonic for publishing staff you cannot count on to read sample chapters. Thirdly, the identification of publisher and editor with your work through such striking examples binds them to you. Next to your implicit promise in the proposal to advance their careers directly by giving them a good book to sell, this is your closest and most personal connection with people you will perhaps never meet but who are nonetheless of great importance to your success. Fourthly, as we have already seen, many publishers of non-fiction books attach great importance to the quality, range and selection of your examples: they can deduce a great deal from them about your command of the subject and your ability to communicate your knowledge to readers.

The purpose of pictures A picture may indeed be worth a thousand words. But the first purpose of a picture in a proposal or synopsis is to answer a thousand questions you don't have the space to answer in words. In short, you must choose your picture by the same criteria you choose your written examples: the one most likely to be startling and/or memorable, the one which will demonstrate your authoritive grasp of the subject and so on, all the factors we have discussed. A picture is different from words only in that it usually occupies less space.

There is however also good reason to include pictures simply to consume space, rather than filling the space with more words. This is a consideration that bears more on the design of your proposal, its visual impact, than in the first instance on its content. Consider a page which has more space left over than the designed white, or which needs to be balanced either in itself or, if presented as part of a spread, with the page opposite, or as part of the overall design of every page in the proposal or synopsis. A solution definitely superior to adding words is adding a picture, assuming that you have something relevant. Don't overdo it to the extent that it becomes obvious you are filling the page—in that case it's better to leave it blank.

Always leave a little surplus white space. It tells executives you said what you had to say, then stopped. People appreciate not having their time wasted.

Never add pictures to a proposal, synopsis or sample chapter for an all-text book. That is mere decoration and editors will find it intellectually offensive. Pictures should be added only to proposals, synopses and sample chapters of books intended to be illustrated, and should relate to the subject, or be a sample of the illustrations intended. In a sample chapter show only those illustrations intended to be shown in that chapter in the proposed or described book; illustrations from other parts of the book that are crucial to your argument for commissioning/buying it should go into the synopsis at the right place. Any particularly striking illustration that is left over after that can be used as decoration for the proposal, with the proviso that one picture per page is the maximum you should permit yourself.

Placement We have seen that additional pictures can be used as spacefillers. But they must not interfere with the impact of those pictures that make important points, that are therefore structural to your proposal or synopsis, and spacefillers are never used in sample chapters. To me that implies that a spacefiller should never be used on any page or spread in a proposal or synopsis where there is already an important picture. You never know what people will see in a picture and the less important picture might raise an echo in the memory of a key executive, causing him to overlook the really important message in the important picture on the same page and perhaps losing you the sale. As a corollary, I try to place an important picture on every page or spread before resorting to filler-pictures. The final, least important rule, is to decide at the start if you will have only the important pictures or if you will have a picture on every spread. If more than half your spreads have one or more important pictures, the other pages might by comparison look a little bare, and you may be forced to use fillers.

This is, incidentally, a much more rigorous standard than is observed even in the best books, where important and merely mildly relevant pictures are often arranged to no better plan than to occupy the space pleasingly because it is difficult to sell books with many blank half-pages.

There is one further consideration, held until last here because it depends not only on the context of each proposal and synopsis and sample chapter but on the author's personal preference as well. Let us say you have thirteen pages altogether that you intend sending a publisher and nine important illustrations (photographs, drawings, whatever) which must go into those thirteen pages to help you sell the project. You have unlimited further illustrations that are less important (in the selling context) from which to choose fillers if required. Because you take my remarks about the unknown effects of pictures seriously, you decide that you will present your combined proposal/synopsis as single pages rather than run the risk of your important illustrations interfering with each other at two to the spread. But you are also faced with another problem: no fewer than, say, seven of your nine illustrations relate to your last two pages of text. Never mind for the moment whether the pictures will look good at any scale or only at a certain size, or the cost of having reductions made. The question is will you pack them in where they belong or will you spread them through the pages to give each space to breathe and make its impact?

Many typesetters, small printers and even high street bureaux can make black-and-white and often colour photocopies to any scale, which you can cut out and paste down. This is usually

cheaper, and easier to arrange, than having photographic repro-
ductions made; though the quality is not reprographic it is
however good enough in most instances to serve as an introduction and saves having to send valuable original material until
a publisher express definite interest. Should you decide to do
this, the better the quality of the reproduction, the more necessary it is for you to mark each and every picture as a photocopy
(Xerox) and note that you hold the original art. If you have a
Macintosh and suitable software, typesetters and bureaux can
give you either proofing quality or professional quality scans
(vast price difference!) on disk for direct inclusion in your text.
The same thing is possible but more difficult on IBM and com-
patible desktop computers used for word-processing.

There are of course cases where packing the maximum number of hardhitting illustrations together magnifies the impact, but
in my opinion that is a high-risk option for all but the most experienced and talented designers. In the case described above, I
would spread my nine illustrations over nine pages, with longish
captions if required, and leave four of the pages without illustration to hammer home the point that the illustrations shown
are very important; I would back up the point by mentioning
prominently in a separate headed paragraph that I already had
obtained x hundred illustrations to choose the rest from.

Something else that I have done on occasion, but that you
may like to think about twice until you have enough track
record for publishers to know such things do not happen
through oversight or laziness, is to use the same illustration
twice or even repeatedly in either the same document, or, more
commonly, across the various documents (proposal, synopsis,
sample chapter, even the accompanying letter) that are sent in
the same envelope to the publisher. Of course only the most
important illustrations will stand this treatment.

In many cases the advice above may not be relevant. You
may not wish to go to the expense of having copies of illustrations made to a suitable size for pasting into your proposal,
synopsis or sample chapter. Alternatively, you may not be able
to, either for lack of facilities or because you do not own the
copyright of the picture until it is paid for, which you will of
course do only after the book is commissioned or sold. In this

case, you should present your material in one of those books of clear plastic envelopes that salesmen use for brochures. Stick a note on it that the illustrative material is original and you would prefer that it not be unnecessarily handled. People can see through the envelopes and those who will, after the warning, take material out of the envelopes are usually those who know how not to damage artwork. Make sure your name is on the back of every illustration. In such proposals you can insert illustrations and sheets of text in any order you choose.

A space-saving trick for illustrated books When your synopsis starts looking a bit long, there are a few tricks you can apply to cut it back without losing the impact. The suggestions here and in the next section have the additional advantage that they lighten up the appearance of the synopsis by replacing large blocks of text by more broken material that looks faster to read.

If a book is largely composed of illustrations, or if the illustrations will be a key element, you can show the shape of the narrative by a list of the illustrations in order.

Chapter chronology If your book will be mostly text, your chapter breakdown can often show its shape, progression and organisation much more effectively than a less structured discussion of what you will include. When chapter heads are explicatory or have clear sub-heads you can often get away with just the two heads and perhaps a brief explanatory paragraph; if you have crossheads and subheads in the text itself, a listing of these is always superior to mere description and need take no more space if you run them on separated by dashes or semicolons instead of listing each on a new line.

The element of surprise All these contortions to squeeze a gallon into a pint pot, and the even more radical compressions that follow, have the beneficial side effect of providing variety and changes of pace, which in turn are conducive to promoting small gasps of surprise even from hardened editors when they come upon something striking in your material. That is all to the good. You should also see if rearranging your material cannot enhance this element of surprise, or at least place it to best advantage for mnemonic purposes by juxtaposing your surprises and your very best points. Often, of course, they are one and the same.

SUMMARISING THE SUMMARY

The job is not finished when you finish writing the proposal, synopsis, sample chapter and the accompanying cover letter, extracts from reviews and publications list. Each of the first three must be covered by a one-page summary. Why?

It is courtesy to your editor to provide a short summary and it is also good business. If your proposal, synopsis and sample chapter are well written and within the editor's publishing brief, you can be certain he will read every word, perhaps more than once. But neither you nor he can be certain that others with decision-making powers will read anything between 2000 and 20,000 words. This requires shorter summaries. If you don't write them, he must. Do you want to run the risk that he has the time?

The first page of the proposal If you have a bullet list on the first page of your proposal that covers the highlights of the proposal in a systematic manner, that could very well be sufficient. Just check that genre and length is also on the front page, and that any sections, which do not feature in the bullet list, especially those to do with markets for the project, are prominently headed in the body of the proposal so that the interested executives can find it easily. If the proposal is more than four or five pages, add a contents list.

If your bullet list is not on the front page of the proposal, then you must prepare a separate cover page. Part of it should be a contents list—annotate it if you have space—plus a very brief description of the purpose and content of the book and the market it is intended for. I used to head this 'Executive Summary' until an editor told me it made his bosses feel I considered them functional illiterates who couldn't concentrate beyond one page. Now I head it 'Very Briefly' or 'Summary' or something similar, and end it with a remark that all these matters are expanded in the body of the proposal. But I have come to believe very firmly that nothing beats the bullet list and contents on the first page of the proposal.

The first page of the synopsis Here you should in a single paragraph, at most two paragraphs, encapsulate the content of the book or project. The question immediately arises of what you should put in the space. You cannot tell the full story, that's for sure.

But every project has a key, one major question it answers. In a novel the crisis in which the characters find themselves is the key motivational element; in a biography it is the reasons why the subject did something crucial; in any piece of contemporary history it is the out-of-the-ordinary and unexpected. You cannot propose a project until you know the key question you wish to answer. This key should drive your covering summary of the synopsis.

All of this sounds extremely theoretical. It isn't. It is actually easy, and made easier because it puts you under no obligation to describe a narrative with a beginning, a middle and an end. You can do that, if you want to, of course, though it is very hard to do in a couple of paragraphs, and has the very great disadvantage that it gives your ending or conclusion away and so discourages busy people from reading the whole.

The easy way is to think of when your book will be in print. The dust jacket front flap or back panel, and on the paperback (pocketbook) the back cover, will contain an advertisement for the book known as the blurb. This is what turns publishing executives on and it is therefore what I advise you to include as a summary on the synopsis.

A draft blurb does not so much represent a book in real life or a synopsis in publishing as raise a fascinating question about it, the answer to which one can only discover by reading the book or synopsis. Publisher David St John Thomas adds a down-to-earth hint about the construction of the blurb: 'Don't start the draft blurb with "This book..."'

For a feature script, think of the poster outside the cinema, or the blurb on the video-cassette and proceed from there.

The first page of the sample chapter On the sample chapter you will put not a summary, which would defeat the purpose of having a sample chapter, but a teaser which should make publishers want to read it all. The teaser is normally a paragraph pulled from the sample chapter and repeated on the cover page. It is the most important element on the cover page, and if it is particularly intriguing it can be the same sample paragraph you used in the synopsis or proposal, which will strengthen the mnemonic links.

There could be two further elements on the cover page, and many writers mistakenly believe that these are more important than the teaser paragraph. For a novel, biography or history, these two additional elements are a paragraph describing how the characters have found themselves in the situation at the beginning of the sample chapter, if it is not the first chapter, and another paragraph describing what happens afterwards, if it is not the last chapter. The second paragraph should not give away your ending or, in the case of a non-fiction book, your conclusion; let them read the synopsis for that.

This single covering page should, like the first and last pages of sample chapter itself, contain your name and address. In addition it should include the number of words in the complete book and of course its title. It does no harm to make a note on the sample chapter and its covering page that it is accompanied by a proposal and synopsis. If you have published or performed work to your credit, add under the title on both pages 'by the author of...' just in case your sample chapter is sent for an opinion to an outside reader who does not get copies of your covering letter, publications list, review extracts and so on.

Under no circumstances add a note that the sample chapter is not typical of the proposed or standing book. If it is not typical, why send it?

FORMATS FOR SAMPLES

Every medium has its own logical, traditional or currently preferred format. In addition, individual producers in films and television may have their own preferred layouts and you should take the trouble to find out what these special preferences are and comply with them. This applies whether you are offering a full-length manuscript or a sample. With a word-processor it is usually easy to recast your text into whatever format is required. Trade publishers are generally less particular, as long as the text is typewritten and doublespaced on one side of the paper, but most of the university and textbook presses have very strict house styles as regards referencing, section or paragraph numbering and layering, and a multiplicity of other matters, which extend even to proposals, synopses and sample texts. It is up to you to discover this and comply with the rules.

A 'trade publisher' is a general publisher of many kinds of books as distinct from, for instance, a strictly educational publisher. Originally the word described a publisher who sold to bookshops ie the trade.

Where no particular rules are laid down, it is still advantageous to show that you are aware of the minimum professional requirements of the medium or the market or even the individual publisher and can work within it.

Layout and format A book sample chapter is laid out just as in any manuscript. The text must be double-spaced, with generous margins, and typed on one side of the paper only with a new ribbon. Do not use your word-processor to right-justify text in manuscript or sample chapters.

Samples of how to lay out a film, a teleplay, and a radio play are harder to come by. The examples reproduced in the samples at the end of this book show the standard layouts that are acceptable at most production companies. The main considerations are

- to offer to producers in each field only samples laid out in the particular style acceptable in that medium, and
- always to distinguish clearly between staging instructions to the director and the dialogue the actors will speak.

6
SAMPLE CHAPTERS
AN ONLY SLIGHTLY CROOKED GUIDE

THIS is not a book about writing—it is a book to help you sell your writing. Keep that in mind when you read this chapter on selecting or writing your sample chapter. It should be obvious where the advice below differs from that in any competent book intended to help you write better, but there is a more subtle effect to look out for: a sample chapter is often tweaked or purposefully written to be much more concentrated than anything you would ever put in a real book, or to contain material that in real life you would place elsewhere, or in some cases not even include.

The purpose of the sample The purpose of the sample chapter is to convince a publisher who likes your concept, as revealed in the synopsis, and believes there is a market for such a book, as you claim in the proposal, that you can in fact write a saleable book. This is a reasonable requirement when dealing with a newcomer to our profession or someone with a short track record, but it is offensive to a writer with twenty or thirty books under his belt. It does no good to send such publishers copies of your other books: they want to see a sample of the particular book you are proposing to them.

If you are an established writer you must make up your own mind how far you will go along with such nonsense. I write a sample chapter for any new publisher only once and then only if I have no other commissioned work at the time; after that I refuse and tell him to read my other books. In practice I tend to think of a sample chapter as my cut-price introductory offer and try to recover cash for the time I spent on it by jacking up the advance on the assumption that a publisher who has seen a sample chapter should, if he trusts his own judgement, be in a position to pay me the full royalty expected to be earned by the first print run (rather than just three-quarters or four-fifths of it as is standard practice).

Select or write? If you don't have a manuscript, you have to create your sample chapter or chapters from scratch. If you already have a manuscript, you have the option of

- selecting a sample chapter or chapters from it and offering them as they stand, or
- tweaking them to sell harder and/or represent the complete manuscript better, or
- creating special selling versions from scratch.

In practice the writer who writes so skillfully that he can select a chapter or three and send them away totally unmodified to represent him and his work—doesn't need to. This writer is normally at a stage in his career where he rarely has a manuscript before he has a contract, or if he has a manuscript his existing publishers and all their competitors will be overjoyed to receive the entire manuscript and read every word in it most attentively.

Unfortunately the writer who most often has an uncommitted manuscript is commonly not yet so skilled that a chapter or three can without modification represent him and his work faithfully, never mind sell as hard as it should. He is also, in my experience, the writer who still has most difficulty ruthlessly altering his work to serve some non-literary purpose. ('What has this to do with art?' one young lady demanded when I told her to cut more than half of her three sample chapters before offering them again.)

The final consideration is that even for a skilled writer it is often more difficult to turn an existing chapter from a book into a selling document than simply to create a sample chapter solely for the purpose of selling.

For all these reasons, and others which *do* have to do with protecting the literary value of the resulting book, I would prefer to create samples from scratch even if I had an unsold manuscript to hand from which to pull sample chapters.

The disposition of specially created sample chapters For exactly the same reasons, with their effects taken in reverse, the tweaked or specially created sample chapter is always more trouble when you try to put it in the actual book than it is worth. It always takes less time to write a new chapter than to make a sample fit back in with the rest or fit with the newly created balance of the book. Either go back to your original, pre-tweaked material or create a new chapter from scratch. In both cases you will of course junk the 'sample' version.

If you don't believe me, put a hard-selling sample chapter back in its place in one of your own books and read it in the middle of the flanking regular chapters. It will make very nervous reading, like an impatient newcomer at a relaxed dinner of old chums. I can spot the sample chapters of other writers too lazy to do the work over from a mile away by the excess tension they generate.

On the morality of the author as a salesman The question arises: is this extremely effective procedure honest? As so often in these pages, it is a matter you must decide for yourself. I can only list a few considerations and then tell you what I think and do.

First, and most important, it seems to me that most experienced editors expect authors to do it. Certainly no editor or other publishing executive has ever reproached me for moving material that he saw in a sample chapter to another, more logical place in the book, or observed that he missed the tightness and pace of the sample chapter in the complete book. One good reason for editors not to complain about this procedure is that it helps them sell the project to other executives whose entire narrative reading may consist of *parts of* sample chapters, who may have forgotten how a whole book works. Editors—and I stress this is a personal view based on my own experience—are accomplices to the dishonesty, if dishonesty it is.

In the second place, everyone agrees that with your synopsis and sample chapter you are supposed to create an image that truly represents the proposed book or existing manuscript. If a true representation cannot be created by selecting only part of an existing manuscript, or a purpose-written part that will fit seamlessly, without alteration, into whatever you create later, surely good sense, perhaps even honesty, demands that you make such alterations as will create a true image. We are not talking about lies, of promising to deliver what you know or suspect you cannot, but of the nip and tuck that makes the coat fit the slimmed-down concept; everyone who is not a fool knows that for the full-length version the concept has to be fattened up again and the tucks let out.

Notice that this is entirely different from agreeing with a pressing editor who wants to over-stuff your book and then finding right on the deadline that you have run out of space. That is an accommodation to his greed or inexperience and a justified negotiating position—who knows, he might be right and there may be sufficient space for everything he wants. But such matters are discussed in the proposal or synopsis, both more negotiable documents than the sample chapter; both of them are in a sense in flux right until the book hits the bookshops. By contrast the sample chapter is almost entirely the writer's baby. In the sample chapter you should not put anything at all you are not certain will find a place in the finished manuscript.

THE SELECTED SAMPLE CHAPTER DISSECTED

Let us suppose for the moment that you will ignore my advice to create your sample from scratch and instead try your hand at selecting and perhaps tweaking a sample chapter or chapters from a standing manuscript.

How to match purpose to available material The first requirement is to select the material to serve your purposes. Your purposes are twofold: to make an indelible impression that will sell the project, and to give a fair impression of its totality. It is obvious that the first chapter you select will be the one that makes the most startling revelation. It is however a mistake to include the chapter that contains the denouement, which is normally the final chapter. After that, anything must be an anticlimax; if all the reader's (in this case an editor's or publisher's) questions are answered, the tension is gone and, perhaps, with it the sale because people don't always act logically.

Thus your first choice of sample chapter will be the one that makes the biggest impression. If you provide more than one sample chapter, the considerations on which you select the rest are somewhat different.

Always include the maximum amount of sample material permitted, because that decreases the impact of the various problems with extracted material.

You don't want to leave the impression you are all fireworks and no backbone, so next select a chapter which shows solid groundwork and patient development; this normally has the beneficial side effect of showing off the depth of your research or the scope of your examples or both. You could note in the proposal or synopsis that this sample chapter is included to show the use to which you have put your special or unique knowledge or research. Remember, many of the people you are addressing may not be experts and may not even notice that your information is special; this applies even to sample chapters from novels if some esoteric expertise or knowledge is involved. Tell them!

If a third sample chapter is required or permitted, in non-fiction it is sometimes fruitful to select one of the necessary appendices—even if it is dull, as long as it will be considered of great importance by users. On one occasion I received no fewer than three offers for a proposal for which my sample was only the bibliography: later I discovered that all three editors had precisely those books on their private bookshelves. If there is an important table, you might show it. If necessary, note on it or nearby, 'This table might appear dull to lay readers but your academic advisers will tell you that to our key market it will be one of the selling points of the book.'

In fiction, this third chapter selected could be the opening chapter or another chapter close on its heels in which the predicament of the characters is most clearly stated; this will be the chapter which states the questions to be answered. Some writers will in fact choose this one before the 'development and research' chapter.

If these chapters can go as they stand, fine. If not, read on.

The problems of a selected sample First, do be certain at least three months have elapsed since you read the complete novel before you read the selected sample chapters to determine if they can stand on their own feet. Any less than that and information that is lodged in your brain from the unsent chapters, ie not available to the publisher, can cause you to overlook lacunae in the flow of the text.

It is worth spending a moment on 'lacunae in the flow of the text'. Suppose for the moment I sent only the present chapter as a sample for this book. Without the chapters that went before, it would appear to any reasonable reader to make very large unfounded assumptions. In the context of the book, it does no such thing, of course, all the assumptions being discussed earlier and, I hope, agreed between you and me; any assumption not specifically agreed by you is however understood by you to be reasonable on my part because I have explained how I came to my conclusion. We share the same information. But an editor seeing only the sample chapter does not share all that prior information. And it simply isn't done to litter your sample with notes such as 'This was underpinned in an earlier chapter'—it looks most unprofessional and in practice confuses editors by breaking their reading-flow.

There is no point in making a depressingly long list of everything that can go wrong with selected samples. Those wrong with your own selected sample chapter(s) should become clear as you work with the text. But, besides gaps in the natural flow, there are a couple of major solecisms even professional writers commit.

The most irritating to editors is the matter of names. When a character or a real person is first introduced, he is normally named in full, first name and surname. Later he might be just a first name or only a surname. It is infuriating to sort out who is who when you have only half the name. It can wreck any narrative for the editor trying to get an impression of it from a sample chapter. The same thing applies in technical or popular how-to texts when the full name of some process or material or group is given in the 'missing' chapters and you are suddenly faced with a meaningless acronym without any explanation.

The other major problem in creative writing is caused by the requirement of all narrative for friction, which might be described as the universal force of literature. A novel routinely takes characters at a crisis-point in their lives, out of sorts with their circumstances or their families or colleagues or bosses. A biography of a man universally in agreement with his times and his contemporaries would be a bore; interesting biographies are normally about men at odds with accepted contemporary wisdom and their achievements in changing public opinion. But friction fluctuates in intensity and direction from chapter to chapter towards the resolution. That is what makes it such a rich source of misunderstandings between writers and editors when only samples are available to the editor. Put yourself in the editor's shoes.

If while reading a sample from a biography of a long dead statesman you do not know that X had a fight with Y in the previous chapter, not available to you, you might well be amazed to find bad blood between two men you always thought had been great friends and colleagues. And, of course, the next chapter is not available either, so you cannot even discover that they made up at the next Cabinet meeting. If 'you' are the editor here, you might easily conclude the writer is at best wrongheaded and probably an idiot—and clip a rejection slip right there.

Friction does not happen only between people; the friction between ideas also makes good books, subject to the same problems as biography, history and fiction when sample chapters are extracted. I recently saw a sample chapter from a book attacking scientists for substituting their method and results for religious faith. Without the underpinning arguments and ideas it seemed simply barefaced assertion of a particularly tendentious kind. When it was published, that particular chapter still failed to convince me, but at least I could understand how the author had reached her conclusions, and agree that they might under certain limited circumstance be arguable.

How to doctor sample-chapter shortcomings Make a master copy of your manuscript, date it, and put it somewhere safe, so that you can return to it. Work on copies of your sample chapters rather than the originals.

Now check the names of people, things and places in your sample. Add text (not a note that the missing information was explained earlier in fully integrated text) so that the names may be clear to those who have not read the earlier chapters.

Double-check the time of events in all creative-writing narratives: year, season, day of the week, time of day. This is often 'lost' in the previous, 'missing' chapter, and can stop the reader in irritation. If necessary, add a couple of words of integrated text to make this clear.

Bring in text to elucidate earlier frictions: 'Their fight yesterday brewed adrenalin which still coursed through his veins.'

Read *only* the sample chapters to identify and eliminate any text that is not required to close the sample, for instance material that establishes or serves as background to events or arguments that will be concluded or brought to climax outside the sample chapters. Such material is unnecessary, confusing, liable to raise questions, and should therefore go.

Now read to see that the sample chapters leave no big questions unanswered except the really major one: how did it all end? I can hear you complaining that that is what the complete book is supposed to do, not the sample chapters. Sure. But the sample chapters are all the publisher has before him. The problem with major questions (except for *the* major one of the conclusion) is that they start to raise doubts about your ability to close the chain of argument or motivation. Of course, you have closed it in the synopsis, but at this moment the editor is reading your sample chapters and he may not have time to read the synopsis again to reassure himself that you actually did tie up all the loose ends in the rest of the manuscript.

Eventually you will end up with your sample chapters plus a large number of key paragraphs from elsewhere in the book which you must somehow integrate to make everything clear. Integrating these seamlessly into text already tightly cut and rewritten to flow like molten gold is such a pain that at this point most writers throw up their hands and either send the extracted sample chapters as they stand or start writing a sample from scratch to do the job right.

When you work with selected and tweaked sample chapters, the before and after linking paragraphs on the cover sheet assume an even greater importance than when you create your sample from scratch, for precisely this reason, that in selected samples it is so much more difficult to close the circle. Those very brief linking passages must therefore answer all the unanswered and unanswerable questions (again, excepting the major one of the conclusion) which is often more than they can bear.

If you have more than one sample chapter, you might be forced to have a page with a linking paragraph between every pair of chapters. Frankly, I wouldn't, because it looks so amateurish. I'd rather start again from scratch.

THE PURPOSE-CREATED SAMPLE CHAPTER

In specially created sample chapter(s) you will not make the same mistakes about names and friction as in selected ones, and you can craft the sample very tightly to the purpose of closing the circle of motivation or argument, leaving no big questions unanswered. That does not mean the purpose-created sample chapter is without problems, simply that I consider them more easily handled by the author.

Tentative tone When you write the book, you write from conviction. In practice, the opening sections of most books or scripts are the parts most rewritten. The reason authors rewrite them is to get their tone of voice right; they then continue to the end in that tone of utter conviction. A sample chapter isn't a long enough document to get the tone of voice right and, even if it carries conviction from the weight of fact or exposition, it may still suffer from a tentative tone of voice. An uneven tone of voice has the same result: a shortfall of persuasive power.

The cure is really quite simple, and obvious from the reason for creating a sample from scratch. The tentative tone disappears if you write your sample as if it is all you will write, so that it is 'closed' in itself. You should think of it as a longish short story or article, less only its climax or major conclusion. This way you can include fully integrated references to all your major points of motivational development or argument, so that any reader will grasp the undiluted effect of your brilliance—everything that is, except the last and greatest denouement.

Of course you have to resign yourself to chucking this appealing piece of work when the book is commissioned, but that is a small price to pay for the saving in time and frustration—for greatly increasing the chances that your work will be commissioned. Unless you are unlucky, you will be able to use in the book itself many of the striking phrases this pressure-cooker style of sample chapter throws up. If for some reason the project is not commissioned at the full intended length, you can always write an ending and sell the sample as a short story or article.

MORE ON EXPLANATORY AND LINKING NOTES

In theory, and as often as possible in practice, your unadorned sample writing should speak for itself. In real life, as we have seen, linking and explanatory notes are often unavoidable.

Do please remember though that linking and explanatory notes are undesirable: they look unprofessional if there are too many or if they are too long, and in the ideal sample they would be entirely absent because the material would be closed in itself. It is hard work to avoid them but well worth the effort: the appearance of professionalism is far more important at the beginning of your career or during your first exchanges with a particular publisher than later when your track record will have earned some allowances.

Here are my own rules of thumb:

- Links on cover pages should not be longer than a short paragraph for *Before* and a short paragraph for *After*.
- Before and after links on cover pages should be separated by a teaser of a paragraph or a short run of dialogue extracted from the sample chapter or elsewhere in the manuscript.
- Explanatory notes should be no longer than one sentence, should be on cover pages rather than in the text if possible, and if in the text should be clearly distnguish-

able from the sample text itself.

- Where an explanatory note highlights a point that will appeal to non-editorial staff at the publishers, it should be repeated in the proposal or synopsis on the page where that chapter (or appendix or market) is mentioned, with a reference to the sample material.
- Other than as a highlight repeat, described immediately above, proposals and synopses should never need to include explanatory notes, and of course their covers are given over to summaries rather than linking notes.

Never, ever, say or imply that the sample isn't typical, or say the finished book will be better, or note that it is a tweaked and combined piece which you intend to split up again for the actual book. That sort of thing just confuses many publishing executives whose expertise relates to non-editorial areas. Your editor will know and, in the unlikely event that he mentions it, of course you will explain how you will divide the material for the real book.

FINAL WORD AND SUMMARY

Let's give the last word to David St John Thomas, a publisher who has seen proposals, synopses and sample chapters, not to mention complete books, from two generations of writers. He condenses all that experience into four simple, embracing points:

- The writer must prove the coherence of his book
- The organisation and order of material must be clear
- The sample must convince the publisher that the writer knows his subject in depth and can make it vibrate with real-life examples
- The writer must prove that he knows the market he writes for.

7

UTMOST GOOD FAITH
WHAT TO LOOK OUT FOR IN CONTRACTS

IT is a mistake for any writer to spend too much time worrying about contracts. This isn't just an outrageous statement, against the received wisdom of the trade, to get your attention. I made the same mistake. My first fiction publishers, Hyland House of Melbourne, allowed me to write my own contract; other writers and agents were astounded that anyone should get such an advantageous contract. Before that, for the publication of my juvenile poems and various monographs and theses, I had been too busy to read contracts and simply signed them after the family lawyer approved them. In neither instance have I been sorry, though in the Hyland case I might as well have agreed the terms on a handshake because in fifteen years there has never been a dispute—in a word, I wasted the time I spent swatting up on contracts in order to write that one.

According to an ex-agent and ex-publisher of mine, I have probably agreed more contracts with more publishers than 99.5% of writers are ever likely to sign; these agreements are with most of the major publishers and many of the smaller ones around the world. But I have yet personally to discover a publisher who is deliberately dishonest in any financial sense, and know of only one who as company policy paid deliberately slowly (which hardly qualifies as theft); publishers' delays and small lies of justification about other matters may be irritating but they are not actionable at law. In fact, it is generally accepted that the vast majority of publishers will bend over backwards to pay authors on time.

Even with half a dozen three-inch ringbinders bulging with contracts, I cannot think of a dozen times over the years when it was necessary to refer to the contracts.

More, on the two occasions on which I took on major publishers, the question in each case was resolved *outside* the publishing contract, on questions of principle decided by common or constitutional law. You have certain rights, guaranteed by the traditions of the form of government under which you live, that no publishing contract can take away from you.

Light relief Publishing contracts are in any event a farce—since the legal world is not renowned for its sense of humour, that really is saying something. The farcical element is easy to demonstrate.

The most draconian clause in any contract is the one that holds the author responsible for libel, with unlimited indemnity to the publisher for any sums a jury might award the injured party plus legal costs, usually for both parties. In theory the publisher, who will have to pay in the first instance, can bankrupt the offending author. In practice it is the poor author of small fame whose libels slip through and the publisher who pursues him will have to spend even more to recover nothing. The rich and important author's books are also important enough to be checked very carefully by the publisher's top libel expert, so in the one case where the publisher could conceivably extract restitution, almost always he has avoided the necessity at his own expense (the lawyer's fee).

Or take the matter of the publisher's option on the author's next book. There can be few authors who don't have some dud manuscript in a bottom drawer that they can show an insistent publisher to fulfil this requirement and so break the contract, should they wish to take their next good book elsewhere. I refuse to sign such an obvious lie: if a publisher messes up the marketing of my book, he will not be offered another opportunity regardless of what I may have been forced to sign. If he markets my book well, it is in my own interest to give him the next one; if he doesn't believe that when I tell him so, and insists on the clause, I go elsewhere.

The right attitude to contracts This book may seem at first glance to be aimed at helping you create proposals and synopses that persuade a publisher to give you a contract to write the book you want to write. That is a wrong conclusion. It is aimed at persuading a publisher to pay you while you write a *publishable* book, to help you avoid the labour and frustration of writing a book that no one wants. The end product should always be a published book. The contract is only a way station and, as I have demonstrated, one rather less important than new writers and professional legalists including agents are apt to assume. Of course the money paid on agreement of the contract is usually important either financially or as a boost to one's confidence!

Two reasons to pay attention to contracts However, especially when dealing with a publisher for the first time (or with an agent who has just sold his first book for you), it makes a professional impression to let it be known that you have read the contract and can make an intelligent contribution if necessary. I consider this quite as important as the second reason, which is that you may be able to negotiate an improvement in the *conditions* of the contract.

The conditions are different from the *terms* which refer to the financial arrangements. The conditions relate to all the other matters you agree which do not cover how much you will be paid and when. It is generally accepted that the author will try to negotiate better terms but publishers try to create an impression, in the first instance by printing their contracts up tidily, that everything else is carved in stone and the author should simply agree to it.

Agents have always rejected this sham. An agent might, and probably will, negotiate a better advance (but rarely a hugely better advance), and almost certainly a more advantageous share of the royalties and subsidiary rights income, and will ensure that you are paid some of these incomes beyond the royalties earlier than might otherwise be the case. But where agents really shine is in deleting conditions not to your advantage, or negotiating the inclusion of conditions very much to your advantage.

There is no reason you should not do the same in direct negotiation with a publisher. Whether you will succeed depends on the publisher, on your relationship with the publisher, on your seniority in our profession, on the book itself, and on your negotiating skills. And, of course, on your knowledge of what is negotiable and worth negotiating.

A MODEL CONTRACT

Various professional bodies for authors publish model contracts and author's annuals also carry lengthy clause by clause discussions. Rather than repeat such widely available examples, I include, at the end of this next chapter a simple, elegant yet comprehensive contract used as standard by one of the oldest publishing houses in the world. It is a contract I have in the past signed almost as it is printed. Anything more than contained in this standard contract simply adds layers of confusion.

Recently, when I entered into a long-term arrangement with this house for myself and many other authors who would be contributing books to a series of which I am general editor, I worked this contract over to reflect more closely my practice when dealing with the meganationals, with whom one has to be careful because you never know when some inevitable change in their management will put lawyers in control. This can have stressful consequences of interpretations that editors and authors never intended. Even a prestigious house (perhaps especially a prestigious house) may fall into the clutches of the financiers...

This particular contract has the added advantage that it follows closely the order of most other publishing contracts. To help you comprehend it more easily, I shall take it from the top, stopping only where a sensible author would take note and perhaps try to improve the printed version; that means that we cannot separate discussion of financial terms from that of the other conditions but the distinction should be clear to you by now. The numbers refer to the clauses.

Agreement Date, names of parties, addresses. Obviously! Also a tautological statement that the parties have agreed to this agreement. The other important point in this paragraph is that the contract is assignable, which means that either party may sell, give or bequeath his rights in the contract.

1. Description of work Name or at least a working title for the book. Sometimes the subject matter or genre. Length either in pages including illustrations or as a number of words.

If a proposal or synopsis is named, it should be a dated or otherwise clearly identifiable version. American contracts departments are more likely than not to want to attach a copy to the contract and make it part of the agreement.

If delivery is to be on disk, you should ask for a keying payment which need not appear on the contract but can be confirmed in a separate letter.

2. Delivery date If you fail to deliver, the publisher may recover the advance.

Some contracts have wording either here or in the payments clause to the effect that the manuscript must be acceptable to the publisher in style and content. This is unenforcable nonsense; if the publisher did not believe you could write a book he would accept, he should not have contracted to publish it once written. Generally speaking, if you deliver a publishable book, the publisher cannot wriggle out just because the market has moved on or his own taste has changed or even because he made a mistake. But if a detailed proposal is part of the contract, he may try to renege by claiming the author has delivered a book that does not meet the synopsis in full. I regret having to report that such attempts are, according to New York agents, on the increase; no cases have been reported in London as I write. If you fear this happening to you, you should insert a clause (preferably drafted by a lawyer or someone at the national author's society you either belong to or that your local branch is affiliated to) to the effect that in case the publisher feels the manuscript does not follow the synopsis, he should advise you in detail of deviation and allow you an agreed time to bring it into line.

3. Payment for copyright material and indexing Who pays for illustrations and quotations. I always alter this to make the publisher pay either for agreed illustrations and quotations or at least up to a certain amount. It is far easier for a publisher to handle copyright requests to the owners of the copyrights (often other publishers), so I normally ask them to take care of that as well, especially if they will be paying.

In my sort of work, I prepare my own indeces, but it is easy to conceive of an author, of a huge encyclopedia for instance, who will want his publishers to pay for professional indexing or at least to share the cost. Indexing can be expensive, so be certain to return an index with the page proofs!

If you create your own illustrations (including photographs) you should make it clear either here or in my inserted clause 5A that the copyright in the illustrations is to be credited to you. (There are variant interpretations around the world but you should be aware that in some jurisdictions, while your copyright in written work will – except in a very small number of cases – certainly belong to you however many times you accept money for it, illustrations are often considered work-for-hire in which the copyright passes to whoever makes one payment for it; the remedy is to claim the copyright for the illustrations as well as the text.)

4. Correcting proofs You must. Turn in a clean typescript and you will not be tempted to make expensive alterations.

5. Indemnity You warrant that the book is your own work. You assume responsibility for libel. You cannot negotiate this clause except for the point about having been published before in the territories granted, which must be altered when you are selling reprint rights, but which does not enter into consideration for commissioned books which are by definition never published before.

5A. Copyright registration This is a clause not printed in this British contract but always found in American contracts. It contains wording to the effect that the publisher at his own expense will where required register your copyright with all the appropriate authorities in all the territories to which you grant rights, will make the same clause a condition of any sub-licenses he grants, and will furthermore at his own expense act to protect and preserve the copyrights granted under the license. Any . income raised by such action should be split 50/50.

6. Publication Alter this clause to set a maximum time limit between delivery and publication: eighteen months is ample. If the publisher does not publish within that time without some good reason, the rights revert to you, you keep the advance, and you can sell the book again.

7. License to publish in English and territory If you can you should limit the assignment of the copyright to the publisher to a period not exceeding seven years. Five years is better. If the book is so successful that he wants to make a new arrangement with you after that period, then you can cut a new deal. Otherwise the copyright automatically reverts to you.

If the territory for the English language volume rights is not worldwide, there should be a schedule to specify the territory granted country by country—*not* some vague phrase like 'the traditional British Market'.

8. Payments in advance, royalties In educational books a fixed fee per edition or impression is relatively common. The better publishers, such as the one whose contract we are considering, top it up with a royalty on any 'trade' copies sold after a certain number; 'trade' is merely jargon for general book shops as opposed to educational institutions and their satellite bookshops.

General authors get an advance against royalties. The royalties, which are calculated either on the book's recommended retail selling price or the amount actually received by the publisher, may escalate after a certain number of copies have been sold; you should certainly try to negotiate an escalation. If the publisher sells the books at more than a certain discount, the royalty rate will be lower.

There may also be provision for a lower royalty rate for small reprints. If it is not stated in the contract, a publisher may later telephone to ask if you will accept a lower royalty because that is the only way he can reprint some small run like 2000 copies just to keep the book in print. I always agree. (If you are agreeable about such matters, you will find publishers agreeable when you ask them for alterations in the terms of a standing contract. For instance, sometimes I want to give chums of mine on the other side of the world minor rights which they cannot afford to buy from the big boys. No publisher has ever refused the request.)

The advance against royalties is usually paid in three parts, on signature of agreement, delivery (or approval) of the manuscript, and on publication. If you have more than one book to your name already, or if you are in a strong bargaining position, you should try to have the advance split between signature and delivery. If there is a payment due on approval rather than delivery, you should include wording to the effect that within six weeks of delivery of the typescript or any alterations to it the publisher must advise you of acceptance, rejection, or his requirements for alterations. The purpose is to avoid the possibility that he delays acceptance simply to keep the money earning interest in his own account. If a payment is due on publication, you should alter the wording to read 'on publication or twelve months after delivery, whichever comes first'.

An advance against royalties is precisely what it says, an advance. It is a loan, in most cases non-returnable (and you should resist attempts to make it returnable except for non-delivery of a publishable book), and must be earned by copies sold before you receive additional royalties.

The payments clause is also where I enter the wording for any rollover I have negotiated in lieu of giving a publisher an option. A rollover is a new book or books automatically commissioned upon delivery of the contracted book. The additional wording should be to the effect that the publisher shall within six weeks of the delivery of the work agree with the author which book (in the series, from your proposals on file with them, to their own idea—whatever is suitable to your relationship with the particular publisher) they wish to commission from him next on terms at least as favourable as in the present agreement.

9, 10, 11 12. Export sales and subsidiary rights These are in most cases also part of the license to the publisher, though in some cases agents handle book club and, more often, translation sales. Income is divided between the author and the publisher in any proportion from 50/50 to what you can negotiate, usually 70% for established authors. I don't waste time on trying to negotiate my cut of the anthology and quotation income because it is mickey mouse money but insist on 70-85% of the translation income because that can make a substantial difference. You should add wording to the effect that income from subsidiary rights should be paid to you on receipt by the publisher. Otherwise such income might be held over and accounted for in the next royalty statement, which can be six months or a year away.

If the printed contract claims film and broadcast rights for the publisher, ask after their track record in selling these; if they have none, scratch the assignment.

12A. Other rights You should, if the contract does not include it as our example does not, add a clause to the effect that all rights not specifically licensed to the publisher, and all rights still to come into existence, are reserved to the author.

13. Author's copies You should receive 12 free copies of the first edition and six of each subsequent edition. Trade price, at which you can buy further copies, is normally a discount on the published price of 35—50%.

14. Accounts The publisher should account to you, and pay you for, income on the books at least twice in the first year and thereafter at least once and preferably twice a year. Some agents like adding to this clause wording to the effect that sums over a certain amount should be paid within a fortnight or a month of accruing but I believe that contingency is adequately covered in the clause about subsidiary rights income being paid promptly. To ask for royalties to be paid more often than the regular interval of twice a year simply causes work and resentment in the accounts department.

15. Revision You undertake to keep the work up to date without charge. Unless you have large unearned advances outstanding,

112

this is always to your benefit because the publisher cannot have the book revised without issuing a new edition, which will earn you royalties as it sells.

16. Remaindering The average life of a book is now months rather than years; only the very best books, a small part of one percent of all books published, survive to become fixtures on bookshop shelves. But your book must have time to establish itself. You can't permit your publisher to panic and sell off all stock at a risible price. The standard contract illustrated generously offers 18 months before overstocks can be remaindered. But this firm is in the business of standard text and craft books at the profitable (read 'expensive') end of a market they know very well indeed.

If you have to add such a clause, or renegotiate an unrealistically short period in a standing clause, you should probably aim for a minimum of six months.

In Britain remaindering means that the publisher allows the trade to sell the book below the so-called Net Price, which is the Recommended Retail Price. In the States, where resale price maintenance is illegal (as it is in Britain for almost everything except books though it is notoriously practiced illegally in new car sales), remaindering means giving such a discount on the jacket price that the book can be sold on bargain tables for a small fraction of the jacket price. In an American contract you should therefore state both the period and the maximum discount the publisher is limited to during that period, say 60-65%. I should tell you that only the most powerful agents and authors are permitted in this way to limit the power of American publishers to behave like bulls in china shops; in New York don't break your deal on this clause.

The point about being able to buy your books at the remainder price is important; add it if absent. I know one author who for twenty years has made a good living selling first his own remaindered book and then reprints of it he ordered to fulfill demand! At the very least you must have copies to offer to potential new publishers.

17, 18, 19. Reversion If the publisher allows your book to remain out of print after a request to reprint, the rights revert automatically. Scratch from this clause any reference to circumstances beyond their control—in the global village they can order copies from where the printers aren't on strike, or where there isn't a war. Scratch also reference to being 'in the course of production for a reissue' which can continue indefinitely and should not last longer than the six months of grace already permitted by this clause. Do not agree to any clause claiming grace for longer than nine months.

You also recover the rights if the publisher goes bankrupt. If either of these important clauses are missing, add the wording (as amended) from the example.

20. Competing works It is reasonable that you should not sell the same work in different form to another publisher but anything else you might write on the subject could be taken by literal-minded lawyers to 'prejudicially affect the sales of the Work'. To tell you the truth, I don't even bother scratching this bit of nonsense. Let them prove it! Of course it will never come to that: if the publisher is competent and pays on time, he will be offered my next book in the same line, and if he is not, who cares that he will scream ineffectually, or waste money on lawyers, because I have gone to his competitors?

21. Option on next book This is an unenforcable crock. I refuse to sign it on principle (why tell lies which benefit no one?) but you can if you like without doing your career as a writer any damage. Or you could use it as a lever to get an automatic rollover, which is precisely what I have done many times.

21A. Jurisdiction The sample contract does not say in which country's courts a dispute will be adjudicated. (The assumption is that a contract drawn in London will be referred to a British court.) Sometimes it is explicitly stated that a dispute under a British contract will be referred to a British court; American contracts almost always indicate a State jurisdiction.

A lawyer friend assures me that there are nuances: that a Scottish or Californian courtroom is a friendlier place to a writer than one in England or New York. If you earn very big money from your writing and you are in addition litigious, you may want to add or change such a clause because one or another jurisdiction may offer you some benefit; but such a writer will already have a competent lawyer and does not need my advice. I am perfectly happy with British, American and Australian commercial and civil justice.

If you live in some other part of the world, you may wish to negotiate with the publisher in which jurisdiction a dispute will be settled, either because it is more stable than the country you live in, or because you understand the customs or perhaps the language better. Any serious publisher will be happy to accommodate you.

And that's all there is to contracts, except for the signatures. No mystery, no mystique, no jargon, no bull. If they cannot explain a clause to you in comprehensible English, scratch it before you sign.

Good luck!

MEMORANDUM OF AGREEMENT

made this .... day of .... 19 ....

BETWEEN ....

of ....

....

(hereinafter called the Author) of the One Part and the Company of NAME OF PUBLISHER of ADDRESS (hereinafter called the Publishers) of the Other Part for themselves and their executors administrators assigns and successors (as the case may be) whereby it is mutually agreed as follows:

1. The Author agrees to write a work provisionally entitled   **Work**

....

(hereinafter referred to as the Work), which shall consist of approximately .... words, including all captions, notes and ancillary material, ... black-and-white photographs, ... colour photographs and .... line illustrations.

....

....

2. The Author undertakes to deliver two (2) copies of the work   **Delivery** (prepared in accordance with the publishers' *Notes for Authors and their Typists*), together with the photographs and line illustrations, to the Publishers by the

.... day of .... 19 ....

The Publishers shall insure illustrations while in their custody or in the course of production up to the value one thousand five hundred pounds (£1500). Should the Author fail to deliver the typescript and illustrations by the prescribed date the publishers may if they think fit decline to publish the Work, in which case the Agreement will be subject to cancellation by the Publisher and any moneys paid shall be returned. If in the opinion of the Publishers any extra editorial work is necessary before the work is ready for the printer and the Author is unable or unwilling to undertake the necessary work promptly, or to arrange for it to be done promptly, then the Publishers shall be at liberty to employ a competent editor to do the work and any reasonable fees paid to such an editor shall be deductible from the sums payable to the Author under this Agreement. If in the opinion of the Publishers any pages of the copy are unclear or unsuitable for the printer the Publishers shall be entitled to have those pages typed or legibly copied and to charge the cost of such typing or copying to the Author.

3. The Author shall at his/her own expense obtain from the owners of any material in the Work including quotations, photographs, line drawings or maps of which the copyright is not his/her own, written permission for the use of such material. **Illustrations Quotations**

4. An index shall be supplied by the author at the Author's expense and sent to the Publishers at the same time as the corrected page proofs. **Index**

5. The Author agrees to correct the proofs of the Work with all reasonable promptitude, to see the Work carefully through each stage of production and to bear all costs of corrections and alterations made by him/her (printer's errors excepted) exceeding ten per cent (10%) of the cost of typesetting. The Publishers shall be at liberty to set off all costs against any sums which may be due to the Author. **Proof Corrections**

6. The Author hereby warrants that the Work is an original work, has not been published in volume form within the territories covered by this Agreement and is not in any way a **Indemnity**

117

violation of any existing copyright, that it contains nothing libellous or defamatory, that all statements contained therein
purporting to be facts are to the best of the Author's knowledge
and belief true, that the Author has full power to make this
Agreement and will indemnify the Publishers against any loss
injury or damage (including any legal costs or expenses and
any compensation costs and disbursements paid by the
Publishers to compromise or settle any claim) occasioned to
the Publishers in consequence of any breach of this warranty
or arising out of any claim alleging that the Work constitutes an
infringement of copyright or contains libellous or defamatory
matter. The Author further warrants that the Work contains no
obscene or indecent material.

7. The Publishers shall, unless prevented by war, strikes, lock- **Publication**
outs or other circumstances beyond the Publishers' control,
produce and publish the Work at their own risk and expense
with reasonable promptitude. The Publishers shall have control of the entire publication. Paper, printing, binding, jacket
and embellishments, the manner and extent of promotion and
advertising, the number and distribution of free copies for the
Press or otherwise, and the price and terms of sale of the first
or any subsequent edition or impression shall be at their dis-
cretion.

8. The Author being the sole owner of the copyright of the **Assignment**
Work grants to the Publisher during the term of unrestricted **of Copyright**
copyright the exclusive right to print and publish the Work in
book form throughout the world subject only to the provisions
of Clauses 9–13.

9. In consideration of the rights and privileges accorded to the **Payment**
Publishers under this Agreement the Publishers agree to
make the following payments to the Author:

For the first and any subsequent impressions a fee of ....

pounds (£   ) payable ....

which shall cover all copies of each printing, irrespective of markets into which the copies are sold.

A royalty of .... (%) shall be additionally payable on the trade edition after the sale of ....
(   ) copies of the Publisher's edition; the royalty shall be calculated on the published price on all copies sold at a discount of less than fifty per cent (50%); on copies sold at a discount of fifty per cent (50%) or over, the royalty shall be calculated on the Publishers' receipts.

9. In consideration of the rights and privileges accorded to the Publishers under this Agreement the Publishers agree to make the following payments to the Author:

Payment

On the first impression an advance of ....

.... pounds (£   ) payable ....

....

....

.... against a royalty of ....

....;

The royalty shall be calculated on the published price on all copies sold at a discount of less than fifty per cent (50%); on all copies sold at a discount of fifty per cent (50%) or over, the royalty shall be calculated on the Publishers' receipts.

On the second and subsequent impressions the royalty shall be .... (%).

10. On copies produced by the Publishers for bulk sale to an overseas publisher or overseas book club (e.g. in the United States of America, Canada, Australia, New Zealand) and sold at a price inclusive of royalty, the Author shall receive

Overseas
Bulk Sales

.... per cent (%) of the Publishers' receipts unless such copies be the subject of Clause 9. Should such copies be sold at a price exclusive of royalty, the royalty shall be divided in the proportion of sixty per cent (60%) to the Author and forty per cent (40%) to the Publishers.

11. On copies produced by the Publishers and sold to a book club in the United Kingdom at a price inclusive of royalty the Author shall receive.. per cent (%) of the Publishers' receipts unless such copies be the subject of Clause 9. On copies sold at a price exclusive of royalty the royalty shall be divided as in Clause 10.

Book Clubs

12. The Author and Publishers shall mutually control all paperback rights in the Work and shall divide the royalties received in the proportion of fifty per cent (50%) to the Author and fifty per cent (50%) to the Publishers.

Paperback

On all copies sold of a paperback edition produced by the Publishers themselves the Publishers shall pay to the Author a royalty of.. per cent (%) of the published price on all copies sold at a discount of less than fifty per cent (50%); on all copies sold at a discount of fifty per cent (50%) or over the royalty shall be.. per cent (%) of the Publishers' receipts.

13. The Publishers shall control all translation and reprint rights (including separate manufacture and publication outside the United Kingdom) in the Work, the receipts from which shall be divided in the proportion of sixty per cent (60%) to the Author and forty per cent (40%) to the Publishers. The Publishers shall also control all digest, serial, one-shot periodical,quotation, dramatic, film, microfilm, anthology, radio, television, audio and video recording rights in the Work and shall divide the net proceeds with the Author in the proportion of fifty per cent (50%) to the Author and fifty per cent (50%) to the Publishers.

Subsidiary Rights

120

14. The Author shall be entitled to six (6) free copies of the first and two (2) free copies of any subsequent impression of the Work on the day of publication and to buy further copies at trade price. The Author shall be entitled to buy, at trade price, copies of any other books in the Publishers' list. **Author's Copies**

15. The Publishers shall render the first two accounts of the Work as at 30 June and 31 December next following the date of publication and subsequently annually as at 31 December. All moneys due to the Author shall be paid within three (3) months of the said accountancy dates except that no account need be rendered, unless specially demanded, nor payment made in respect of any period in which the sum due is less than twenty-five pounds (£25), in which case the amount will be carried forward to the next accountancy date. **Accounting**

16. In order to keep the work up to date the Author shall, if called upon by the Publishers, without charge to the Publishers edit and revise all editions of the Work during the currency of this Agreement and shall supply any new matter that may be required. In the event of the Author neglecting or being unable by reason of death or otherwise to edit or revise the Work or to supply new matter the Publisher may procure some other person to edit or revise the Work, or supply new matter, and may deduct the expense thereof from all sums payable to the Author under this Agreement. **Revision**

17. Should the Publishers at any time allow the Work to go out of print or off the market and being given six (6) calendar months' notice in writing by the Author fail to re-issue or reprint and put on the market (unless prevented by circumstances beyond their control or because the Work at that date is under revision or in the course of reproduction for re-issue) an edition of the Work, then all rights granted by the Author in respect of the Work shall revert to him/her. **Reversion**

18. The publishers shall, not less than twelve (12) months after publication, be entitled to sell surplus stock at the best price such stock will fetch. The Author shall be offered the **Overstocks**

121

right to purchase such stock at the estimated sale price; if the average price achieved within the royalty accounting period proves to be lower, the Author shall be entitled to an appropriate refund.

19. Should the Publishers go into liquidation other than voluntary liquidation this Agreement shall thereupon terminate and the Author shall be free to license any other person to print and publish the work, notwithstanding anything to the contrary contained or implied in any part of this Agreement. **Relicensing**

20. The Author shall not, without the written consent of the Publishers, publish or cause to be published any abridgement or expansion or part of the Work in serial or book form, nor shall the Author prepare otherwise than for the publishers any material which shall effect prejudicially the sales of the Work. **Completing Works**

21. The Author agrees to give the publishers first option on the publication of his/her next full-length work. **Option**

IN WITNESS WHEREOF the Parties hereunder set their hands the day and the year first above written.

By or on behalf of the Author   Witnessed by ....

....   Address ....

....

....   Occupation ....

For and on behalf of the Publishers   Witnessed by ....

....   Address ....

....

....   Occupation ....

8
HOW TO DO IT
EXAMPLES FOR ALL PURPOSES

In all the examples the dates, contact addresses and telephone numbers have been removed. Remember to add them to your own proposals, synopses and sample chapters!

Non-fiction examples start on page 124.
Fiction examples start on page 140.
Film, television and radio examples start on page 177.

NON-FICTION

We'll start with the proposal for this book. You will be able to see for yourself how the proposal matches the finished book.

Writing Book Proposals and Synopses that Sell
by André Jute

About 70,000 words. The tone will be personal, from-me-to-you, as in the rest of my books for writers. Here is some of what I shall put in the chapters; snappier titles for the chapters will be worked out on hand of the final content. If I seem to have missed anything important, let me know and I will include it.

1. Who is this book for and how can it benefit you? Two classes of writers:

a) New writers who cannot get their complete ms read by editors and are often required to send sample chapters and a synopsis; all the yearbooks and the best how-to books for writers now advise the inclusion of a synopsis even when the full ms is also sent. Many writers (including a surprising number of experienced ones) believe naively that this synopsis is similar to those written in literary appreciation classes—it is not: it is a sales tool and should be so approached.

b) Established writers who can have books commissioned at a point when little or nothing of the book is written. These writers' skills of writing narrative or expository prose are a hindrance rather than a help when it comes to writing what is in effect a sales presentation that must persuade not only literary or semi-academic types but also sales, marketing and promotional staff.

Brief note on using the book intelligently and innovatively rather than slavishly.

2. Who counts in Babel? A brief history of recent publishing, explaining why it is a business and demonstrating that the type of person in editorial positions is changing. What do these editors and publishers want? Who else in the publishing house is influential? (In the last year alone, one book of mine depended on the acceptance of the production manager, and another on the approval of the design manager; and at another house my most dependable partisan is the director of publicity.) How is their time allocated? Their performance judged and rewarded? Why should this matter to an author?

3. Samples of good synopses. Samples in several fields including at least one for a novel, one for prose non-fiction, one for illustrated non-fiction, and definitely one for a how-to book (for some reason a very common failure). If space permits, bad examples as well, probably in a separate chapter.

4. What *your* proposal/synopsis *must* do. Purpose of synopses. Selecting the keys that will open doors. Relevant personal experience. The most concentrated document you will ever write. Churchill's 'a single side of a sheet of paper'. A full circle of motivation is essential. The problem of apparent completeness in a tight space. The key of memorability. Mnemonic hooks for committee members. The problem of saying more than you need to. How the over-detailed proposal or synopsis will later kill the quality of your writing. (This chapter may have to be split into two parts to keep it short.)

5. The style of your proposal and synopsis. Future tense and active voice: 'Will.' Synonyms for 'show'. The soberly extravagant promise.

6. Order and layout. The purpose of illustrative examples, the purpose of pictures. Placement. The advantage of chapter chronology for minimal proposals. The trick of demonstrating the shape of your book by a list of its illustrations. The element of surprise. Mechanicals (length, etc). The mistake of using too fine a paper, printing, etc: concentrate on content rather than flashy context.

7. Selecting or writing your sample chapters. The catch-22 of 'we know what you want to say but not how you will say it.' The purpose of the sample. How to match purpose to available material. The problems of a selected sample; how to doctor them temporarily, keeping a master copy. The 'tentative tone' of purpose-created sample chapters. The cure (write them as if they are all you will write, so that they are 'closed' in themselves, and resign yourself to ditching them completely when the book is commissioned). Undesirability of introductory and linking notes to samples.

8. Putting your proposal/synopsis in the right hands. Selecting your publisher. The problems of the new multi-national, multi-glomerate publishers for the writer. (Recently a proposal of which I sent six copies to Longman divisions was not forwarded to the correct division by five of them. Of the five executives responsible, four did not know of the existence of the correct division!) Their internal communications failures. The specialisation of various editors, the problems of discovering the name of the right one. The telephone. The letter of introduction and inquiry. Building a relationship with an editor.

9. Contract and latitude. The undesirability of having the proposal included in the contract with a certain class of publisher. The amount of deviation generally accepted; when the writer must advise his publisher of changes, when he must ask permission.

To ease you into the rhythm of proposals, here is another one, for a set of three handbooks for writers, of which two, Start Writing Today! *and* Keep on Writing! *have been published. The titles were changed because the sales department thought the title of the first one carried sexual overtones. Note the 'Quick Guide to This Proposal' on the* first *page.*

A proposal by André Jute

This is a proposal for three books, which together will offer the creative writer comprehensive guidance at each stage of his or her career.

CREATIVE URGES: Essential Foundations for the Writer will guide the absolute beginner by steps to his/her first complete novel and finding a publisher.

GROWING TALENTS: Skill Development for the Writer will help the writer who has a book or two finished, the serious amateur and the semi-professional, to improve his/her work and to market it on a continuous basis.

COUNSELS OF PERFECTION: Advanced Strategies for the Writer will provide a professional basis for a writer's work and his/her relations with the publishing world and its multitudinous ancillaries.

A QUICK GUIDE TO THIS PROPOSAL
General Description
Outlines for
CREATIVE URGES: Essential Foundations for the Writer
GROWING TALENTS: Skill Development for the Writer
COUNSELS OF PERFECTION: Advanced Strategies for the Writer
Samples
Draft sample text: INTRODUCTION to CREATIVE URGES
Writing a Thriller —a copy of an earlier book for writers

General Description of Set

Each of the books will be about 50,000 words.

The layout and progression of subject level will make them suitable for use in creative-writing classes. The style will be informal and anecdotal where suitable. These books are intended to be read right through at once, with some pleasure, and then kept beside the writer for reference, each in its turn as he progresses in our profession. Each will have a bibliography. Detailed indexes will be included.

I am suggesting three modest books because one monster volume is too clumsy to handle and keep beside one's typewriter; in addition, writers at different stages of their careers ask completely different questions about the same subjects, finally, three separate books will be not only easier to digest because more immediately relevant but more affordable than one over-thick volume.

A suggested skeleton outline by subject matter for each book follows to demonstrate the shifting emphasis and intensifying levels of engagement of the three books as they answer to the needs of the writer at different stages in his career. (A comparative listing showing how the various chapters in the different books meet the writer's needs over the span of his development is available on request). I am of course open to suggestion on including other necessary subjects, or moving sections about if it will make a stronger or better balanced book or set.

To demonstrate the intended style and the method of expanding from the outline, both of course open to suggestion and alteration, draft text is included for the Introduction to the first book.

A copy of an earlier book for a special class of writers, *Writing a Thriller*, is also included. Besides dipping passim, the chapter on Character, p24, and the chapter on Writers' Blocks, p70, might repay perusal, though in the proposed books the treatment will have a somewhat different basis and will of course be much more thorough.

Volume 1: CREATIVE URGES
Essential Foundations for the Writer

Introduction
Whom this book is for. Can *you* be a published writer? The philosophy behind this book. The writer as professional. Importance of perseverance. Limits of approach. How to use this book.

1. Reader, Writer, Market, Reader: Novel, Genre and Creative Non-Fiction
Hobby or apprenticeship for future profession? The writer as a reader; reading influences the writer. Choice of subject matter not free; constraints imposed by marketing channels and editorial preoccupations. Your choice of genre and level. Why your choice should extend your present skills. Politics and commitment — barrier or opportunity? The women's market. The maverick. The multimedia society.

2. Intimate Relations: Theme, Concept, Plot and Character
Why it is an error to separate these except notionally; how they relate; why Character must enjoy primacy and how to ensure that it does. The problem of breaking down your initial insight into digestible pieces. The importance of writing everything down. How to avoid being confused by the fecundity of your own mind — keeping control of the threads.

3. Transmuting Reality: Discovering Your Plot and Characters
Sources of themes within and without the writer. Building on perceived reality. Universal plots and unique characters. Too-popular plots. Problems of libel, hidden censorship, the received wisdom of publishers, changing public standards and taste in relation to violence, sex and obscenity.

4. Constructing a Detailed Outline
Techniques for controlling and channelling imaginative insights into a large-scale long-term project. Structure as creative tool. Theme and concept via event into plot. Character-generated

plot. How the writer develops, then keeps control of the elements of his story. Construction methods and plotting tools that work for various media. Formal formats and academic mirages. Beginnings and endings. Check for the primacy of character even at this stage. Plot as potential framework for tension; actual tension achieved in writing by reader identification with character. Mechanics of tension: hooks, starts, etc. The ending. The Ernest Hemingway/John Braine method described; its advantages and disadvantages.

5. Creating Living Characters
Sources of characters. Creating a character from scratch. Vital alterations to those taken from life (libel again!). Care required because plot flows from character (several examples should be given here rather than just one as elsewhere). Creating living characters. Character names. Naming minor characters. Character v. pace. Compound characters. Dull characters. Baddies. Runaway characters. How do you know when your characters are over the top? 99% of writers' problems originate in their fictional characters: solutions to character problems.

6. Cutting and Rewriting
When, what, why, where, how. Recognising the essentials of your work; detailed techniques for removing superfluities. Seamlessness versus the episodic narrative. Too much "establishing" explanation. Why rearranging material suggests cuts. Problems with pace. Recognising the permitted luxury. Style not as something learnt but what is left after the excess baggage has been jettisoned.

7. Research
How not to let research take over your life. When, why and how to research. What to research. How much detail is required? How to use research. No-noes. How to let others do it for you. Identifying under-researched writing and rectifying the problem. Getting your research done free of charge. Getting free trips. The 5% of essential facts and the single telling detail that establishes the writer's authority. Impressing specialist knowledge without intrusion; fudging unknowns. Settings you

have not visited and other dangers. Recognising the over-researched book — refer back to chapter on cutting and rewriting. Hazards of having a technofreak editor.

8. A Writer's Day and Difficulties
Routines, techniques and shortcuts to actually finishing a novel. Blocks identified, classified and described; detailed methods for avoiding or overcoming each block, with a description of its probable causes. Which blocks are genuine and which result from bad work practices and are therefore avoidable. Protecting an artist's sensibilities in a commercial environment. Importance of routine, a room of one's own, thinking time.

9. Discovering and Cultivating Your Editor
Finding professional help before you approach a publisher. On agents, editors and publishers, finding and keeping them. The agent and the unpublished writer. Selecting your publisher. The ms and the synopsis. Building a relationship with a publisher over several unpublished books. Also a brief (3pp) introduction to the bare essentials of contracts and subsidiary rights.

Bibliography
A very few recommended books.

Index

*No need to go into the second and third books of this set—you have the idea! When the second of the books proposed in the example was due for publication, I supplied the jacket copy that follows. The jacket blurb is exactly the same as was **supplied with the ms as a summary**. Note how suggestions to the editor and designer are distinguished from the text to be reproduced by square brackets.*

[[[DUST-JACKET FRONT-FLAP BLURB]]]

KEEP ON WRITING!
From Creative Writer to Professional Writer
André Jute

You can be a professional writer but only if you have the right attitude. André Jute, who has written nearly thirty books issued in over a hundred editions, comprehensively surveys and explains those elements of attitude, technique and presentation that build into the image of a talented professional writer which inspires publishers to pay special attention to your manuscripts and to offer you commissions for as yet unwritten work.

He progresses naturally from your ideal reader (a person much like yourself) to the characteristics publishers wish to see in writers they take on for the long haul. An entire chapter is devoted to the sources of new themes and ideas for professional writers, the use of the serial theme or character, and the concept of ensuring your future as a writer by aiming for the very top of the profession. New ideas are so important for the constant writer that plotting techniques are also thoroughly covered from the most basic to the most advanced.

The heart of this helpful and supportive book for all levels of serious creative writers is the long chapters on creating and developing characters, and on the essential art and craft of cutting and rewriting. Here those critical creative and technical problems are canvassed that every writer must overcome if he is to survive in the profession.

The experienced writer turns his blocks to advantage and André shows how this is done, and how the writer can develop his own personality to do better work and more of it.

Many are called. By identifying and demystifying the essential steps that lead from occasional writing to earning a full-time living, André Jute helps you become one of the chosen.

In proposing a non-fiction book, you should normally begin by pointing to the market you intend to reach. Notice how I start off—bang!—with a new market publishers are likely to be aware of, the desktop publishing market, even though it will soon become clear that it is not my main aim. This particular proposal for a forty-three book series was commissioned by Batsford with me as general editor.

a proposal for a series
Graphic Design in the Computer Age
André Jute

The set of books in this proposal is aimed at professional designers as well as that large group of pseudo-designers created by the desktop publishing and presentation capabilities of the personal computer who are keenly aware that they need to inform themselves of the first principles of design. The education market is not a primary target but most of the books will be suitable for use in colleges, which may provide a profitable secondary market. The books in the basic set will also attract laymen.

The phrase 'in the computer age' in the series title has a double meaning: it can mean 'with the aid of computers' or it can mean, and it probably does so mean to the majority of designers, nothing more than 'modern'. I intend the second meaning: modern design, to which the computer is a handy aid as long as one remembers that command of design principles combined with vision and talent is always more important than any tool. The viewpoint throughout will be from the creative rather than the technical perspective.

The series is structured to build into a standard library on all aspects of graphic design so that the designer with one of our books who wants a refresher or update or greater depth on some specialised subject can with confidence buy another volume.

But computers are going to be important, aren't they?
Pundits predict that within three years over eighty percent of

133

graphic design will be done on computers and that over sixty percent of designers will do all their work on the computer. Some of their supporting statistics are more convincing than others. Three items in particular strike me as valid:

The first is an economic argument. The state-of-the-art graphics design machinery in 1991 will be the NeXTstationColor with a street price well under £5000 including a double-page colour screen. Apple's LC, including colour screen, brings high-level design abilities to anyone with £1500 (RRP — less at the discounters). Even at the higher prices, electronics need make existing designers only marginally more productive to present an unanswerable case for buying the equipment rather than putting on more staff.

The second argument is educational. It is already difficult to find a design school without computers. At these prices, the computer will very shortly become the tool of choice for students and new graduates (in fact, we can already hear complaints that the new kids don't know how to use a Rotring and a scalpel). Your new professional will take a computerised workplace for granted and design shops that want to attract the best and the brightest will offer them what they expect.

Finally, design is an intensely competitive business. The main advantage of electronics is again economic: that the designer can do so many things which before were either impossible or too expensive for all but a handful of the best-heeled clients. It is likely that more and more specialist functions now concentrated at the blockmakers and other ancillary services will be brought into the design shop itself. Even if they are not, designers will require far more expertise in design areas hitherto handled by experts to instruct the satellite bureaux to do what they want.

In sum, while the computer will make many jobs easier, quicker, or cheaper, designers who wish to survive its arrival and probable hegemony will in fact require higher levels of expertise over a wider area of the first principles of graphics, design and production than is currently the case. That is our opportunity.

Where current design books fall flat

There are three kinds of current design books:

a) Desktop Publishing Books: those of a general nature assume the reader is a design-idiot. In most instances they are right. The median user of these books has no design training and has been catapulted by the computer into performing design functions that were previously undertaken by experts. However, he is usually well-educated and accomplished in some other field and resents being patronised by ex-printers and longhaired paste-up artists. He is also habituated to expanding his horizons through self-education by books. More specialised DTP books assume that the reader looks to the book in his hand for a commonsense tutorial on the software he will use to apply pre-existing design skills—good examples are the books by McClelland and Danuloff on the computer drawing program Illustrator. Both classes fall into the 'gee-isn't-the-computer-wonderful' trap. All are found on computer book shelves rather than on art and design shelves, despite the fact that on any Saturday morning you can start a computer club before the design shelves in Waterstone's. (Specialist bookstores, either for designers or computer people, are not a good test. If a designer can't find a book where he expects it in Foyle's or Waterstone's, there is something wrong with its marketing. In any case, you won't find real designers in computer bookstores.)

b) Nuts-and-bolts books, the kind that pretend to show you how to use a guillotine. (My contempt isn't for the genre itself but for its misuse as a tool to communicate with graphic designers.)

c) Books of first principles applied, the better ones showing design in action so the designer learns by example. The very best of these are essentially sourcebooks with structured analysis of the creation of graphic designs. What's wrong with those on the shelves or forthcoming is that they treat the computer as something distinct, often in a separate, tacked-on chapter. Good though many of these books are, they will not survive because their authors have the wrong attitude which will make them seem old-fashioned in a year or two. Objectively, they also have the problem that those new procedures made possible by the computer are treated as optional add-ons to the graphic designer's armoury whereas in reality they are already necessary commonplaces at all levels of design. (This is why our books will take the computer for granted as a tool the designer may choose to execute the ideas we're illustrating.) Furthermore, many books ignore the real-world fact that much graphic design must work across many different media, a problem that makes them seem irrelevant even without considering computers. But with the arrival of the so-called multimedia applications which put the designer at his desk in charge of what goes out on video for the price of a heavy-duty photocopier (rather than some engineer in control of a king's ransom of machinery), hitherto esoteric cross-media pollinations will be important all the way down to junior designers.

Are these then going to be 'computer design books'?
No. They will be what I have above called 'Books of First Principles Applied'. The difference is that they will take the computer for granted, and therefore go that extra step so that they will be useful to all designers, including those whose work must be adapted across many media. They will be useful to the designer who resists a computer on his own desk as much as to the computer enthusiast, precisely because they will be *design* books.

It would be a desirable triumph of marketing to sell these books into the specialist computer bookstores—and some are aimed specifically at making that possible as can be seen in the listing of possible titles—because I think there is a big market of people hungry for proper design principles out there; these people think of themselves as graphic designers. However, in general bookshops I fancy our books should be where designers would normally look, in the Graphic Design section somewhere between Art and Craft.

So, to summarise the target market
In order of importance, working designers plus those who think of themselves as designers (the large group, usually called 'desktop publishers', created out of non-design professions by the advent of the personal computer) plus students plus inter-

ested members of the general public*.

Size, length, production

Around 144pp, square (probably your nearest standard size to 8inx8in), bleed across the gutter, all-colour where appropriate; several require only one spot colour.

Delivery on disk in appropriate formats or printed to disk as PostScript ready for RIPping. There's bound to be stripping required but it will vary from book to book; at a guess I will say that on average 15% of pages will require stripping with some books requiring none and others requiring as much as 50%. Other details will have to be discussed for each book: an instance of what I have in mind here is that any proper book on type almost requires an insert printed on a letterpress because it feels different...

Unified jacket design with enough variegation possible to separate and distinguish units in what could eventually be a very large series. Uniform spine design, possibly with colour key to specialities. I shall design the jacket grid and colour scheme at the appropriate time.

Presentation

These are books a designer might have open on his desk semi-permanently as instant references. All books will therefore avoid big chunks of running text and be presented where possible as annotated worked examples or illustrations with extended captions taking in all the necessary information. Obviously the design of the books will be used to project their message. I chose this 'worked workbook' style because most designers I know doodle and make notes on their sketches but are not great readers of unalleviated chunks of text. Because designers think with their eyes, we want a book in which they feel at home at whichever page they open it either in the bookshop or at their desk.

Can we split a complicated subject into discrete small volumes?

No problem. Graphic design never was a unitary art; its very creative variety and technical complexity is what attracts so many challenging minds. We will simply follow the logical splits, as if dividing responsibility between unlimited staff in a large studio.

For our own publishing and marketing convenience only, the series will break into two classes:

1) **Key titles** which will

a) give working designers, and other interested parties who may think of themselves as designers, ideas by worked examples (including fully integrated examples of how their skills can be applied and expanded by the computer either on their desk or at a bureau) and

b) give students a brisk once-over of first principles in the subject as they are applied in real-world solutions (i.e. there will be no theory by numbered paragraphs to be learned by rote).

2) **Advanced titles** aimed at:

a) designers of skill and experience looking for a quick refresher in a specialised subject/new ideas/detailed applications and

b) more advanced students or students who specialise.

There is no compelling reason to distinguish key and advanced titles on the jacket but they are separated here because in some cases it might be logical to publish the key title in a subject before the more specialised titles. This is not to say that the advanced title may not in some instances enjoy the biggest sale of all. If it weren't so hackneyed, we could title all the key books 'Basics of...' to distinguish them. 'Applied...' is possible but it closes out a lot of potential sales to interested laymen. The advanced books can be explicitly titled without fear of losing any part of the target market. Note that our lead market, professional designers, will not make the distinction between the key books and the advanced books; whether a book is basic or advanced will depend for each designer on his experience: a designer who has spent all his career creating corporate images might find our basic books on illustration, retouching and publications most refreshing but the two advanced books on image control quite tame...

KEY TITLES

Typography History, nomenclature, typestyles, the importance of restraint, intention and choice, matches, worked examples including some wrong ones, markup, mechanics of type, considerations of reproduction method, manipulating type, designing your own fonts.

Design Typography and illustration, mass and balance, message and impact, colour, medium (it infuriates me that most writers on design seem ignorant of the reality today that most designs must work across several media) and reproduction, all done through worked examples.

Colour What it is, how it works, how it affects us, how the designer's informed motivational and creative choices are restricted by medium and reproduction method. A very basic book with virtually each chapter to be followed by a booklength in-depth study in the advanced section of the series. It seems to me that colour is becoming such a cheap communication method that soon black-and-white could be the specialist subject.

Illustration Types of illustration (these samples will take up half the book), sources, articulating and refining concepts, commissioning, working back from medium and production limitations, copyright.

Presentation This book is aimed mainly at those executives who make presentations on overhead projectors or slides to colleagues and customers, and print out notes and other sales aids from this material; however, designers working in advertising or public relations or in-house design groups will also find it helpful in preparing slide presentations for themselves or their clients to give.

...and on and on for several more pages of thumbnail sketches

139

Fiction examples

In fiction the publisher normally knows the market. Here is an extended proposal for a series about a continuing central character, complete with part of its sample chapters. You might think it odd that a proposal for an American publisher does not explain why American readers would buy books set in Europe – but the setting was suggested by the commissioning editor himself. The 'guide' to what is after all a substantial wad of paper should be nowhere else but on the front page.

BEN BRADLEY
a hero for the 1990s

a proposal for a series
by André Jute

accompanied by a
15,000 word sample
from
The Shanghai Sting

Contents of this proposal

2. On the Character of Ben Bradley
5. Regular Characters
9. Ten Plot Kernels
12. **THE FERNEY-VOLTAIRE STING**—detailed proposal
18. **THE OSAKA STING**—detailed proposal

(separately)
THE SHANGHAI STING—15,000 word sample

140

On the character of Ben Bradley

A whole series of possible plots follow directly from Ben Bradley's character, his outlook, his prejudices, his Sicilian-Irish blood tempered by a Harvard Business School education and some extremely formative years mismatched to the corporate structure of what he now calls 'the three Generals' —General Motors, General Dynamics and General Foods, all three of which eased him out because his brand of lateral thinking made them uneasy. They will never admit it but Bradley disturbed them not so much by overt anarchism in appearance or manner, or even in theory, as by brilliantly apt unpredictability in action. For such employers dull consistency is safer.

Bradley, fired by three of the Fortune Top Ten, is virtually unemployable by the only class of organisation he has been trained to serve. This is weird, because when we first meet Bradley, jobless and almost broke in Europe (he was last let go by Vauxhall, the General Motors subsidiary in Britain), he looks like Organisation Man: black Brooks Brothers suit, buttondown white Arrow shirt, plain red Countess Mara silk tie—and that is the giveaway, even when his face is blandly in repose: a real organisation man would never wear such an aggressive colour, would choose the compromiser's blue instead. And there's his Corvette: at GM the fellows who will make it to the top progress from Buicks to Cadillacs (I wrote in a motoring journal on the day that Bob Lutz joined GM that he would not last, citing as evidence of nonconformity his ownership of several motorcycles—I was very shortly proved right). Worse, Bradley can drive his Corvette, as it should be driven; in environmentally conscious corporate America a taste for driving an automobile hard is not only an offense against the projected image, it is next of kin to outright criminality.

And the key to Bradley: cursed with honest, hardworking parents, he missed an opportunity to spend his life in the freebooting pursuits his temperament suits him for: the Mafia, the CIA, Aramco or Occidental Oil. But, while at 32 it is too late to join these 'early entry' organisations, a kind destiny will allow Bradley to stumble into a profession entirely suited to him. We

141

will enter Bradley's life at this crisis: the first two books will show how Bradley almost accidentally enters the trade of industrial espionage. In later books we shall see how his own special kind of unpredictable initiative, so undervalued at the Generals, helps him solve the thorny problems of each 'sting' even while having to deal with treachery from all sides.

A word about Bradley's other skills. He is no James Bond or Matt Helm. He doesn't know any karate though he is handy enough with his fists. And he has big hands—one way of short-cutting all the damage a karate tenth dan can do you is to grab him by his testicles and squeeze steadily until he passes out. This forte is lateral thinking or, better still, Japanese water logic (a Japanese life-and-management theory of flow and adaptation as opposed to confrontation by the book as in Western 'rock logic'). Bradley can fly a twin-engined light plane well enough to earn an instrument rating and drive a fast car very well indeed—the latter he learned from some good ole boys while exiled to the Atlanta office of General Foods. He can shoot a rifle well enough to hunt effectively and learns pistol shooting on his new job because he must; but he considers having to use a gun a failure because he'd rather outsmart his enemies. Bradley is not macho at all in attitude, and in action only when forced into a corner. But he does have a ruthless streak: neither forgive nor forget until your enemies are dead; this does not mean that he will act profitlessly for revenge, because he understands the other guys are in business too, but that he will promptly repay those who do him damage additional to that required for the protection of their specific interests. And Bradley is by nature relentless: once he has his mind set on something, he never gives up, whatever the cost of achievement. Bradley is stubbornly utilitarian: he smokes panatellas because he likes them, not to enhance his image; if a girl scoffs at doing espionage in a reference library, Bradley ignores her and goes ahead to the library—what works is what counts. Bradley will eat and drink well (I tour from restaurant to restaurant and can never resist putting all that expensive expertise in my books) and otherwise live well when he can afford it or someone else is paying. Bradley is also good with women, because he makes them laugh, but less good with men (if he were a leader of men in the accepted lowest-com-mon-denominator sense, he would have done better at the Generals).

Bradley, in a word, is rootless; in a phrase, he is slightly dis-oriented; and in a concept, Bradley is that twentieth-century man who knows he has only himself as a reference point for morality and survival. Nothing will be made of this explicitly in the novels but the reader will deduce it and conclude it is just and meet that Bradley, pushed out by the big guys, should rip off their military-industrial complex for the benefit of the lit-tle guys and the also-rans.

But most of all, Bradley does it because he likes doing it. Note that Bradley is at least nominally a Catholic, and geneti-cally half a Latin; the sense of guilt his idleness arouses is therefore a graft from his American childhood and education in a Calvinist environment rather than inherent in his immediate family heritage. It is one of those ironies that, in small doses, produce interesting characters.

Bradley is deeply moral in the sense that he never betrays anyone who has not betrayed him first; in a Bradley operation innocent bystanders are always safe, at least from Bradley. He is not a paranoid cynic who assumes everyone is trying to kill him and therefore always shoots first.

At first Bradley, forced into the unknown by threats to his life, fights only to survive. But (from the third book on) once he dis-covers his métier, he does his work well because he cannot bear to do anything badly. That, if he isn't killed, it will make him rich is incidental, a convenient way of keeping score.

More or less regular characters

Intelligence agencies are characterised by two tendencies that are reinforced in times of overt or apparent friendship between nations, and also in times of transition when new alliances are being struck, as in the 1990s:

•intelligence agencies spy on friendly nations equally with unfriendly (until early in 1942, gathering information for a possible war against Britain had a higher priority in the American military than gathering intelligence for a possible war against either Germany or Japan, a fact understandably not now given much prominence)

• much of the intelligence gathered is not military, or even military-industrial, but plain economic intelligence aimed at gaining a commercial edge; there is nothing new in this—the first modern spy, Elizabeth I's John Day, operated in the age of mercantilism, and his brief was to keep England out of any possible war while gathering all information that would enrich it by trade

It goes almost without saying that in such unsettled times as ours plausible deniability becomes the key concept of any operation—and men like Bradley all the more important to the official spies, of which three, thumbnailed here, will feature more or less regularly:

Kerensky, the youngest colonel in the KGB, is executive assistant to Kurusov, a member of the Politburo and a survivor. Kerensky is tall, blond, elegant, cultured (he spent his early years travelling with the Bolshoi to make sure the dancers didn't defect). He is no mad killer but he is utterly ruthless. He rather likes Bradley and Bradley rather likes him—they are very much alike, mavericks in stultified organisations, the difference being that the KGB is changing in Kerensky's image while the multinationals are growing ever more conservative. Sometimes Kerensky is Bradley's client, sometimes his opponent (the KGB also handles counterespionage).

Drexler is oldline gung-ho CIA. Political considerations force him to hire Bradley to do a job he believes he can do better himself. Besides, he thinks Bradley should do the job from patriotism; to Drexler, a WASP snob from a banking family, Bradley is no better than an educated immigrant-gangster. Drexler cannot understand that, if he had not first endangered Bradley's life, Bradley would never have worked against American interests, nor will he accept that his own interpretation of American interest is open to question by the likes of Bradley. If he can get away with it, he will betray Bradley and get him killed without even considering advantage, merely to teach him a lesson. Drexler is a closet sadist and one day soon Bradley will have to settle scores with him—permanently.

Newton-Boult is the youngest son of an earl. He tries to patronise Bradley and resents Bradley's apparent ignorance of being patronised (Bradley knows, of course, and is storing up little black marks on his shit list against Newton-Boult's name). But what really eats Newton-Boult's liver is Bradley's contempt for British incompetence, and the casual way Bradley always delivers and right on time. Newton-Boult, quite a young man, can still remember when the CIA treated British Intelligence with great respect as the founding fathers of the trade. He too will sacrifice Bradley on the smallest pretext.

Bradley also does straightforward industrial work and in this regard he runs up against national counterespionage services (who are interested in protecting industrial information thought to be in the national interest either commercially or for security reasons) and private security firms. Sometimes he has to deal with criminal elements either selling 'protection' or trying to steal something for themselves. Here are a few of his enemies:

Ohira, a yakuza (Japanese crime boss) Bradley has crossed more than once, in the process unforgivably causing Ohira to lose face. Ohira will have him killed if he can. What's more, Ohira is in the business of offering Japanese companies 'protection' for their confidential information, and by the nature of things Bradley's targets are often Japanese.

Toshida, chief inspector of industrial security for MITI (Japanese ministry of trade and industry).

Suma, MITI's boss of 'honourable economic information' who is in charge of stealing technical information wherever it can be stolen and therefore in direct competition with Bradley.

Schweitzer of the Swiss fremdenpolizei (roughly equivalent to MI5 or the counterespionage section of the FBI) who hates spies using Switzerland as a football pitch, but especially the ones who make a lot of money at it and allow their enemies to disturb the *Swiss* money-making peace.

Tang Chiang of the Chinese Seventh Bureau who reckons Bradley always gets the good stuff and considers it easier to take it from Bradley than from the original owners.

Kristensen of the International Corporate Security Coordination Bureau (ICoSCoB), who considers Bradley a rabid dog to be shot on sight.

Scarlatti of the Mafia, who feels Bradley shows insufficient respect in refusing to pay over a percentage of any profits he makes in Scarlatti's fiefdom. But Scarlatti, who was in Bradley's class at the HBS, is not a mad killer: he will merely send his men to foil Bradley's plans until Bradley learns his lesson and pays up.

TEN PLOT KERNELS

In all of these you can take the girl and the sting in the tail (Bradley's lateral thinking) for read.

THE FERNEY-VOLTAIRE STING Bradley is involuntarily, under threat of his life, dragged into a battle between intelligence agencies for a privately developed supergun commissioned by the Iraqi.

THE OSAKA STING Bradley, who is hiding from the spooks he stole millions from, is blackmailed by the suave Kerensky into stealing a prototype fighter jet fitted with an anti-Stealth radar from the Japanese. He discovers that industrial intelligence is his métier. *Detailed outline attached.*

The above two books have to be written first, as they establish the character development and milieu that underlies the rest. The further eight ideas starting below can be used **in any order** but there should be a balance between commissions Bradley undertakes for private enterprise and intelligence services, and also a balance between geographic locations. (I think it very likely that over the next few years the main enemies of popular perception, to replace the red menace, will be found in the Middle East, the Balkans, among the new Muslim republics in what used to be the USSR, and on the Pacific rim.)

THE GAUGUIN STING The French, culturally invincible in everything but their judgement of painting, lock fakes in a rock cavern at a secret location, just in case they are later discovered not to be fakes. Bradley undertakes to help a Texas millionaire, who has bought a painting, now discovered fake with the original presumed in the French cavern, to discover the location of the secret vault and is then involved in the raid on the cavern to liberate the real thing. Too late he finds Scarlatti wants all the paintings in the caverns...

THE TAI STING The Dallas Zoo has bought a breeding pair of rare marmosets for millions from Chinese freelancers.

Unfortunately, the marmosets have been highjacked by war-lords. Bradley is suckered by the pretty lady director of the zoo into ransoming her little pets and bringing them out. But there are other treacherous bandits who want them, not to mention Ohira-san, the yakuza, keeping his hand in on holiday by negotiating for twelve tonnes of raw opium, and not at all averse to a little abduction and torture to discomfit an old enemy.

THE PALERMO STING The old gangster wants to give himself up but he doesn't trust the corrupt Italian police. His nephew, Scarlatti, recommends Harvard Business School classmate Bradley as an intermediary and the Italian government reluctantly agrees. If Bradley had known how many mafiosi wanted the old man dead, and how treacherous Italian politics are, he would never have taken the job.

THE WEIMAR STING Let nobody call Bradley a racist, or even a snob. When the Libyans approach him to liberate from a German firm the chemical formula for a liquid nitrogen that will make the Libyan desert bloom, Bradley agrees. But when he discovers it is to be used for chemical warfare preparations, he tries to duck out. But the Libyans have strong feelings about the sanctity of contracts...

THE TRIPOLI STING Kerensky, always persuasive, makes it sound very simple. A State visitor has palmed a priceless Fabergé egg from the Hermitage. Bradley will please steal it back. Bradley finds himself nodding agreeably—until he finds out that the thief is Gaddaffi, who has ordered Bradley killed, and that the egg is now in the madman's tent in the Libyan desert.

THE MULLAH STING A beautiful widow has been ripped off by a conman. Bradley promises to get her money back—before he discovers the conman is a nephew of a top Iranian religious leader and now living in Teheran under his protection. But he has promised, so he must go ahead.

THE SHANGHAI STING The Chinese have captured a Russian submarine. They deny having it, of course, but send Bradley to make a deal with the Russians: sub and crew in return for high technology the Russians received from the US. The Russians are in a bind—they always bring their own people back, having a far better record in this regard than the Americans or the British—and agree. But Drexler tries to foil the deal to protect the American technology and it all explodes into treachery and violence with Bradley in the middle and virtually every nation with an intelligence service also trying for the technology. (*The sample chapters available relate to Bradley trying to find out who has abducted his live-in girlfriend, the Swiss-American Geneva-based banker Linda Sheri Unterberg.*)

THE ISTANBUL STING Bradley has had enough of Drexler's attempts to have him killed. He has wind of an enormous transaction Drexler's family bank is involved in, and, to celebrate his first year in business, decides to cut himself a large slice of it to teach Drexler a lesson. But the deal turns out to involve Drexler and some even badder-ass oldstyle KGB types in bed together on a monstrous drugs-into-Russia deal. (Drexler wants to use his profits to finance operations his superiors have forbidden, and the Russians want a new hold on their citizens now that independent thought is no longer a crime.) Bradley finds himself on the same side as Kerensky—with most of the good guys in the KGB...

On the front cover of each of the detailed outlines there is a quick take of its content.

THE FERNEY-VOLTAIRE STING
by André Jute

FERNEY-VOLTAIRE IS NOT A NEW BRAND OF FRENCH
SPRING WATER.
IT IS A SMALL TOWN
EVERY INTERNATIONAL CONMAN,
INTELLIGENCE AGENT,
OFFSHORE FUND PROMOTER
AND HARVARD BUSINESS SCHOOL GRADUATE
KNOWS ABOUT.

FERNEY-VOLTAIRE IS WHERE
BEN BRADLEY, 32,
GREW UP.
VERY SUDDENLY.

Ben Bradley was never cut out to be a pinstripe executive. He had been on the fast track at the three Generals (Dynamics, Motors and Foods) and each had decided such a fertile mind was hazardous to its corporate slumber. Essentially his Harvard Business School education was an expensive waste because that august institution trains administrators, the sort of fellow who can as easily make a career as a Russian commissar as flying a desk at Ford—and Bradley is a lateral thinker.

That's how come Bradley, 32, very well educated, happens to be in Europe with six Brooks Brothers suits, two dozen plain white button-down Arrow shirts, no job and no money once his savings run out. But the only job going for a thrice-recycled executive is offered by the decidedly shady George Charpentier (who has come to inspect the Corvette Bradley is advertising for sale so he can pay the rent). Bradley reckons that reorganising a warehouse outside Brussels, even if it is the warehouse of an armaments designer and merchant, is no more morally reprehensible than organising a tobacco warehouse to maximise profits. Bradley, it should be said, smokes long thin cigars which make him look extraordinarily like Dean Martin, whom Bradley's mother, an Italian, had fancied; from her he has also inherited enough Sicilian blood to forgive his enemies only when they are dead. From his father Bradley has inherited his Irish temper and ability with his fists. Nobody has ever accused Bradley of being a hypocrite, another reason why he did not flourish with the Generals.

When Iraqi terrorists torch Charpentier's warehouse, Bradley stuffs the most valuable papers into his briefcase and runs before the fire and the exploding bullets and rockets. The Iraqis intended to destroy the plans of the supergun Charpentier designed for them, which had meanwhile been uncovered piecemeal by the British, Italian, Greek and Turkish customs authorities as it was shipped to the Ministry of Industry in Baghdad from the various foundries and machining mills in Europe. The Iraquis see Bradley open his briefcase to show his boss the rescued papers... Fortunately for Bradley, they don't make the connection until later–until after they have murdered Charpentier.

Bradley is in serious trouble. The Belgian police and examining magistrate (something like DA, Grand Jury, and Judge all rolled into one) believe Bradley fingered Charpentier for the kill—otherwise why did the assassins not wipe out the only witness who can identify them?

The Iraqi assassins, descendants of the Hashshishin of legend, know Bradley has the plans which prove that the Iraqi president, Saddam Hussein, is an outright, knowing liar. More, the Pentagon and Frunze St (Russian Army Intelligence, the GRU, is headquartered there in an architecturally notable building though the business is done in the ugly Stalinist seven-storey annex across the road) know Bradley has the plans of a new type of super-cannon capable of being constructed with only the basic smelter, rolling mill and machining mill you can always take over in any moderately industrialised country you invade. The reason the big powers don't have superguns is that they are impossible to transport. Previously, big guns had to be made in one piece on truly sophisticated equipment. Now, because of the genius Charpentier's special flanged, bolt-together construction, they can have superguns made on the spot (or back home in pieces for local assembly) in only a few days—and, with the imminent removal of nuclear weapons, they might yet need them to replace the negotiated-away cruise missiles.

The big boys want the plans partly for themselves and partly to keep them out of the hands of unreliables; European unification of 1992 and the continuing breakup of the Russian bloc have destroyed many of the old trade barriers. And the French, who are members of the Community but not of NATO (and will therefore keep their nuclear weapons), would like to destroy the supergun plans so that their *force de frappe* is the only credible deterrent (especially against a newly reunified Germany, the nightmare of every Frenchman who ever read a history book). And the Iranians, against whom the Iraqi supergun was intended, also want the plans to build their own to further the holy war against Iraq. And the Israelis—of course! And the PLO. And Albania on behalf of themselves and their Chinese paymasters. Not to forget the Belgians themselves, now awakened by their own armaments manufacturers (the major Belgian industry, far more so than aerospace in the US) to the commercial possibilities of grabbing the plans and registering the patents; and the peaceful Swedes, who sell almost as many guns to whoever has the money as Uncle Sam and Uncle Joe (US light infantry special assault troops, 'lightfighters', carry a licensed, modified copy of the Swedish Carl Gustav automatic rifle).

'It's a convention of assassins,' Bradley says to Sari the Indian girl who is running with him because the assorted thugs shoot at her as well. Of course she is with Indian Intelligence and wants the plans too, but on the other hand she is a Buddhist and Bradley doesn't believe she will kill for the plans if she can take them by stealth. And she's smart. 'You're a negotiator, so negotiate,' she tells Bradley. 'Even killers have their price.' The problem is that all these killers have the same mutually exclusive price: exclusive possession of the plans plus, just in case he memorised them or stashed a copy somewhere, the opportunity to torture Bradley until he reveals his knowledge. After which they will shoot him just to make certain. Bradley also wants to lessen the odds that some disappointed low bidder might kill him from pique. Here are some of the set pieces of the story:

—The Iraqis set fire to the warehouse. Bradley escapes with flames licking from his coat-tails and heatseeking rockets trailing after his dodging form. His boss is murdered just as Bradley tries to hand over the rescued plans. Bradley is roughly handled by the Belgian police and accused by the examining magistrate of complicity in arson and murder, as well as industrial espionage (in Belgium a more serious crime than either arson or murder, in that the same penalty applies as for high treason: death by firing squad). The police, believing him to be in cahoots with the killers, refuse him protection. Because the examining magistrate (who uses the police like an American DA uses the police or his own assigned special investigators) hopes Bradley will lead them to his accomplices, the police refuse to lock him up even after Bradley publicly slugs magistrate, arresting officer and several attending policemen. Bradley, who had once been arrested in Cambridge, Mass, for being drunk in charge of a bicycle, cannot believe how difficult it is to be arrested in Belgium.

—Bradley went to school with a fellow now high up in the State Department and posted to London and, like any American who gets into trouble in foreign parts, he expects his government to send a gunboat. His chum promises protection but on the drive into the British countryside Bradley discovers his own countrymen intend holding him prisoner for a year or so until they have tested the design. After that, who knows? Bradley can guess. The car is attacked by French Intelligence agents and in the confusion Bradley escapes. A car chase ensues across England, a fight on the ferry, where Bradley meets Sari when she 'rescues' his briefcase, and another highspeed chase across the German autobahnen. In Geneva the Iraqi, the PLO and the Israelis all catch up with Bradley. Once again he and Sari extricate themselves from the dangerous battleground between the competing forces but now Bradley has an idea. In the spirit of European unity, he will put all his tormentors to negotiating with each other just as they have been negotiating with him: at the point of a gun.

—At Harvard one of the key case studies involves acquiring Swiss legal protection and prestige while avoiding Swiss labour costs by chartering and operating a company from Geneva but billeting staff who cannot get Swiss residence permits in the French village of Ferney-Voltaire just across the border. The village is both the scene for the shootout and on the line of Bradley's escape route: just off the end of the airport runway, where anyone with a pair of wire-cutters can cross the border if they have the nerve. (And it is proof Bradley's parents didn't waste the money they spent on his education.)

—The climactic shootout proves that the United States of Europe is a lot less united than the United States of America; but nobody is as united as a man and a woman in love. When it is all over, Bradley grabs the millions belonging to the bidders and lets Sari take the plans to the most populous democracy in the world, India. He shrugs off the death threats the survivors make as they are led away by the Swiss police to rat-infested cells — the only part of Switzerland that isn't hygienic, and on purpose.

'You tried to screw me and got screwed instead. Where's the

profit in revenge? Think of it instead as a lesson in American know-how—and be grateful.'

Now you can understand why the Generals, the commercial ones, not the military intelligence ones Bradley just screwed out of millions and in some cases their lives, thought Ben Bradley should come with a government health warning stamped across his Brooks Brothers suits. By now only one of his suits would meet the Generals' exacting standards. The other five have been burned, rocketed, bullet-holed, slashed by a razor-wielding Armenian, torn when its wearer was being thrown out of speeding cars, or spotted by lobster thermidor in the Tour d'Argent and blood on the High Corniche not to mention sheepdung on the South Downs.

'It's tough being an international businessman,' an Egyptian tells Bradley in a bar at the beginning of our story. 'There are risks. But the rewards are commensurate.' I'll leave the reader to make the connection.

Sample chapters are preceded by a page describing what happened before.

15,000 words
Sample for the Ben Bradley series
from

**The Shanghai Sting
by André Jute**

What happened before these sample chapters

The Chinese have captured a Russian submarine. They deny having it, of course, but send Bradley to make a deal with the Russians: sub and crew in return for high technology the Russians received from the US. The Russians are in a bind—they always bring their own people back, having a far better record in this regard than the Americans or the British—and agree. But Drexler tries to foil the deal to protect the American technology. It all explodes into treachery and violence with Bradley in the middle and virtually every nation with an intelligence service also trying for the technology.

Drexler sets the Palestinians (who believe they're working for the Russians) to abducting Bradley but they capture only Sheri. Bradley stashes the high tech information (and some embarrassing titbits he has found out over the years) in a public database, set to print out at United Press and Associated Press if he misses sending a password every few hours. Then he tries to blackmail the various services into helping him find his love.

In the sample we enter the story at the lowest point in Bradley's life, where everyone but he is convinced Sheri is already dead. They are wondering whether it wouldn't be cheaper and faster all round to kill Ben Bradley as well. On the plane he reads a probability study from Shin Bet (Israeli intelligence) pointing to Drexler's sidekick, Mark Diehl, as the brains behind the abduction.

Now read on...

Wednesday, 27 October
England

'Goddammit! Will we Americans never learn?'

'We're here,' Herriot said inconsequentially.

The plane was at a standstill. I rubbed my eyes. I had dozed for a while after reading straight through the various scenarios, then woken with a start from a nightmare so terrifying my subconscious censored it in the moment of waking: I was drenched with sweat. I had sorted the scenarios into two piles, the incredible and the all too-credible. In the latter category there were only the three scenarios I now held in my hand, having packed the others in my bag when the stewardess told me to fold the little table away.

'Stay in your seat until everyone else has gone,' Herriot told me.

It was impossible to believe. I still didn't believe it. In many ways, it would be easier to believe that Braymore was destroying the world because his job was too big for him and his wife was a bitch. Or that Kurusov's ego craved one last grand gesture and bugger the cost. I wished fervently I had Yum and Yo or even Kerensky and Niminski to discuss my discovery, to weigh the pros and cons. I also knew I had made a potentially disastrous mistake in coming to London. I should have read the printouts and considered the implications before rushing off into the wild blue yonder like all these action-prone idiots I keep condemning so roundly. Men who live in glass houses... I vowed to stick to what I do best, sifting facts and drawing logical conclusions, and immediately broke my resolution by digging my arm in Herriot's side. He was a poor specimen intellectually (Marlborough and Sandhurst, he had told me proudly when I asked) but there was nothing wrong with his eyes.

'Where did you start tracking me, Herriot?'

'Tel Aviv,' he said without looking at me. He was studying the other passengers, some of whom were trying to hang on to their seats much to the chagrin of the hostesses.

That was no help at all.

'I hope you enjoyed your flight with us. This is London,' said

...and so on. For reasons of space we have cut the rest of this sample chapter, the whole of the second sample chapter, most of the third sample chapter, and continue with the last page of the third sample chapter...

wisdom of that choice.' I swung my foot in a bigger arc, though staying carefully out of his reach. I was still not entirely convinced that he was as helpless as he tried to make out.

His head slumped and frothy stuff trickled out of the corner of his mouth. I decided to change tactics—to gamble. I stepped up boldly and kneeled next to him, raised his head and wiped the froth from his lips. 'You have punctured lungs. Unless you get medical attention soon, you'll die. Tell me where to find Sheri and I'll take you to hospital.'

'Less gerout tahere'n'wec'n makadeal.'

'Now you're talking sense. But first you tell me, then I drive you to the nearest hospital.'

'Nobody's everngon lief you did this to mearlone.'

'If you tell me where to find Sheri I'll tell them there was a whole platoon of us.' He was slipping away from me fast. 'Don't you have family, boy?'

He nodded weakly.

'Then, for their sake, tell me. If you do not, I will seek them out and kill them one by one. Father, mother, sisters, brothers, wife, children, all. You must know I have Sicilian blood.' I was desperate. Mark Diehl, despite his scything arms and bright chat and obstinate resistance to what must be excruciating pain, was dying. Of that I was convinced. I shook him, then grabbed at his lolling head to support it. 'Tell me. For your family.'

'The farm,' said Mark Diehl clearly. Blood spurted from both his ears and trickled down the sides of his face onto HarBat's suit, which I still wore. 'At the farm,' he repeated. Then he died.

'What farm? Goddamn you, where is the farm?' I shouted, but I knew those staring eyes belonged to a dead man. I laid his head on the road and pummelled his chest with my fists. When it was clear that my overwhelming fear and anger would not resurrect him, I sat and wept for Sheri now surely lost to me.

The three sample chapters are followed by a sheet describing what happens afterwards.

What happens after these sample chapters

The Russians won't help either but Bradley has a convincing argument: do they want him to be the cause of American secrets splashed over the media? They let him go—on the gold plane to Zurich from where he makes his way to Rome where Scarlatti, his mafioso classmate at the Harvard Business School, is kissing the Pope's ring.

Scarlatti is willing to help, for a consideration, of course. Bradley tracks down Sheri to Camp Peary and with a bunch of Mafia on standby for muscle, blackmails the CIA into giving her back. Simultaneously he arranges the handover of the Russian sub and its crew by the Chinese while he hands over the American technology...

Another deal concluded, though many of those who gained would like to kill Bradley. 'So what?' says Bradley. 'This isn't a popularity contest. Next month they'll need me and then they'll be back. Nothing personal, only money.'

I'm considering ending all the books in the series with Bradley saying, 'Nothing personal, only money.' That would make it both a leitmotif and his personal motto, and also serve as a marketing link, reminding readers that more adventures by their favorite character are coming.

From Andrew McCoy we have this detailed proposal for a novel. Note how the definition of a helix, in parenthesis, is in fact also a suggestion—'predictable spiral'—that it is important to the narrative; it implies a thriller. And 'specialist' is not bad either, implying as it does specialist knowledge, which publishers love.

THE MEYERSCO HELIX
a proposal for a novel by Andrew McCoy
about 100,000 words

(To most people, a helix is a spiral; to specialists like biochemists and series-mathematicians it is a predictable spiral.)

In the opening scene we find the President of the United States being awakened and pressed on the telephone by the Chairman of the Joint Chiefs of Staff for a decision which in four minutes ('and counting') will become irrelevant. The President asks: 'How did we ever get to where the President of the United States has four minutes to decide if he'll nuke Boston or instead let the world go insane?' The rest of the story tells how a series of minor and major coincidental misfortunes, flaws in people and systems, plus the admirable qualities of others, have inexorably combined to create the catastrophe.

Near the remote village where he grew up Alexander Ribicoff, a sometime football star and now a civil-rights lawyer, and his fiancée Stella Christopher, who is director of clinical testing for the Meyers Ethical Pharmaceuticals Company, camp in the forest and try to capture a female Gillian's Redhaired Mole, a near-extinct species of which Ribicoff has a male in the 'zoo' he keeps in their Boston apartment. Just as they succeed, the men who own the luxurious duckblind nearby turn up and, mistaking Ribicoff and Stella for conservationists interfering with their out-of-season duck hunting, become aggressive. One of them, Kee (whose path has crossed Ribicoff's once before in Vietnam where Ribicoff wrecked Kee's career because of drug smuggling) casually blows the rare mole apart with his shotgun. When Ribicoff tries to protect the mole, there is a flash of violence. It turns out the men are security officers from a nearby military installation and, against Stella's protestations, Ribicoff decides to go to the camp and lodge a formal complaint with their CO. ('Every time Army men behave like thugs, they're spitting on my Silver Star.')

On the way to the camp, he is nearly run off the road by the three officers returning from visiting their colleague Kee whom Ribicoff put in hospital, but the senior man realises that, once they have Ribicoff on Army property, civilian law no longer applies and they let him proceed. When Ribicoff is inside the camp, they arrest him. Ribicoff knows that, once they have him in their stockade, he will come out a vegetable. He resists, knocks two of them out and, with his back to a glass wall before a laboratory, finds the remaining officer shooting at him. A bullet passes through the glass (hurricane- but not bullet-proof) and into a flask inside, from which gas leaks, killing first the scientists inside and then the officer outside with Ribicoff. Ribicoff himself, whose excellent reflexes have already set him sprinting away, survives. Almost immediately liquid white phosphor (imagine napalm but two hundred times hotter — this stuff even melts tungsten alloy Crucible 165H) is automatically sprayed over everything; those who aren't killed by the gas are burnt. From town, Stella sees the army installation suddenly consume itself in flames and the forest catch fire all round, then the windstorm hits the little town and it is virtually flattened.(White phosphor sprayed thin enough burns its own weight in oxygen every .008 seconds at temperatures hot enough to vaporise the resultant H_2O so that it doesn't drown and simply goes on and on burning while slowly consuming itself, drawing in vast volumes of air very quickly indeed.) Stella, as a physician, obviously helps with the injured from the town and among the firefighters — until the townspeople, considering her as guilty as Ribicoff for the disaster that has overtaken them, refuse any further help from her.

At this stage she believes the President's explanation of a fuel dump exploding. What she does not know is that the President has had an explanation from the military for killing six hundred of their own: a rogue department of the Pentagon has siphoned off a little money to carry on biological-warfare research in defiance of international agreements and presidential orders and has succeeded in making a gas that will not kill people, merely affect their brains to make them 'a little simple-minded' and swell their joints; the gas is particularly fast-disseminating and once released, bonds with the most common of all elements, water, to enter all living things; more frighteningly, it is totally indestructible by anything but very high heat, which accounts for the white phosphor and the lack of a warning or any attempt to evacuate the site, and it is self-propagating. But the Pentagon is on top of it now: all the gas has been destroyed, there isn't any more anywhere in the world, and those responsible will be punished.

Grieving for Ribicoff, Stella heads back to Boston, past the men in spacesuits and special vehicles digging up the earth and putting it in lead barrels, going down to the underground vault to recover the films of what happened... When the films are screened in Washington, the full danger becomes clear for the first time: Ribicoff got away, the film shows clearly that he breathed some of the purple gas. He could die anywhere and the poison will enter the drinking water and the breathing atmosphere from his decomposing body...and from there into people to grow again, until the whole population is made up of mad monstrosities.

The FBI and Army Intelligence start a no-holds-barred manhunt. Gotham, who asks to be put in charge for the FBI, was Kee's prosecutor all those years ago; unlike Kee, he feels Ribicoff protected Kee against the full force of the law's retribution ('The Army looking after its own'). Meanwhile, back at the wrecked backwoods town, a woman is raped by what to her looks like a giant monster at just about the same time as Ribicoff, autistic from the effects of the gas and with his joints horribly swollen, comes stumbling out of the forest, another mole in a cage in his hand. In the uncertain light of the fires, he looks like a monster-rapist. The rednecks, already convinced he was responsible for the destruction of their town's source of income, the army installation, and the consequent flattening of the town itself, are easily persuaded by Kee, ironically put in hospital and so saved by Ribicoff, to beat him up and, when he escapes, to form a posse to hunt him down.

Stella tries to sink herself in her work. She cannot understand why the FBI keep pestering her with questions and following her around. Then she comes home to find two Gillian's Redhaired Moles in Ribicoff's 'zoo' and she knows Ribicoff is alive. As he steps through the door from the balcony, she is horrified by his appearance. He cannot speak but points to the answering machine: he was about to leave after delivering the female mole when he heard on the answering machine her doctor calling to say she is pregnant. As she cleans him up, the FBI bursts in and, in escaping, Ribicoff kills two of them. They arrest Stella and, before her boss — Meyers, a survivor of the Holocaust — gets her released, she finds out about the gas and the danger from Ribicoff. She realises that the FBI and Army Intelligence men intend shooting him on sight and incinerating his body immediately. They will not believe her that he is not violent or that he can be kept in isolation until a cure is found; killing Ribicoff is a policy decision taken way above their level.

Stella, working at her desk, with her terminal, driving her brilliant young associates to put their minds to the problem, soon decides there is indeed the possibility of a cure. Ribicoff has been saved from the worst effects of the drug because of the massively abnormal amounts of adrenaline his athlete's body secreted while defending himself. (I have a bio-chemist giving me chapter and verse on the technical aspects.) Stella thinks she can use this coincidence to save him, drive the poison from his body, and even repair his mind to a certain extent. But she can reach no one to get them to call off the dogs because the FBI blocks her at every turn. When, in desperation, (and anger because she has discovered many of the scientists at the destroyed installation were not chemists but series-mathematicians, which proves that they knew the nature of the gas and that its unstoppable growth was not a mistake as she had been assured but planned from the beginning) she sends a young colleague to talk to a reporter who has been digging into the disaster, both are brutally murdered.

Meanwhile the vigilante group, led by Kee ('This is almost as good as being back in Nam'), is making its own brutal way through the country and the city after Ribicoff. The FBI, seeing an opportunity too good to miss, ascribes some of the vigilantes' sins to Ribicoff, so setting off a public manhunt for a 'mad killer'. Ribicoff hides himself in the violent and incompetent public edifice for dealing with the criminally insane; when he is ready, he will escape. When they try to arrest Stella, she knows they are closing in on Ribicoff and escapes to the only place they have not yet searched for him, Meyers' boat moored opposite their wharfside condo. And, indeed, Ribicoff does appear but with Meyers on his heels — Meyers has been persuaded to betray them by a promise that Ribicoff will not be killed. But, as the FBI and Army Intelligence close in, the vigilantes also arrive and start shooting. Meyers steps in front of Stella to protect her and takes a shot in the shoulder. He falls overboard and is chewed up by the props. In the uncertain light, the FBI and Army Intelligence think it is Ribicoff's body spreading blood in the water. How can one possibly burn the Channel and the Bay? As they helicopter out, the decision is passed to the JCS, where they have contingency plans for exactly such an occurrence... The Chairman calls the President to tell him that unless he burns downtown Boston with a nuclear device, the poison will spread and the earth will soon be inhabited only by simpleminded, swollen monstrosities. Everyone must take water...

Of course the President must choose the lesser evil, though I will make something of his moral dilemma (how many may one kill to save all?). From the flybridge, Stella, crying for all her dead, watches the nuking of Boston. When she goes below, she finds Ribicoff lying in the saloon, unscathed except for a bump on his head which had knocked him out. What's more, he can speak haltingly and the swellings in his joints are receding; he'll be all right. Boston has been destroyed on a false assumption.

*This is the complete proposal from which this novel was com-
missioned by an editor who has known me a long time. The
purpose of this kind of proposal is not so much to provide an
outline with a beginning, a middle and an end as to prove to
non-editorial publishing executives that the author knows what
he's talking about—his editor already believes in the author's
wisdom or he would not even consider so skimpy a proposal.
The proposals for the other two novels in the commissioned
trilogy were so similar it is not worth reproducing them; the
only noteworthy point about them is that the similarity rein-
forces the concept of a set of related books, something every
publisher likes.*

DZERZHINSKY SQUARE

First in the trilogy
An Intelligence of Patriots
by André Jute

Lubianka was an insurance company whose headquarters
building Feliks Dzerzhinsky's Cheka took over for office space.
It is still inhabited by the highest officials of the KGB because
it is more convenient for the Kremlin than their huge modern
offices seventeen miles from the town centre on the Moscow
Ring Road. There is an inner courtyard, backed by another
building containing, among other things, the torture and execution cells (Not in the cellar of the main building, as often
claimed). The main building has green linoleum on the floors;
the execution cells out back are said to have had rubber mats
on the floors to catch the blood. The street side of No 2
Dzerzhinsky Square is painted olive-green, with white facings
to the window surrounds. The front door is guarded by two
members of the elite First Kremlin Guards Division, the ones
with the double red tabs to their lapels. They look across the
square to the world's largest department store, GUM, and,
incongruously, to the world's largest toy store, Detsky Mir (Our
World). They can also see the onion domes of St Basil's and
the Clock Tower near the Spassky Gate to the Kremlin, just
along from Lenin's Mausoleum. The Lubianka is a centre of

power, and power has been wielded from it from the very beginning of the Revolution; Dzerzhinsky moved here from the Smolny Institute in St Petersburg immediately Lenin transplanted his revolution and capital to Moscow.

Our story is nothing less than the sweep of humans (and inhumans), inquisitors and victims, who make up the history of the KGB from its beginnings as the Cheka in the Smolny. It will be told in the first person by three generations of KGB officers: the Extraordinary Commission from the beginning—and from the inside, motivated by its own imperatives of fear and fanaticism, through the murders of whole professional classes, the massacres of the kulaks, the betrayals of friends and family, the show trials of colleagues, the psychiatric tortures of dissidents, right up to glasnost, when the fourth generation must answer the question: Was the result worth the effort?

The story will abound with real characters, the great, the mad, the lethal, even the chill technocrats, from Lenin to Stalin to Beria to Chebrikov. The historical detail will of course be impeccable. And the tension, the tragedy, the final ray of hope and humanity in the realisation that oppression cannot work forever, all is inherent in the material.

•200,000 words.

Authors can sometimes obtain a copy of the publisher's reader's report, which can be very useful for selling into subsidiary markets. Here the report as well as a personal note from the reader is used to sell the novel proposed above after it was written and edited.

The accompanying manuscript incorporates detailed editorial suggestions by Andrew Taylor, winner of the John Creasey Award for his first novel *Caroline Minuscule*, Golden Dagger nominee and Edgar Scroll holder; his recent 'big' novel, *The Second Midnight*, was widely acclaimed. Here is the introduction to his report on:

Dzerzhinsky Square
by André Jute

**From the reader's report
by Andrew Taylor**

'This is a long, impressive and often powerful novel which serves up seventy-five years of modern Russian history in the guise of a combined espionage novel and family saga (on a very grand scale). It is meaty stuff. Jute is particularly good at showing how the revolution carried within it the seeds of its own downfall and at describing the KGB cog-wheels in the Soviet power machine.'

Further extract from a personal letter to the author

'Well—what a book. I thought the range of your narrative extraordinary, and I certainly know more than I did about Russian history. What will stay in my mind I think, are those explosive vignettes (like the Railway of Hands) and the carefully selected details (like Babe noticing that the only clean windows in Moscow are at the Lubyanka, with all that that implies). It is certainly the best book of yours that I have read.'

Once Dzerzhinsky Square *was written, the draft blurb for the dust jacket did service as a summary of the contents. Even a commissioned novel should be accompanied by some kind of summary on one side of a sheet for the possible use of executives other than the editor.*

**THE GREATEST CONSPIRACY
THE WORLD HAS EVER KNOWN
STARTED WITH THE
STORMING OF THE WINTER PALACE**
In the beginning
they were impassioned young revolutionaries risking only their own lives for justice. The prince, the soldier and the peasant became the patriarchs of three families whose generations are enfolded in the sweep of humans and inhumans, inquisitors and victims, that tell the story of the KGB—which *is* the story of Russia in our century—from the day Lenin created it as the Cheka in the Smolny Convent: the Extraordinary Commission from the beginning and from the inside, motivated by its own imperatives of fear and fanaticism, through the murders of whole classes, the massacres of kulaks, the betrayals of friends and family, the show trials of colleagues, the psychiatric tortures of dissidents, right up to glasnost, when the fourth generation must answer the question: Was the result worth three generations of suffering and sacrifice?

If you read only one novel this year, read this the epic historical saga of three intertwined families who live and die by their love for their Russian motherland and the searing passions they arouse in each other.

**First in André Jute's trilogy
of major suspense novels
AN INTELLIGENCE OF PATRIOTS
comprising
DZERZHINSKY SQUARE
LANGLEY VIRGINIA
100 BROADWAY**

It is good insurance if you have them to send extracts from reviews with every manuscript. These extracts are tailored to a thriller.

[[[EXTRACTS FROM REVIEWS FOR DUST JACKET]]]

Reviews of the novels of André Jute

'Wild but exciting. A grand job with plenty of irony.'
New York Times Book Review
'So bizarre, it's probably all true.'
London Evening News
'This is an important book.'
Sydney Morning Herald
'Keeps up such a pace and such interest that it really satisfies.'
Good Housekeeping
'A masterly story that has pace, humour, tension and excitement with the bonus of truth.'
The Australian
'Jute has clearly conducted a great deal of research into everything he describes, investing the novel with an air of prophecy. His moral concerns are important.'
Times Literary Supplement
'He gets on with the job of telling us exactly what it is like in the Heart of Darkness. He has the soldier's eye for terrain and the soldier's eye for character. This has the ring of truth.'
John Braine/*Sunday Telegraph*
'Like the unblinking eye of a cobra, it is fascinating and hard to look away from, powerful and unique.'
Edwin Corley/*Good Books*
'I found this work excellent. I recommend it as a book to read on several planes, whether as politics, history or just as a thriller — every episode is firmly etched on my memory. It is certainly a most impressive work of fiction.'
'H.P.'/*BBC External Service*

This is a synopsis of a novel already completed. Such a synopsis serves both to help to sell the novel and later to demonstrate to secondary purchasers such as film producers the high points of the story.

Synopsis

IDITAROD
by André Jute

Briefly

Iditarod tells of a grudge match of a man and a woman against each other, against the forces of nature, against Alaska, against a wolf pack — but most of all against themselves. It is a love story and a great adventure.

Narrative

Rhodes Delaney is practising for a local Colorado dogsled race when James Alderton Whitbury III, a Winter Olympics skiing hopeful also out practising, crashes into her. Her dogs savage his wrist; angry words follow. They meet again that evening at the country club where James's awkwardness, aggravated by Rhodes's abrasive best friend, Margery, leads to a challenge: Rhodes against James in the toughest race on earth — the Iditarod: 1200 miles running behind a dogsled across Alaska in winter. Rhodes refuses James's $10,000 bet but Marge's father, Harvey, takes it.

(The Iditarod is an annual event commemorating a race against death to deliver serum by dogsled to the children of Nome during the diphtheria outbreak of 1925. It is generally recognised as the ultimate endurance test for athletes: *The Very Best of Everything* describes it as 'the only true modern equivalent of the Ancient Greeks' Marathon'.)

Meanwhile Rangers on Isle Royale in Lake Michigan kill the last wolves in the lower forty-eight States; one wolf escapes and makes his way to Alaska where he establishes another pack.

When James wins an Olympic Gold Medal, he tells journalists how he got the wrist wound that nearly kept him out of the team. The journalists find out about the grudge match and the $10,000 bet, and descend on Rhodes at her father's Colorado ranch, offending her sense of privacy. She escapes them only when she leaves to work in a salmon factory in Alaska to earn money for the race. (James has developed a lightweight alloy sled which he sells to the pipeline maintenance company sponsoring him in the race.)

At the start of the race Rhodes is almost injured when James loses control of his dogs. Then on a frozen river she crashes her sled into poles frozen into the ice. James arrives and attempts to help her mend her sled but Rhodes, thinking he's trying to have her disqualified for accepting help against the rules, whacks his sore hand with frozen rawhide. As they race on, more of the small but potentially fatal accidents of the trail happen to them or other racers: wrecking sled and dogs over sharp rises, dogs fighting over buried meat, becoming lost, overturning the sled on a steep slope. Rhodes loses her post-packet (symbolic of the diphtheria serum — without it the runner is disqualified) and is delayed at a checkpoint; James arrives with it but very late and she suspects he took it to delay her. She almost is delayed 24 hours before Rainy Pass — with a storm approaching that would put her out of the race — but a checker points out a loophole in the rules and she runs on. In the night a bull moose charges her and, to give her dogs a chance of surviving, she runs into the forest to lead the moose away from them. As it is about to trample her she runs into a tree and is knocked unconscious.

James meanwhile is running up Rainy Pass, falling off the narrow trail over a precipice, having hallucinations from his exertions. Near Rainy Pass Lodge his dogs take off after wild horses; he can only hold on desperately until the dogs lose interest. (The dogsled racer — 'musher' — has no reins, controlling his dogs by voice alone.) At the Lodge a journalist tells him he is the leading rookie but Rhodes, whom James thinks should be 24 hours adrift, is only 12 hours behind him. He hears the story of how two long-ago mushers, Chittick and Jacobsin, died on the mountain. At the top of the mountain, where he has decided to camp before starting the perilous descent at dawn, his dogs run after wild Dall sheep. James runs after them, hallucinating in the aurora borealis, thinking Chittick and Jacobsin are chasing him. Reaching the bottom of the mountain safely, he is blown up in an explosion on a frozen river.

When Rhodes recovers consciousness the moose has lost interest and is grazing nearby; she creeps away. She jogs up the trail, looking for her dogs. Another racer, Bloody Bobby Franks, is holding them. She runs on up Rainy Pass. Going down it in daylight, she sees only the hair-raising beauty. She finds the crater in the frozen river and thinks a musher went down in it but race officials will not believe her and no one has been posted missing, though James, who had left Rainy Pass Lodge before her, has still not arrived. Rhodes runs on. On Lake Veleska, fatigued but determined to go on, Rhodes sees her own aura (there are many recorded instances of Iditarod racers and other ultra-endurance athletes experiencing this). She arrives at Farewell and sleeps at last, to be woken with news that James died at the explosion on the river. She runs on, for herself and for him. (There is a visual symbol here of a rising flock of ptarmigan.)

James has been flung back from the explosion, recovering consciousness after the trapper who caused it has gone. (The trapper blows up the river to kill the animals in it, then takes them out downriver; all this is explained to Rhodes in the previous section. Here we see that the trapper is unaware of James's presence.) James resigns himself to freezing to death but then finds fuel drums left behind by the trapper. But his fingers are near-frozen and he cannot handle tools. After great effort he punctures a drum with his axe and lights the fuel to dry himself and his dogs. He runs on: concussed, fevered, he misses the checkpoint but must continue — if he stops or falls off the sled he will die. At last, blinded by pain, he stumbles upon Farewell. When he wakes 24 hours later, the doctor is against letting him continue but race officials, in view of the explosion, are prepared to overlook the missed checkpoint. He runs on, into a blizzard in which he loses the trail.

In McGrath (a town containing 'two of the three bars between Anchorage and Nome'), Rhodes is waiting out the storm with the leading racers. Marge has formed an attachment to Dave Cohen, a dog breeder employed by James. When James arrives, Rhodes accuses Dave of trying to keep her there so James could catch up. 'When you're in that mood, sane men will admire you from afar,' James snaps. Rhodes runs out into the blizzard, intending to return when her anger has cooled. But her dogs lead her back to McGrath. Rhodes, to keep mastery of them, must run or scratch, blizzard or no. She loses the trail in the whiteout; immediately she recovers it, a hungry bear just out of hibernation finds them. As Rhodes tries to outrun it, it ambles alongside, eating one of her dogs still in its traces. Rhodes, who mostly cannot see the bear in the curtain of snow, stops the team and unharnesses her dogs one by one, getting nearer to the bear all the time. The bear attacks her: James arrives and frightens it off by firing his revolver. They camp to wait out the blizzard. They make their explanations to each other. James invites her to run near him; she accepts. He is worried about wolves on the trail; she is not.

In quick cuts we see the Alaskan pack established by the wolf from Isle Royale: eating a survivor of a plane crash; driven from their territory by salvagemen; drifting northwards onto the tundra after migrating caribou; remaining there when the caribou return to the southern forest; growing hungrier as winter closes on the tundra; finally, starving, they attack the fierce musk oxen who kill many of the wolves.

James and Rhodes run on, their relationship developing. On the Yukon they meet vicious headwinds and a chill factor off the bottom of the scale. Their dogs have to be led from the front, where the cold soon causes hallucinations — James, a native New Yorker, imagines that the Yellow Cab Company is trying to kill him, Rhodes that wild mustangs are stampeding over her. At Kaltag they discover they are the leading rookies, running in the top ten — but the hard men of the Iditarod are closing on them... Onwards across the ice, ever onwards into the blizzard. At the next checkpoint Eskimo hear James explaining the importance of the wolf in Alaskan ecology; they tell him of a huge wolf pack skulking on the trail, so desperately hungry it will attack men — and the only men out there are the racers. Officials think the Eskimo are joshing a rookie... Later they hear more about wolves but Rhodes believes they are an obsession with James. Onwards they run, beyond fatigue. Starting the last stretch they abandon all but the regulation gear to save the fatigued dogs' strength for the final sprint to the victory arch. Among the gear they discard are their firearms.

Near Port Safety the wolves attack them: they try to outrun the pack but fail. Rhodes falls back and James stays with her despite her shouts to save himself. A wound, cut on one of her dogs by the bear, opens — spraying Rhodes with blood. A wolf jumps at her, grabs her mitten; another hangs onto her parka. She rams her axehandle down its open throat; its weight pulls her under the wolf pack. James axes a wolf and drags her clear. Rhodes, enraged by seeing a wolf chewing the bloodied axe-handle handcarved by her father, runs back to grab the axe, leaving her too near the wolf to retreat: she uses the axe to chop off its head, then retreats while the other wolves devour it. She and James stand between their dog teams, watching the circling wolves; when the wolves start howling, Rhodes howls with them. The wolves attack again. James pushes her down but a wolf knocks him sliding on his back across the ice beyond the circle of dogs. Rhodes runs after him to stand over him swinging her axe. A helicopter and snow machines appear on the horizon but already the wolves, having tested James and Rhodes, are heading south to their forest.

But the race is not over: on the horizon they can see Bloody Bobby Franks, one of the hard men of the Iditarod, rapidly closing on them. Rhodes and James and their dogs run on raggedly. Almost in the chute on Nome's Front Street, James has a last trick — but Rhodes too has one. Their hands slap the victory arch almost together. They roll in the snow, laughing, their dogs jumping on them, the announcement of placings lost in the hubbub.

This example, also from Andrew McCoy, is for a complete novel. Note the page references to the key or set scenes, the ones where a film producer might find his 'production values'. A similar synopsis for a busy reader or editor included with your manuscript sent in on spec might ensure that your best bits are read!

CAIN'S COURAGE
Andrew McCoy
a brief synopsis

The novel's main theme is of American and Israeli Jews striking back at the South American Nazis who finance and train Palestinian terrorists. Here are a few of the high spots, with the page numbers referring to the HarperCollins paperback edition; the bold page numbers are recommended reading for film executives:

1. Motivation, pp**9-38**: Right after a rocket attack on the kibbutz where American businessman Mark Bern spends his holidays, he kills a blond German young man from South America in the dark. Rodzoventsky, an emeritus professor from the Sorbonne, has a theory the South American Nazis are financing and training the newly-efficient Palestinians but nobody believes him. Mark carelessly suggests to the rabbi that the Jews should apply Hitler's methods to their tormentors and is asked to leave the kibbutz because of it. In the morning, before he goes, two schoolbuses full of children are blown up by explosives planted under the diversionary cover of the rocket attack. Sarah, a kibbutz teacher and Rodzoventsky beg Mark to do something.

2. Planning, training, recruitment, logistics, determining beyond doubt that it's Max Spitz they want, establishing other characters in the Paraguayan milieu, setting up bases, pp41-104.

3. First strike, pp**104-173**: Their plan is to break the Nazis' secret bank. To find it, they abduct Maximilian Spitz's granddaughter Hilda (who turns out to be a sex-mad problem

teenager) and demand three truckloads of gold. Following the trucks leads them to the secret bank in the Paragauyan outback. But the exchange of Hilda for the gold goes wrong when Muller, Spitz's exhibitionist right-hand man, starts a firefight. Mark's party ends up with both the gold and Hilda. When they release Hilda, she signs herself into Madame Rosa's brothel — where she is discovered by Max Spitz being auctioned as the virgin of the week.

4. With the gold they buy the support of the local revolutionaries. They are told to lay off by Israeli Intelligence. Pp174-217.

5. MAIN CLIMAX — attack on the vault, pp**217-289**: This sustained action-centrepiece of the novel describes the attack on an almost impregnable fortress guarded by men, Rottweilers, a moat with snakes and piranhas, spraying acid, a guillotine door, an electrified tunnel, a falling roof, a Götterdämmerung explosion, und so weiter. After defeating all these obstacles, our heroes are betrayed by the revolutionaries, who make off with the gold and leave them locked up for the rapidly approaching secret-police torturers to find. Meanwhile Rodzo finds that the real wealth of South American Nazis was not the mountain of gold, but the contents of a plain grey filing cabinet full of title documents to holding companies based in Liechtenstein that own half the industrialised world (the post-War inflation as Hitler's real revenge). They fight their way out once more, carrying this filing cabinet with them.

6. They give the money to Israel but are despondent; they have hurt Spitz but he is selling land and carrying on training Palestinians. They arrange a meeting with Spitz in the training camp, fully aware that he will break his promise of safe-conduct... pp289-303.

7. The final climax, pp**303-316**: Spitz's betrayal, the final fight, Spitz, captured, digs his own grave — but now none of them can kill in cold blood. Spitz dies of anger when Muller, trying to bargain for his own life, betrays his employer's real identity: Bormann.

TELIVISION, FILM & RADIO

The length and appearance of a sample script for television, film or radio determines whether it is read at all. If it is too long or too short for the intended time slot, it is not read. If it does not appear professional to a quick glance, it is not read.

The appearance of the page is important because various creative and technical people on the production team must be able to grasp by merely glancing at a page whether it contains any instructions of relevance to them.

Parts much smaller than pages are numbered so that they may easily be found in rehearsal, or for substitution when rewritten. (In the film and broadcast industries rewrites are much more certain than either death or taxes.)

In films and television the largest unit separated from another by a new number is the scene, which ends any time the location shifts or the time of day changes; that is why film and television scenes carry headers defining the location as interior or exterior and describing the time of day (essential information for the chief lighting cameraman, the one credited as the cinematographer).

In radio the speech is the smallest numbered unit; every time a new actor speaks or new sound effect is introduced a new number is required.

It is imperative that you clearly distinguish:
• description of the set from instruction to the actors about how they should move
• dialogue from instruction on how it should be spoken
• camera instructions from the 'business' of the actors.

Above all it is crucial that nothing which is not dialogue can be mistaken for dialogue.

I demonstrate an accepted method for each of television, film and radio in the pages that follow. There are other ways

177

of doing the same thing but my illustrations have near-universal acceptance, with this small exception: the BBC, which is the largest market in the world for radio material, prefers speech-numbering to restart at 1 on each page rather than continuously from the beginning of the play, as in my version. However, if your word-processor insists on numbering paragraphs from the beginning of the document, the BBC will generously forego their preference. Do not count on any other producer to be so tolerant!

Note that, unlike in book manuscripts, single spacing is used. Leave large margins. Type on only one side of the page.

Synopses for film and television are constructed by similar principles as those for narrative prose. The main difference is that for film and television synopses the chain of motivation is absolutely everything. Even novices need only one written episode plus an outline for the rest to propose a major series. The exception is comedy, where producers demand to see several and sometimes all episodes for fear that you have used up all your jokes in the sample...

For television, a large-scale worked example:

DOMINOES
what if Britain proves ungovernable?
a teledrama in six one-hour episodes
by André Jute

OUTLINE: EPISODES 1-6

CONTENTS

THE STORY
2. SYNOPSIS:
3. NOTES:

        a) symbols
        b) location dialogue

EPISODE OUTLINES:

4.	1. May you live in interesting times
7.	2. Conflicts of interest
10.	3. Minute margins
13.	4. Blessed are the peacemakers
17.	5. The flick of a fingernail
20.	6. A fall of dominoes

THE SCRIPT
Episode 1: *'May you live in interesting times'* is bound separately.

DOMINOES

SYNOPSIS

DOMINOES asks, 'What happens if Britain proves even momentarily ungovernable?' and offers a partial answer (who could possibly offer a complete answer?) by depicting what happens to a group of people placed in contact and conflict by family, work, ideals and the events themselves.

The tale starts with a British Christmas, made vaguely uncomfortable by industrial action and with the hint of international concern that worse may come and set the dominoes tumbling... but what else is new? A few people have died of cold and hunger. Their deaths happened not because of the evil of men but because the conciliatory leaders on both sides of the dispute cannot muster a majority against hardliners who see the fight as a matter of principle. The vile weather is not helping and forecasts are for worse.

A National Government is formed and Sir Oliver recalled as Cabinet Secretary; he brings his son Adam, an economics lecturer at the LSE, with him as his personal assistant. Sir Oliver is a man who believes it is often better to take the wrong action, take responsibility for the consequences and learn from your errors, rather than to do nothing and let things slide into chaos. He is, however, no authoritarian and believes that, even in an emergency, government must proceed by consultation and consent, ie talk, the one commodity of which there is always too much in an emergency. But nor is it likely that those in command of para-political groups (here Buller's British Bastion, a conflation of Mosley's Blackshirts, National Front and Britain First ideas) will in the event be able to cause planned disruption on a decisive scale because they are hidebound by their own conventions. Moreover they are subject to governmental checks and to violent reactions from those they attack (and they always do attack some class or race before any attempt at a coup is made, if ever — in this play coups are threatened but not attempted). That leaves the power of the unions and the power of the government representing parliament or the will of the people. And, more sinisterly, it leaves the effects of chance events or of the malicious actions of insignificant individuals. In any society larger than a village, all eventualities cannot be foreseen and not all those that may be predicted can be controlled (even if one is willing to pay the price of Stalinist near-perfect control).

There are no evil men here. Tom Coburn and Beresford Marne are men of goodwill but both must persuade committees — they follow majorities. Buller may be a bigot but he is personally charming and courageous; he is willing, indeed keen, to go to gaol for his beliefs (and the greater glory of martyrdom). Even Terry and Jack, who cause an enormous amount of harm, do so for some twisted ideal of improving the human lot, though both are tainted by a taste for violence. Even so, their unpredictable acts of violence are rendered harmless by the crisis managers, except that repeatedly a bystander innocently starts a fatal chain reaction in good faith or ignorance. The bang in each episode is therefore set off in the main by the 'little people', those the men of consequence and power cannot even see, never mind regulate: the admirable nurse Sally, the unnamed soldier, a lowly Army Captain, even a small dog. Unpredictable consequences are by definition uncontrollable: of the central characters, only one does not survive and he is a blameless bystander, by nature an onlooker. Even Terry and Jack's masterstroke of disruption — flooding London — has the perverse effect of uniting people in defence of the capital. The dominoes can fall the other way as well, with magnanimity as a self-regenerating force.

SYMBOLS
Big Ben is used as a symbol throughout, both for the narrative in general and for Sir Oliver personally. This is not shown in these brief episode outlines, but can be seen applied in the script already written, Episode 1, '*May you live in interesting times*'.

LOCATION WORK
There is no reason the scripts should not be written to minimise location work requiring lipsynch as in the standing script.

EPISODE 1

MAY YOU LIVE IN INTERESTING TIMES

This episode is written. The master scenes here listed do not carry the same numbers as in the written episodes: master scenes have been split and intercut for narrative purposes, pace and tension.

MAIN TITLES OVER:
1. EXT. WINTRY COUNTRYSIDE. DAY. LOCATION.
Sir Oliver walks home from church on Christmas Day. His family pass him in their cars — and are typed by their cars and characterised by brief verbal exchanges.

2. EXT. SIR OLIVER'S HOUSE. DAY. LOCATION.
Adam arrives in a spectacular slide on the snow, with Siren, a beautiful American girl who is an ambitious journalist, something of a woman's libber, and who carries a chip on her shoulder despite being the daughter of the American Secretary of State.

END MAIN TITLES.

We learn that there is serious international concern that the trouble in Britain will 'be the start of the new Dark Ages for the whole world'.

3. INT. SIR OLIVER'S LIVINGROOM. DAY. STUDIO.
The family is gathered for the traditional Christmas Day meal but some have not come: Tom is saddened and angered that Jack has chosen to attend a picket line rather than the great family occasion. There is no electricity or heating fuel. Establish other characters: Siren watchful, sardonic; Adam aware that his views are respected despite his youth; Beresford a little stiff with strangers, dispassionate, impassive, controlled even in small things; Tom caring but frustrated

....and so on, scene by scene.

The layout sample for a teleplay is from Dominoes, *for which we just saw the proposal and outline:*

20. EXT. TILBURY DOCK GATE. DAY. LOCATION.

OWEN REACHES THROUGH THE HOLE IN THE FENCE, GRABS JACK'S ANKLE, TOPPLES HIM AND DRAGS HIM THROUGH THE HOLE.

CAMERA TIGHT ON THE HOLE IN THE FENCE.

INSPECTOR KERTIN'S LARGE BOOTED FOOT IS PLANTED FORCEFULLY BEFORE THE HOLE.

TERRY, JACK AND OWEN RUN AWAY TO THE SKYLINE OF CRANES.

KERTIN: Let them be now. They can't go anywhere. We'll pick them up later. (RAISES VOICE) Hey, Doc, here's one for you.

21. EXT. WHARF WITH CRANES. DAY. LOCATION.

HIGH ANGLE BUT ZOOMED TIGHT ON TERRY, JACK AND OWEN.

TERRY, JACK AND OWEN ARE RUNNING ALONG A WHARF UNDERNEATH CRANES.

WIDEN ANGLE AND TILT TO SHOW ROW OF CRANES STANDING NEATLY IN LINE ABREAST.

TERRY'S VOICE: Like ninepins, my old son.

22. EXT. WHARF UNDER CRANE. DAY. STUDIO.

TERRY, JACK AND OWEN STAND CLOSE UP TO THE

MASSIVE LEG OF THE CRANE, THEIR CHESTS HEAVING FROM THEIR EXERTIONS. TERRY GETS TO WORK STRAIGHTAWAY, PUTTING HIS KNAPSACK DOWN GENTLY AND TAKING A BATTERY-POWERED DRILL FROM IT. HE DRILLS A HOLE IN THE METAL WHILE OWEN LOOKS APPREHENSIVELY OFF IN THE DIRECTION OF THE FIGHTING.

SFX: DISTANT FIGHTING.

JACK WATCHES CLOSELY AS TERRY POURS A COLOURLESS JELLY INTO THE HOLES HE HAS DRILLED.

OWEN: Where'd you get that stuff?

TERRY: (NOT LOOKING UP) Melted it down from dynamite.

OWEN GASPS. HIS FACE IS A STUDY IN INCREDULITY AND SHOCK.

TERRY HOLDS HIS THUMB CAREFULLY OVER THE HOLE AND LOOKS UP.

TERRY: You know about dynamite and nitro, do you then?

OWEN: Yes, I work on the Thames barriers. Are you a docker?

TERRY: Naw, a lorry driver.

OWEN: Hey, you can't blow up other people's workplace.

TERRY: Tomorrow, Boxing Day, the wharfies are going to unload those ships.

The film and radio layout samples are from Pivot *and show Harry Luce and Ed Murrow on their way to persuade General Eisenhower to run for President. For film:*

32. INT. AIRPLANE. NIGHT.
TECHNICIANS SLEEP OR PLAY CARDS OR TALK
QUIETLY. DAVID SCHOENBRUN READS A SCRIPT.
HARRY, MURROW AND MURRAY HAVE GLASSES.
MURRAY HAS A BIBLE OPEN ON HIS KNEES.

MURROW
Answer me this, Harry. Under what
circumstances would you use *Time
Magazine* as a political instrument?

HARRY
(unhesitatingly)
If the Republic were in danger.

MURROW
When Wilson replaced Teddy
Roosevelt as President, the
Democrats had been out of power
for fifty-two years. It hadn't done
democracy any lasting harm.

HARRY
I know. But things move a lot faster
now. Look at how quickly weak
opposition parties damaged
Germany, France, Italy and Britain
between the wars. Are you so
certain American democracy is
indestructible?

MURROW LOOKS THOUGHTFUL BUT DOES NOT
ANSWER.

MURRAY
Forgive my ignorance but I thought
that a declared Republican like
Harry as a matter of course uses
his magazines to promote his
political outlook.

HARRY GRINS, THEN RAISES AN EYEBROW AT
MURROW.

HARRY
(chuckling)
I wish it were that simple. Ed's
good at this.

MURROW
(to Murray)
No, you're confusing objectivity
with truth and fairness. Harry
doesn't pretend to be impartial,
objective, uncommitted. But he
does undertake to tell the truth.

MURRAY
Which means what?

MURROW
That he presents the truth as he
determines it, on balance of
evidence, plus as much of the
opposing side's argument as is
necessary for his readers to make
a fair judgement.

MURRAY
(amazed, to Harry)
You'd give the Devil a fair hearing?

...and for radio:

1450 **SFX** THEY ENTER THE PLANE, THE STEPS ARE
WHEELED AWAY AND THE HATCH CLOSED.
1451 INSIDE THE AIRPLANE.

1452 **HARRY** Ed, this is the Reverend John
Courtney Murray. He's my moral support. John,
this is Ed Murrow.

1453 **MURRAY** Ed introduced himself.

1454 **STEWARD** **(shouting from back of plane)**
1455 Will you fellows sit down! We're rolling.

1456 **SFX** THE STEWARD STRIDES DOWN THE AISLE
TOWARDS THE THREE MEN.

1457 **STEWARD** Oh, I didn't know it was you, Mr
Murrow.

1458 **MURROW** **(easily)**
1459 I'm sure the same rules apply to everyone.

1460 **SFX** PLANE TAKING OFF.
1461 CROSSFADE TO:
1462 PLANE CRUISING.

1463 **MURROW** Answer me this, Harry. Under what
circumstances would you use *Time Magazine* as
a political instrument?

1464 **HARRY** **(unhesitatingly)**
1465 If the Republic were in danger.

1466 **MURROW** When Wilson replaced Teddy
Roosevelt as President, the Democrats had been
out of power for fifty-two years. It hadn't done
democracy any lasting harm.

1467 **HARRY**   I know. But things move a lot faster now. Look at how quickly weak opposition parties damaged Germany, France, Italy and Britain between the wars. Are you so certain American democracy is indestructible?

1468 **MURROW**   Mmm.

1469 **MURRAY**   Forgive my ignorance but I thought that a declared Republican like Harry as a matter of course uses his magazines to promote his political outlook.

1470 **HARRY**   **(chuckling)**
1471   I wish it were that simple. Ed's good at this.

1472 **MURROW**   No, you're confusing objectivity with truth and fairness. Harry doesn't pretend to be impartial, objective, uncommitted. But he does undertake to tell the truth.

1473 **MURRAY**   Which means what?

1474 **MURROW**   That he presents the truth as he determines it, on balance of evidence, plus as much of the opposing side's argument as is necessary for his readers to make a fair judgement.

1475 **MURRAY**   **(amazed, to Harry)**
1476   You'd give the Devil a fair hearing?

1477 **HARRY**   No, damn it, I would not, and you know it.
1478   **(suddenly laughs)**
1479   Anyway, not unless one of my editors backs the Devil.

INDEX

Active voice 72ff
Agent 38
Author as salesman 95–96
Author's mini-biography 59

Book publishing 15ff
Bulleted marketing points 59–60

Colour 54
Commissioning 9–13
Competition 51
Contracts 104ff
    example 116ff
Costing books 54–55
Cover letter 34

Editor
    features 28–29
    function in books 18ff
    function in magazines 27
    managing 27–28
    reading habits 67
Editorial functions
    see also Publishing functions
Examples
    Fiction 140ff
    Non-fiction 124ff
    Television film and radio
    177ff

Fiction examples 140ff
Film
    see Television, films and plays
Formats for samples 91ff

Genre 39–40

Illustrations 56-57, 84ff

Layout 91–92
Length 81, 55–56
Length of proposals and
    synopses 70-72
Libel 26
Links 102–103
    see also Sample Chapters

Memorability 68–70
Motivation, chain of 62ff

Non-fiction examples 124ff
Novels, market for 45ff

Pitch 40–42, 53–54
Plotting methods 82ff
Presentation 81–82
Proposal
    defined 32, 33
    dated 39

Publications list 35–37
Publicity 24
Publisher's reader 16–18
Publisher, the 24–25
Publishing functions
  in books 15ff
  in magazines 27ff

Reviews 37

Sales director 23–24
Sample chapters 93ff
  purpose 93–94
Size of book 55
Style of proposals and synopses
  72ff
Subsidiary rights 20–23, 47–51

Synopsis defined 32, 33

Target market 44ff
Television, film and radio examples 177ff
Television, films and plays
  11–12, 29ff, 91–92
Theatre
  see Television, films and plays
Tone of writing 101–102
Translations 50–51

Word count 55–56
Writer
  established 10–11
  new 9

SHARING THE STRANGENESS

For 37 years now – ever since Bob Rickard launched a modest publication called *The News*, soon to become *Fortean Times* magazine, back in 1973 – we've been collecting accounts of the unusual, the intriguing and the anomalous; the sort of stories that, if they make it into the mainstream newspapers, tend to be sidelines rather than headlines. As the world's foremost journal of strange phenomena, though, we can leave the workaday world of politics, gossip and sport to the others and concentrate on the far more interesting world of weird stuff; and over the decades we've followed the evolution of all kinds of oddities, from UFOs and crop circles to alien big cats and claims of psychic powers.

And through bringing these subjects to the fore, and talking about them in a rational way, we've also found that people are encouraged to come forward and share their own accounts of high strangeness. Now, you might not want to tell your friends, family or workmates that you've encountered an eight-foot tall tinfoil man or fled in terror from a pub loo because there was *something* evil lurking in the shadows – but you can tell *Fortean Times*.

And people continue to do just that, particularly since we introduced a dedicated 'It Happened to Me' section in the magazine and started an online forum where folks could share, compare and discuss their own strange experiences.

So, welcome to this third instalment in our ongoing overview of a very weird world; we hope you find plenty to make you reel in amazement, shiver in terror or just scratch you head in bafflement.

And, of course, if it's happened to *you*, do tell us about it...

David Sutton, Editor, *Fortean Times*

It Happened To Me!

REAL-LIFE TALES OF THE PARANORMAL
VOLUME 3

Ordinary people's extraordinary stories from the pages of FORTEAN TIMES

EDITED AND COMPILED BY
David Sutton and Paul Sieveking

PHOTOGRAPHY AND DESIGN *
Etienne Gilfillan

EDITOR IN CHIEF
David Sutton

COVER IMAGE
Etienne Gilfillan

PUBLISHING & MARKETING
Russell Blackman
020 7907 6488
russell_blackman@dennis.co.uk

BOOKAZINE MANAGER
Dharmesh Mistry
020 7907 6100
dharmesh_mistry@dennis.co.uk

* all photography by Etienne Gilfillan unless otherwise indicated

It Happened To Me!

REAL-LIFE TALES OF THE PARANORMAL
VOLUME THREE

ORDINARY PEOPLE'S EXTRAORDINARY
STORIES FROM THE PAGES OF **FORTEAN TIMES**

CONTENTS

CHAPTER 1   P8

UNCANNY ENCOUNTERS
Eerie entities and mysterious monsters

CHAPTER 2   P22

WEIRD WILDLIFE
Bizarre beasts and unusual animals

CHAPTER 3   P34

INVISIBLE FRIENDS
Children and their otherwordly companions

CHAPTER 4   P50

UFOS
Strange things seen in the skies – and their occupants

CHAPTER 5   P62

UNNATURAL WORLD
Forces of nature and spirits of place

CHAPTER 6   P74

UGLY RUMOURS
The scary side of urban legends

GHOSTLY GOINGS-ON

Haunted houses and horrifying hospitals

CHAPTER 8   P98

PARANORMAL POWERS

Premonitions, psychokinesis and SLIders

CHAPTER 9   P110

STRANGE SOUNDS

Disembodied voices and spectral screams

CHAPTER 10   P122

NOW YOU SEE IT...

Mysterious appearances and weird vanishings

CHAPTER 11   P134

NIGHT TERRORS

Waking dreams and unwelcome bedroom visitors

CHAPTER 12   P146

THE TWILIGHT ZONE

More tales of high strangeness

1 *Uncanny encounters*

Some of the most unnerving letters we've received concern encounters with beings that appear to be not quite human. These aren't the usual ghosts or spirits, more like interlopers from some other dimension or from our dreams and nightmares: a spooky harlequin, a salesman from another planet, a monster made of grass, or even the Victorian bogeyman Spring-heeled Jack.

EERIE ENTITIES

MEETING SPRING-HEELED JACK

I was making my way to Farringdon train station after having spent an evening out with friends in the Clerkenwell area of London. Not knowing the place very well, I got a bit lost and ended up walking the streets, looking for someone to ask directions.

London seemed strangely deserted that night and I freely admit I was starting to worry, about missing my train home more then anything else, but I also had the feeling of unease you only get if you are totally unfamiliar with your surroundings. If you were ever lost in a department store as a child, you will know what I mean. If you are acquainted with London, you will know that one minute you can be in the most modern metropolis then turn a corner and you are in a Dickensian cobbled alleyway. Well, it was down one of these alleys that my attention was drawn. Out of the corner of my eye, I noticed a darting figure and turned instinctively to look. The alley was lit sporadically by old-fashioned street lamps, and it was behind one of these lamps that I thought I could make out the shape of a figure trying to conceal himself. I pondered for a second on what it could be. I decided I would react to it in the traditional English manner – avert my gaze and pretend nothing was happening. As I was putting this plan into action, I heard a burst of shrill laughter. I turned to face the alleyway once more. Coming toward me in great lolloping movements was a tall, thin figure. It moved silently and was dressed in what looked like tight black leather. I could not make out its face, but I was transfixed by this apparition. It moved as if it were dancing in reverse, coming closer toward me, moving like a giant string puppet. Just as I gathered my wits enough to run, it issued another ear-piercing laugh, crouched on the ground, then shot off upwards out of my view. I did not try to see where it had leapt to – I ran as fast as I could until I found a main road. I followed the main road to the station and only just got the train home.

I have no idea what it was – probably a practical joke of some kind. However, a search on the Internet the next day brought up the name 'Spring-heeled Jack', not seen in London since the Victorian era.
Kevin -- , London, 2003

THE SHAPELESS ONE

The following experience is hard to classify, and I have never heard anything quite like it, although the "Shapeless One" or "Boneless" (described in McEwan's *Mystery Animals of Britain and Ireland*, 1986, p183) has some features in common. It happened around 11.30pm on 21 June 1975, when I was 19. I can pinpoint the location to the nearest yard, as I know the area extremely well. A friend and I were spending the night in a local nature reserve as part of a survey of a local badger population that we had begun at school, and after a fruitless examination of a sett which turned out to be abandoned, we laid out our sleeping bags on a dry spot and prepared to sleep.

It was a warm, dry and starlit night, very dark under the trees as there was, I think, no moon at all, but the nearby lights of Birmingham made the open ground slightly less dark. I went for a short walk before going to sleep, and on emerging from the woods onto the edge of the adjoining golf course, I saw a white shape under an isolated tree about a 100 yards (90m) away. My first thought was that the golf club had erected a notice on the tree, and I walked towards it to investigate. The silhouettes of the trees were visible against the sky, but very little else could be seen, and although the white shape didn't appear to be luminous it was surprisingly prominent. As I got closer, I could see the shape more clearly and, becoming uneasy, picked up a long stick and approached as quietly as possible. There seemed to be a very faint hissing from the direction of the object, but as I knew there was a waterfall a few hundred yards away to my

❝ All I could think of at the time was a spider writhing under a blanket ❞

right I couldn't be sure that the white shape was really the source of the sound.

The shape was by now clear, but it remained indescribable. All I could think of at the time was a spider under a blanket, for the surface was ridged as though by legs radiating out from a central shape, but the analogy was not exact. The ridge facing me was writhing as if what was underneath was more wormlike. The whole thing was about 4ft (1.2m) across and situated at the base of the tree as if stretched out on the ground. I advanced to within about 4ft of it, getting no reaction from it, and stood for a while trying to identify it with something I knew, including some sort of joke with human figures under a white sheet. Factors against this were the general shape, its almost complete silence (it occurred to me that I might have surprised a courting couple, but I could not reconcile this with what I saw) and the fact that its edges seemed blurred and indistinct, as if it faded out rather than just stopping. Having failed to account for it, I became nervous and retreated backwards, not taking my eyes off it until I was back in the woods. Altogether I must have watched it for five minutes, and apart from the writhing visible from close range it never moved.

I have been back to the site at night since, in an effort to identify something that could have caused the phenomenon, but have never seen anything similar again.

Chris Peters, Erdington, Birmingham, 1988

THE HARLEQUIN

About 40 years ago, I lived near a very small city in upstate New York. For about two years, whenever I was on the main street of the city, I would see this person dressed like a harlequin. This was very strange for such a conservative city, although, to my recollection, no one else on the street showed any reaction.

As a kid, I recall walking past this person (or whatever it was) and getting the most uncomfortable feeling from her – I think it was a 'her', since 'she' was dressed in dirty pink satin and stripes and wore filthy ballet slippers. Her face was also painted up like a harlequin. Her behavior was odd, too. She never blinked, but just stared vacantly into the distance. The other weird thing that used to frighten me was that I'd turn to get another look at her and she would suddenly be on the other side of the street. She was always dressed the same way, always behaving the same way, no matter what the weather. She acted strangely enough for me to be afraid that she would even look at me. I still get chills when I think of 'her' today.

Dave Tiger, by email, 2010

THE GRASS MONSTER

I asked a friend of mine if he had any ghost stories as he spent a few years working for British Rail in the UK. While nothing happened to him at that time, he had experienced two unaccountable incidents during his teens. This one is from October 1984, when he was 14.

He was with about eight school friends one dusky autumn evening, walking along a grassy path that runs at the side of a park in Didsbury, Manchester. It is called Sandhurst Road and, although it is properly surfaced at either end, there is a grassy dirt path, lined with trees but no houses, for about 200 metres (660ft) in the centre section. My friend was lagging behind the others by about eight or 10 steps over a part of the path that rises over a long-disused railway line. He wandered off the path, but only by a step or two, into a minor grassy area, say 8ft by 3ft (2.4m by 90cm) alongside a fence. He says that he was dawdling a little.

As he looked at the ground in front of his feet, he saw a series of normal, everyday, healthy grass stalks, about 10in (25cm) or 12in (30cm) long, only they were lying flat on the earth and not pointed upwards. As he watched, four of these stalks simultaneously "snapped" upright. They were so arranged that they formed the four corners of a square. He said they jerked upright but were arched slightly, bowed outwards. Then, in unison, they each bent at the middle and pointed inwards to join at what would have been the centre of the square. Without any kind of uprooting, the 'thing' started moving towards him.

My friend turned on his heel and ran the way he had come, away from his friends. Being then tall and athletic, he ran the 70 or so metres back down the path at top speed. The whole time he was running he said he felt something "buzzing" at his feet, first the left (being the side he saw the "grass monster" on) then the right. He almost fell and came off the path at one point, but soon reached the road proper and a wall with a house behind it. The whole time he had been running, he dared not look at his feet. When he reached the wall/house, he had the impression that the thing was gone, perhaps off to one side of the path into the undergrowth.

When he had calmed down, he checked his shoes and found that the laces on both of his shoes, at the knots, were unnaturally frayed in a way he had never seen laces frayed before, on what were practically new running shoes. He waited a moment and then ran back up the path, past the point where he had first seen the "grass monster" although without looking at the spot, and joined his friends, none of whom had seen anything. When asked what had happened he said that "a beast" had nearly got him.

My friend is well balanced, if a little creative and with a vivid imagination. I have no doubt he was telling the truth. He says at the time it happened he was a happy, untroubled kid and there were no drugs involved. He's open-minded enough to accept what occurred without questioning it too much.

Henry da Massa, Manchester, 2008

MYSTERIOUS MEETINGS

THE IMMORTAL COUNT

In 1972, shortly after I married a Dutchman and went to live in Holland, my mother visited me for a holiday. The day before she left, we were sitting in a small cafe on the edge of the red light district in Amsterdam. It was empty apart from a man sitting in a poorly lit corner. My mother was laughing and joking as usual. Suddenly, the man was standing next to our table. "Would you ladies mind if I joined you?" he asked in English with a slight French accent. My mother, in her usual friendly manner, said: "No, not at all. Please sit down." By way of apology for the intrusion, he said: "Your laughter was more than I could resist."

So began a long conversation, lasting three hours or more, taking in Amsterdam and her history, art, flowers, gold and jewellery. He seemed to know a lot about paint mixing and said that he spoke many languages. He talked a lot about diamonds and said he used to work in a factory around the corner. He talked as though he could even make the things!

When she could get a word in, my mother asked if he would like some coffee and cake. "No thank you, I don't eat," he replied. "I'll just have some mineral water." I noticed he was dressed all in black with small pieces of fancy white lace around his neck and wrists.

It was only years later that I came across references to Count St Germain, named by Madam Blavatsky as one of the 11 adepts who are always present in the world at any one time. In one source he is described as "all in black with touches of white linen at neck and wrists". He is said to have repaired a diamond for Louis XV, something unheard of. He worked in a diamond factory in Nieuwe Uilenburgerstraat – which happened to be just around the corner from the café where we met our 'man in black'. The Count could converse in nine languages and only ever drank mineral water, allegedly having discovered the secret of the Philosopher's Stone and eternal life. While he lived in Holland, he had a number of laboratories where he experimented with paint, improving the brightness of pigments and dyes. Had we really met the eternal Count?

Pauline Barbieri, Eastbourne, East Sussex, 1999

AN ANGEL CALLS

I am now 24 years old and am referring to when I was approximately three or four. I was living in a small, 100-year-old terraced house in a small town called Alnwick in Northumberland. It's strange, as to this day I still have relatively clear recollection of what happened...

In the kitchen of the house I had a blackboard and had been drawing a picture of my house with my mother, father, my newly born sister and myself. It was a bright sunny day and I guess around noon. I remember turning round to find my mother to show her what I'd been doing and right there in front of me was an angel. Now I don't know why I thought it was an angel, other than that's

what it told me it was.

It was around the same size as me. It didn't look like a person though, but like it was made up of clouds – there's no other way to describe it. I remember chatting to it – no words were said back to me out loud, but I kind of knew what it was thinking. It asked me about what I'd been drawing and if I was happy. I must have stood there for a good few minutes with it, then for some reason I got really excited and started bouncing up and down (I was only three or so!) saying it had to meet my mother. The angel said it couldn't do that, and quickly floated up and vanished. My mother came out from the front room only to be met with an over-excited kid trying to get upstairs to see where the angel went.

I was chatting to my mother years later about it, and she remembered the incident, and said around the same time some strange things had happened. A few times she'd woken up in the night to see me standing by her bed, but when she turned on the light nothing was there. One night she told my dad. He seemingly woke up, looked at the small figure said something along the lines of "Have you had a nightmare, John?" and fell back to sleep. My mother put her arm out to touch the figure and it just disappeared.

She likes a good story does my mam, but when she told me this she was deadly serious and, it seemed, quite reluctant to tell me.

John Pickard, by email, 2001

PEANUT SALESMAN FROM URANUS

At about 7.30 pm on 26 January 1986 I was watching TV when the doorbell rang. It was a tall, deeply tanned man wearing an olive-brown suit and a homburg, who said "Hello, sir, I am a representative of the Uranus Peanut Company. Would you like to sample my wares?" I said yes, whereupon he opened a shiny black suitcase and produced a brown paper bag full of peanuts. I took some. "They are delicious, aren't they?" he asked, smiling. I agreed and asked how much a bag was. "Two dollars forty-six," he replied. I gave him three dollars and told him to keep the change. "Thank you. The Council will remember you favourably. Good night."

He turned round and descended the stairs. After about five steps up the drive he seemed to vanish, because I couldn't see him after that. After a few minutes of perplexity, I thought 'he' must have been a spectral Man in Black.

Paul Rebek, Epping, New South Wales, Australia, 1986

> # " *The doll looked at me, with those big, black, empty Raggedy Ann button* "

HORRIBLE HOUSEMATES

RAGGEDY ANN

My wife and I, along with our five-year-old son and our new baby, shared a single bedroom and loft in San Francisco, near the beach. The bedroom opened directly to the living room, and had no door. One night, some time around 1995, I came home from work and walked through the living room towards the kitchen where my wife was cooking dinner. Our older son was in the backyard and the baby was asleep. As I passed the bedroom, I noticed a new addition to my wife's collection of stuffed animals. A large (at least three foot tall) Raggedy Ann doll sitting on the bed, facing the bedroom entrance. I walked to the kitchen, said hello to my wife, and made some small talk. After a moment or two, I asked where she had gotten the new Raggedy Ann doll. My wife looked at me blankly. She had no idea what I was talking about. She gave me a look as if there were large lobsters crawling out my ears. I repeated myself, but she still didn't understand, so I dragged her to the bedroom doorway to show her the doll.

There was no doll. The hair on the back of my neck stood to attention. Less than five minutes earlier, a rather large Raggedy Ann doll had been there, and no one could have moved it, as they would have had to walk past me to get to the bedroom. The more I thought about it, the more freaky the whole scenario seemed. The doll had been looking right at me, with those big, black, empty Raggedy Ann button eyes, and smiling in the way for which that type of doll is famous.

I have no explanation for this occurrence. If I had hallucinated a stuffed animal, what on earth would have made me see that doll? Why not a bear, a cat, or any number of animals? Raggedy Ann dolls have a distinctive look, and are not easily mistaken for another doll. I have never been able to look at Raggedy Ann (or Andy) quite the same since then. These dolls now creep me out, and probably always will!

Dirk Pierce, Palm Harbor, Florida, 2010

THE MAN IN BLACK AND THE WOMAN IN WHITE

What follows is what happened to me as a boy. My parents divorced when I was six years old. My mother took us from our house in Melbourne, Australia, to a series of temporary accommodations in Brisbane, her (and our) place of birth. When I was seven, we finally moved into a house. It took my mother a long time to find a place both big enough for all of us and cheap enough for a single mother to afford. It was an old place, a timber 'Queenslander'. I have no idea just how old it was, but there was an old coal burner kitchen that was blocked off from the 'modern' gas kitchen. This meant that the house must have been built a minimum of 50 years earlier, and could have been much older.

As the youngest (I had three older sisters at the time), I got the smallest room – just big enough for a bed and not much else.

From the beginning, I didn't like the place. I don't remember at what point I realised it was haunted, but I have early memories of closing my eyes before entering rooms, particularly at night. When alone in my room during the day, I saw shadows dancing around the corners of my vision. I got used to it in the end. I was too scared to try and talk to the 'ghosts' – I knew they weren't friendly and were teasing and mocking me. At night, I would sleep with the sheets over my head, too terrified to open my eyes. Occasionally, I would feel them touching me with probing fingers.

One day when I was nine years old, I was talking to my mother who was watching television, and I entered the hallway leading to my room without closing my eyes first. I looked directly into my room and saw something that burned into my consciousness and has stayed with me to this day.

It was a man, dressed entirely in black. He was rather ordinary looking – balding, with a narrow strip of hair around the back of his head – but everything else about him was far from ordinary. He was draped in a transparent black veil that covered his whole body, under which he wore a black tank-top. He was bent over, and doing something with his hands on the wall. I saw him side-on. He heard me, and turned his head to face me. He stared at me for a whole second. His eyes were bright red, like a modern red LED. He had no expression, but unlike the other shadowy figures I would see during the day, he was completely solid and looked 'human'. Abruptly, and without a sound, the man ran directly into the wall and vanished. I was left standing, speechless with terror. I told my mother what I had seen, and she just laughed at me.

I moved from that room shortly after, when my eldest sister moved out, into the room on the other side of the hallway. I was very careful after the incident not to look towards my old room without showing myself first. I never saw the creature again, but the occasional 'touching' continued until we finally left the house in 1977 when I was 11 years old. As an adult, I have been back to look at the outside of the house, but even now I would not be game enough to go inside again. But the story doesn't end there.

We moved into another house, after my mother and I had lived in a flat for a year and my sisters had all left home. I reverted to my old habits of closing my eyes before entering a dark room and sleeping under the sheets. Then, after we had been in the new house for a few months, I had some friends around for a sleepover. We all slept together in the lounge. I woke in the middle of the night, and felt a peace unlike I had ever felt before in my short life. It was a calm that went completely through me. I opened my eyes, and saw a woman.

She was standing in the doorway, and dressed in a long white dress that covered her feet, a lot like a bride on a cake. There was a pattern on the dress, but I couldn't make it out. She stood about five feet (1.5m) tall and had curly, light brown hair. She was looking directly at me, and was smiling. I looked at her, and smiled back. She was lovely, and I have never felt like that before or since. And then, before my eyes, she slowly vanished. I looked at where she had been standing for a few minutes, and went back to sleep, feeling wonderful.

To me it was obvious why the lady had appeared. I have always believed that she knew what I had gone through over five years in the other house and was telling me that I was safe in 'her' house. It changed my life, and I stopped being frightened. I never saw the lady again.

Many people will dismiss my experience because of my age at the time. All I can say in reply is that I know that this is how it happened. I am not the sort (not now nor then) to imagine events and pass them off as real. I can't explain the events, or the reason for the first house's haunting. Neither my sisters nor my mother saw anything strange in the house, to my knowledge.

Perhaps some of the events were simply the imaginings of a frightened little boy. Even the woman in white could have been a fragment of a dream (although I do not believe so). But the vision of the man in black was real, without the slightest doubt in my mind. I always believed it to be a demon, or perhaps a lost soul. I don't know if I really want to know the answer.

Robert Euston, by email, 2002

THE SHADOW PEOPLE

When I was a girl I was brought up, until the age of 10, in a maisonette block in Southampton. I lived there with my mum, one older and one younger brother, and later a stepfather. I used to see 'shadows' quite often, especially walking up and down the stairs. I remember them being human-shaped, but like silhouettes and semi-transparent, and with very round heads. I asked my older brother a few years ago if he had ever seen anything there, and he described the figures to me perfectly.

There were at least two other odd events connected to this place. Every night in bed I would hear a certain noise and got so used to it I'd wait to hear it before I dropped off to sleep. It was the sound of three 'grandfather' marbles (the really, really big ones) dropping one by one and making a sound as if they were rolling across a wooden floor. I was reminiscing with my mother in 1993, when I was 19, and told her about those noises. She was gobsmacked. She said that when I was very young, before my younger brother was born in 1978 (so I would have been three or four and my older brother four or five) the old lady that lived below us came up one day and angrily accused her of letting us play with marbles very late at night. My mother assured her that it wasn't us, and as the family above us had children, set off to ask them. They claimed they had not heard the noise and it certainly wasn't their children.

The other incident concerned my younger brother, who was about three at the time. One night he woke my mother with the utmost urgency. He claimed he had seen a man and some pigs walk into the bathroom! Well, the maisonette was built on old farmland, and the dairy next door still existed and was in use!

Amanda-Jayne Sherwood, by email 2002

The animal kingdom throws up constant surprises, from unusual behaviour we'd normally associate with humans – cats or birds holding what seem to be meetings and even courts – to creatures that flout the laws of nature, like gigantic rabbits and flying snakes. And then there are those curious critters that simply defy description and are perhaps best left to the cryptozoologists...

CREATURE CONVENTIONS

MAGPIE MENACE

On 4 October 1997, I was on board my boat moored on a sharp bend midway between New Bradwell and Great Linford on the Grand Union Canal. Hearing a sharp squawk that I took to be an alarm call, I saw three moorhens running swiftly along the ground and making no attempt to get airborne. I then saw that they were being menaced by a crescent of about 20 magpies, each about five or six yards from its neighbour. They advanced at a steady pace so that the 'sweep' extended the full width of the visible pasture. Despite the fact that the birds passed from view without a 'kill' being observed, I have no doubt that the magpies were engaged in an organised hunt for live prey. I don't know if this was unusual, but I have never heard of such conduct before.
IR Harrison, Ewhurst Cranleigh, 1998

BIRD BRAWL

On Monday 20 April 2005, my wife and I were travelling into Dublin along the N11 dual carriageway. At the Stillorgan bypass section, we were approaching a set of lights when we noticed what we both believed to be a large black umbrella lying on the ground at the junction to our left. As we drew closer, the 'umbrella', which I assumed to be flapping in the breeze, revealed itself to be a mass of magpies and hooded crows physically attacking another hooded crow which was lying on its back, apparently fighting for its life. The magpies and crows (from previous observation, not the best of friends) were working in conjunction in their frantic assault. Our observation of the event only lasted perhaps 30 seconds, but left me with a sickened feeling, much as if I'd witnessed a street brawl. My wife, who is far more pragmatic than me, admitted that it was weird.

Malcolm Blacow, Dun Laoghaire, Dublin, Ireland, 2005

CROW THUGS

I live in the Cornish China Clay area and often use the country back roads. One Sunday evening towards the end of the summer of 2002, I decided to go to the cinema in town, and took my usual back route through the clay industrial area. It was a warm, muggy evening. I turned off at a junction and as I made my way towards the brow of a hill, I noticed a commotion up ahead. I saw three large black objects, which I took to be black bin-liners blowing around in the wind; but as I approached I saw they were three large crows trying to subdue a large rat. When they saw my van approaching, they abandoned their quarry and took off, with the rat scuttling into the hedgerow. I have often seen magpies scavenging rabbit road-kill, but this spectacle was really bizarre.

James Sherriff, Fore St, Nanpean, Cornwall, 2006

SCHOOL FOR BIRDS

One day in the early winter of 1998, I set off to work at around 6.30am. It was just about daybreak as I approached my local private hospital in Harrow. Near the car park, around 30 magpies were gathered together under the streetlights. They seemed unconcerned at my close proximity as I stood still to observe. All of the birds were quiet, apart from an occasional clucking sound, which appeared to be coming from the 'senior' magpie at some distance from the others. It seemed to be addressing the attentive and watching birds. I remember thinking the scene resembled a school assembly. As I had to be on duty, I couldn't stay to watch what happened next.

Bryan Fraser, Ealing, London, 2009

> **❝ It was obviously some kind of ritual, and I was a privileged observer ❞**

CAT CONVENTIONS

At the age of about 14, I was awakened in the small hours one morning by incessant noise from a number of cats nearby. Our back garden was enclosed by a high wall, and beyond one side was a road. The noise seemed to be coming from that direction, so I grabbed the top of the wall, hoisted my head above the brickwork and peered into the road, which was lit with street lamps. I was astonished to see a large circle of cats surrounding two cats who appeared to be facing each other off. The proceedings appeared to be under the authority of a large ginger tom sitting in the circle to one side of the other two, overseeing the confrontation. At my appearance over the wall all of the cats ran off, apart from the large ginger tom who looked at me for a few seconds, then slowly got up, very disdainfully turned his head away, and walked off slowly down the road with his tail erect.
Patrick Foord, Bexhill on Sea, East Sussex, 2010

My half-Siamese cat fetched me from the house and took me down to shrubbery at the bottom of the garden. There I found five other cats in a rough semicircle. She took position facing the other cats and after a period of 'cat talk', where it was obvious I was being introduced, each cat took it in turn to caterwaul and receive response from each in turn. The vocal session lasted at least four or five minutes, after which the visiting cats dispersed and I was taken back to the house. It was obviously some kind of ritual and I was a privileged observer. I have discussed this event many times over the years, but never got any meaningful information.
Don Parish, Brendon, North Devon, 2009

I am a police officer and routine night patrols are part of my regular duties. One quiet midweek night in early December 2009, my colleague and I were doing our usual local burglary prevention patrol. As we turned a corner into a well-known local estate at 2am, my colleague braked sharply. In front of us was a big fat white cat, with patches of tabby in various places, facing a semi-circle of smaller cats, all wearing collars. For a few seconds we just stared at them, then laughed as the big moggie in the centre, who appeared to be holding court, was not sitting in a normal position like the others, but in a relaxed manner almost on his tail with his legs spread apart. We joked that all he needed was a hat and cane and he would look like a pimp or gangster. None of the cats moved or even turned except the big white cat, which stared at us looking nonplussed, then opened his mouth. The engine noise didn't allow us to hear if he made any sound, but at that moment all the other cats sauntered off in different directions. Mr Big waited, then lazily got up and swaggered off into the night. The whole incident lasted approximately 10-15 seconds. Had we disturbed a cat underworld meeting? Has Mr Big now put a contract out on us? I'll await the fish-bone head on my doorstep.
Andy -- , by email, 2010

We've experienced a couple of 'cat conventions' in our own suburban back yard. As far as I can recall, this occurred in the summer of 2006 when our two female cats were about a year old. We like having our cats in at night and as the twilight was deepening and they were still out, I went out to look for them, figuring they would be hanging out in our yard. I discovered not only our two cats, Shadow and Dusty, but every cat at our end of the block: Prescott, Charlie (British shorthairs), and Mouse (American tortie) who belong to a British family across the street, and Pizza (calico barn cat) who lives on the street behind. These cats rarely get along under normal circumstances and it was unprecedented to find them all in the backyard grouped in a loose circle. It looked for all the world as if they were having a meeting, although I didn't notice any cat particularly 'in charge'. They were all relaxed – there was none of that body tension that is so apparent when cats are irritated by other cats. When I came suddenly into their presence, it seemed to break a spell and they started wandering off in different directions as I collected Shadow and Dusty. There was still no running or slinking or other startled cat behaviour. It was really weird. There were other evenings that summer when I would look out and see them all in the backyard, but I tried to leave them to get on with it.
Tracey Serle, Alexandria, Virginia, 2009

I was walking home about 10.30 one dark night three years ago when I saw a gathering of about 15 cats sitting close together in a circle around a wild rabbit, about 100 yards (90m) from my house in Bridgend, South Wales. I stopped and watched them, and after a few minutes they slowly dispersed.
Ron Brain, Bridgend, South Wales, 2009

CRYPTO CREATURES

THE BIG BUNNY OF BANBURY

Last autumn, my family and I went with friends on a canal boat along the Napton-Banbury route. Heading north on 24 October, on the highest stretch of the canal we saw a huge creature on the sloping field to the right of us. I thought it was an adult deer with its legs tucked under, as they do. The colour and size were right, though the ears were rather big. My friend David and Mandy my wife both saw it through binoculars and got very excited as they described it as a giant rabbit. We saw it turn and hop/bound into a nearby hedge – too chubby and rounded to be a hare, not really like a wallaby or kangaroo... just like a domestic rabbit, only bigger.

Have you had any sightings of a reddish-gold lagomorph at least as big as an adult golden retriever? Local people seemed unmoved by our report.
Tim Hill, by email, 2007

With reference to The Big Bunny of Banbury: I too have seen this kind of animal while living in Wendlebury, 20 miles (32km) south of Banbury, in summer 2005. Driving home one evening around 5pm, I saw at the side of the road what can only be described as a giant rabbit, perhaps as big as a large dog, light brown, and with a rather pointed face. My brain seemed to refuse to process this image, and, as I drove by, it just sat on its haunches and looked at me. After a few seconds, I realised what I'd seen, stopped and reversed, but I didn't see it again. I know what I saw, and – after much ridicule – I'm quite relieved to discover that other people have seen it too.
Clive Parker, by email, 2007

KING HARE

In the hot summer of 1976, I set off with a pack-pony and greyhound from Stow-In-The-Wold. I was starting a long-distance trek as a sort of pilgrimage and also to explore ancient trackways. The journey took me through the Cotswolds, the Wiltshire Downs, west Dorset coastal areas and then ended in Butleigh, near Glastonbury. It took me a couple of months.

During early September, I was travelling through the hamlet of Uploders, near Bridport in Dorset. I had permission to put my pony in an orchard there and after erecting my tent, I decided to head off up into the neighbouring hills to see if my dog could catch a rabbit or hare for the pot. On a lonely track I met up with two gypsy men and their lurchers and we decided to combine forces. We walked in the evening sun, enjoying the views and we came across a valley. There we saw a group of around 10 hares, an unusual sight for the time of year, as they are solitary animals, only congregating in early Spring. With them seemed to be a roe deer, until we looked a little harder and saw that it was an enormous hare. We stood and watched, absolutely dumbfounded. We obviously didn't loose the dogs and after a while we walked quietly away.

Louise Hodgson, by email, 2008

CAR PARK LIZARD

I have been interested in cryptozoology since I was 16 or 17, some 30 years ago, but have always considered myself an armchair cryptozoologist, one who read and researched the subject, but not a field investigator who might actually get to see a crypto-creature for himself. All this changed dramatically one hot summer day in 1984 in Miami, Florida.

I was on vacation in Bal Harbour, near Miami, and decided to take a tourist bus to the Miami Seaquarium for the day. The Seaquarium has many fine attractions, including a shark channel stocked with big sharks and rays. I spent an enjoyable three or four hours looking at the porpoises, manatees and tropical fish, then headed out to the parking lot, where I expected to catch my bus for the return trip to my hotel.

As I walked across an open area with a few bushes and trees, I saw an enormous lizard, 4ft (1.2m) long or more, walking towards me. It had huge jaws, a long tail and very impressive claws. My initial reaction was to wonder if the lizard might be an animal from the Seaquarium, but it hardly seemed likely that such a dangerous-looking animal would be allowed to wander around loose.

Also, it was no longer inside the grounds of the Seaquarium.

I happened to have a small Kodak Instamatic camera and took several pictures of the animal as it walked past me, paused briefly in the shade of a tree and disappeared into some high grass in the direction of a rubbish dump alongside a wire fence. Although I am no expert, it looked to me like a giant iguanid. In fact, it looked most like the now nearly extinct Rhinoceros Iguana.

This odd experience changed my attitude towards people who report strange animals. When one has had such an experience, it is no longer possible to accept the derision of the sceptics at face value. It seems that unexpected sudden appearances are precisely the way most unknown or out-of-place animals are observed. People don't expect to see them, and they can hardly believe it when they do. It will always be the bored driver on a lonely road at night who will be the one to see Bigfoot. What could be more unlikely than seeing a giant lizard in the middle of a huge city? It would be easy to doubt the truth of my experience, yet I know it happened and the photographs I took back me up. I didn't imagine the lizard and I didn't exaggerate its size.

Cryptozoology relies for much of its validity on the credibility of witnesses. Yet only one who sees a strange animal can really appreciate the bizarre quality of the experience and be ready to listen with an open mind to the accounts of others. This need for a personal initiation before one can truly accept the possibility of the unknown is characteristic of all fortean phenomena. There will always be a gap between those who are interested but sceptical, and those who have seen for themselves. When I looked into the matter, I discovered that the Crandon Park Zoo, which formerly occupied Virginia Key, was rumoured to have 'dumped out' some snakes and lizards when it closed down. It's hard to believe though that any zookeeper in his right mind would have let go a lizard as big as the one I saw in the middle of a city. And while some large lizards have turned up in southern Florida, they have been monitor lizards, not iguanids like the animal I saw. I suppose those inclined to psychic explanations might say that my intense interest in unknown animals conjured up for me my very own 'monster'.

Experiencing fortean phenomena alters one's ability to believe in the experience of others. As Ivan T Sanderson wrote of poltergeists: "It is no use saying these things don't happen, because they do." The same is true of unknown animal sightings. Now I know that it is no use saying they don't happen, because I know they do.

Ronald Rosenblatt, New York, 1996

“It had a black pointed head with a frilly ruff around the short neck part”

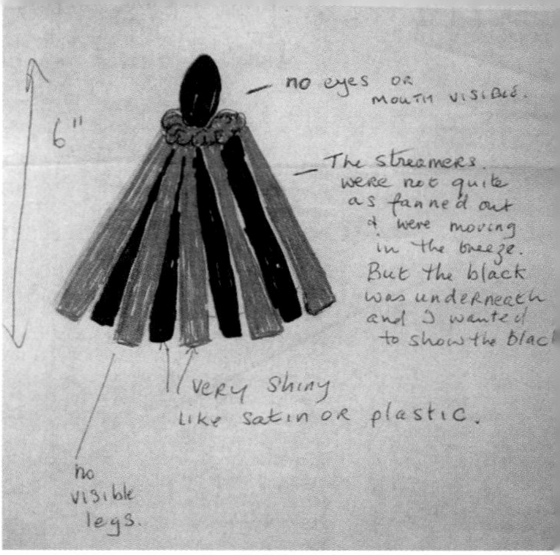
6"
no eyes or
mouth visible.
The streamers
were not quite
as fanned out
& were moving
in the breeze.
But the black
was underneath
and I wanted
to show the blac
very shiny
like satin or plastic.
no
visible
legs.

FLYING ARROW

In 1960 or 1961, when I was 11 or 12, I was living near Acomb, Northumberland. I fancied myself as a painter (I'm not). One lovely sunny day in July, when my parents were out, I set up my easel and was painting away when I heard a kind of whistling and whooshing sound behind me. Turning, I saw something flying towards me. I remember thinking that someone had fired an arrow at me. I threw myself to the ground and whatever it was passed over my head. When I stood up, I saw that the 'arrow' had flown across the yard and stuck nose first into the front door. I went to investigate and when I got to within a couple of feet, the 'arrow' settled vertically beside the doorknocker, which it approximated in length (6in/15cm).

The thing had a black pointed head, with a frilly ruff around the short neck part. The body was black and very shiny, about as thick as my index finger. Hanging from the neck were about six very shiny red, ribbon-like 'streamers', about half an inch (12mm) wide at the end and tapering towards the neck to about a quarter-inch (6mm). There were similar black streamers underneath. To my extreme fright, the thing then moved and started whirling and spinning, making a whistling sound. I ran from the front door, jumped a 4ft (1.2m) dry stone wall with ease, with the thing whistling behind me and following me around the back of the house. I went inside, locked the door, and dragged a heavy dresser across the doorway. I hid in the pantry until my parents came home. Of course they laughed at me and said I had seen a dragonfly or a hornet; they just didn't listen, so I stopped talking about it.

One day I delivered some eggs to an old guy in the village and we got talking. I told him what I had seen and he said: "I haven't seen one of those things for over 50 years. They're called flying arrows." I don't know whether or not he was just humouring me. I have looked in many insect books and have never seen this thing described or portrayed, and it has bothered me ever since. Can anyone suggest an identification?
Ruth Summersides, Qu'Appelle, Saskatchewan, 2007

CORNISH CRITTER

I currently live and work in Falmouth, Cornwall. Between 4pm and 5pm on 4 February, I went for a walk along the Maenporth coastal path from Swanpool after I'd finished work. Coming up the path round by the coast, I saw something moving in a bush ahead of me. I assumed it was a bird or maybe a dog being walked, but as I got nearer I realised it was neither. It was a little bigger than a dog and had a cat's face with eyes that were glazed over and luminescent like a lion's at night. When it saw me it walked away, apparently on two hind legs much like a kangaroo. It had a bushy tail like a fox. Has anyone seen anything similar?
Sam Bradbury, by email, 2009

FLYING SNAKES

I was about five years old in 1957, living with my family in Pikeville, eastern Tennessee. As I played alone near our house, a deafening rattling, clacking noise came up behind me, from above. I looked up and plainly saw a black snake, maybe 3ft (90cm) long, travelling in a side-to-side S motion, as if it were swimming in the air. It had small, dark wings near the front – bat-like and oddly rectangular. The snake quickly flew out of sight over our one-storey house. I didn't see its head, or any patterns on its body. I was absolutely frightened out of my wits and I don't know if I told anyone about it.

My rational mind offers two suggestions. Maybe I saw a hawk fly off with a rattlesnake in its claws. As an adult, I witnessed a hawk carry off a squirrel, and the twisting of its long tail as the hawk flew away did remind me a bit of my childhood experience. My second idea is that a helicopter flew over me, which I'd never seen before. The sound, to my adult memory, almost seems loud enough to have been a helicopter (although more like a rattle), and I know one did take aerial photos of our town when I was a small child. But that leaves me wondering how and why my five-year-old mind would have turned a helicopter into a flying snake.

A final note: I recently read a book on the mythology of the prehistoric Native American tribes who lived in what is now Tennessee and the surrounding area before the Cherokee; it was full of illustrations of the winged rattlesnakes which decorated their pottery and which were apparently sacred totem creatures.

Julia Morgan Scott, Chattanooga, Tennessee, 2009

The accounts of flying snakes brought to mind a story told by my mother, Mrs Hazel Göksu, who is now 73. She lived in a village in the mountains of Bulgaria until 1950, when she emigrated to Turkey with her family at the age of 15. Her life in Bulgaria had not been easy. She had to leave school at 10 to support her motherless family of six.

"When I was a little girl," she said, "I used to go and fetch fresh water from the spring 200m (660ft) from our house. One lovely summer evening (when I was 12 years old), I picked up two buckets and started to walk towards the spring. After about 40 metres (130ft), I noticed what looked like branches on the path, but as I got closer I saw them moving. They were black, grey and white, thin and one or two metres (3ft 3in to 6ft 7in) long. I stopped, thinking they might be snakes, but they were moving in a straight line, not like snakes at all.

"As I got closer, something alarmed them and they noticed me. They gave the weirdest cry I have ever heard before taking off and flying two or three metres (6ft 7in to 9ft 10in) above the ground, straight as arrows. They flew all the way to the spring about 150m (490ft) away and disappeared behind the trees. I don't remember seeing any wings on them. Whenever I remember that cry, it makes the hair on my arms stand on end. I returned home and never went to the spring alone again."

As she told me this story, I clearly saw the hairs rising on her arms. She remembers that one of the snakes was longer than the others, which were probably juveniles. They flew stiffly but made crawling-like movements in the air. She has never seen such snakes again and hasn't heard similar stories from anybody else. She is healthy and sane. The story is hard to believe but I think she is telling the truth.

Izzet Göksu, Bursa, Turkey, 2009

3 Invisible friends

Many of us, or our children, have experienced 'imaginary childhood friends' – those curious companions, usually invisible to adults, often said to be dreamt up by lonely kids with overactive imaginations. But what if these strange, surreal, and sometimes rather spooky, entities – which have been dubbed 'Quasi-Corporeal Companions' – are more than just childish fantasies?

QUASI-CORPOREAL COMPANIONS

LOST TWIN?

I had a sister three years my junior, so although I was a very shy child I was never consciously lonely. When I was seven, we shared a bedroom and I would make up stories until my sister went to sleep. I had a quasi-corporeal companion (QCC) called Doreen who was truly invisible. My mother always had to set an extra place at table for her, and she slept under my bed. I did see her sometimes in my mind's eye – a little girl with auburn hair in plaits – my double, in fact! I only connect her with one house we lived in: it was in Enfield, north London, when I was about five to seven years old.

I went to a very religious (Church of England) boarding school. Doreen didn't follow me there, but I was conscious of 'eyes' looking at me from above and I used to lie in bed reaching up to these presences. Articles in an old book about Spiritualism in the school library set me on a path – and I do have some psychic ability. So was Doreen a manifestation of early psychic development, and the way my guardian spirit chose to manifest at that time?

I have another theory, rather off-the-wall. According to Charles E Boklage (Laboratory of Behaviour and Development Genetics, East Carolina University): "One of every eight human conceptions begins as a twin conception, and for every twin pair born alive, 10 to 12 twin pregnancies that begin as twins result in a single birth." (The missing fœtus is absorbed into the womb.) Spiritualists believe that such children grow up in the spirit realm even if not born on Earth. As Doreen seemed to be my double, was she a 'lost' twin? (I know this reads like an *X-Files* script.)

Diana Lyons, Sheepscar, Leeds, West Yorkshire, 2009

BASEMENT ELF

When I was a child, my family lived above the family business in a house with many rooms ranged over five floors. At the rear of the building there was a trap door set into the floor, which led to the basement. The stone steps were very old and worn and my parents considered them too dangerous for my younger sister or me to use. In any case, the trap door was too heavy for a four-year-old to lift, so we never went down there.

I remember the first time I encountered my own QCC. I was sitting on the stairs about 6ft (1.8m) from the entrance to the basement when to my surprise the trap door began to open. There emerged from the basement an elflike creature, about as tall as I was at the time, dressed entirely in green and brown with a pointed hat. As soon as the trap door had begun to open, I was completely paralysed, able neither to move nor speak. The creature came over and sat next to me on the stairs. He spoke to me in a strange clicking and whistling language that I couldn't understand, but somehow I knew his name was Frick Frick. After he had said all he had to say, he went back to the basement entrance and waved goodbye as he pulled down the trap door. The instant the trap door was shut, the paralysis left me and I was normal again.

I met Frick Frick many times in the next three or four years, always in the same circumstances, always in the hall of the house. I was paralysed at each encounter, but no longer afraid – after all, Frick Frick only ever sat next to me and spoke softly, occasionally tapping me on the arm as he spoke his strange language. We moved out of that house about four years later when I was about eight, and I never saw Frick Frick again.

In the years since then, I have spoken about Frick Frick to both my brother and sister. Neither of them remember being visited by Frick Frick, but my brother, who is two years older than me, remembers often seeing me sitting on the stairs by the trap door just staring into the distance as though in a trance.

John Burke, London, 2009

" *Jack used to talk about the North Pole and his friends there frequently* **"**

JACK AT THE NORTH POLE

At the age of two, my eldest son Jack started to tell us all about his visits to the North Pole. Of course, he met Father Christmas there, but he also had a whole range of other friends, and there was a vague impression that Jack himself was in charge. He had a dog called Sally, a badger called Stocktaking (who taught the cuttlefish to climb trees, apparently), a strawberry farm that was very high up (so no one could steal the strawberries) and therefore a diplodocus that harvested the fruit (as no one else could reach). There were also two shops: The Dying Shop (we never really managed to clarify what went on there), and The North Pole Shop, which sold everything else you could want. There was a tap which, when turned on, poured out sweets instead of water.

Jack used to talk about the North Pole and his friends there frequently – a dozen times a day we'd get updates on what was going on there. A bit like some kind of bizarre soap opera. The strangest conversation I ever had with him, when he picked up an odd-shaped container in the bath, went like this:

Jack: "Oh! It looks a bit like a steedle pot!"

Me: "What's a steedle pot?"

Jack: "We have them at the North Pole. When the sea starts running out of water, we all get our steedle pots and fill them with water at the tap. Then we all wade out into the sea and say 'one two three go' and tip them into the sea. Then we all go back again with no paddling."

Me: "And why are they called steedle pots?"

Jack: "Because they're covered in steedles."

Me: "And what is a steedle?"

Jack: "Well, it's a bit like a present, only not wrapped up."

Jack's relationship with the North Pole continued for over six months, until he was almost three, when it was superseded by his farm, which became as fixed a part of his life. It wasn't the most conventional of farms. It had a windmill and ducks and sheep, but it also contained, – among other things – a marble-making machine that could make marbles bigger than itself. This continued for another six to nine months, and then gradually faded out, perhaps because by then his younger brother was big enough to play with – or perhaps for some other reason...

Roni Jay, Great Ambrook, Devon, 2009

MR NOBODY

I had my own QCC as a three-year-old in 1977. He was a snowman about 2ft (60cm) tall with a bright orange carrot nose, black coal eyes, coal buttons and black hat – but as far as I can remember there was never a scarf. He would never talk or play with me – I seemed to know that it was a he – but would just sit at an odd angle up near the ceiling or on top of the front room light shade (never on the floor), and just watch me play. I was never frightened of him, just accepting that he was there, and nothing out of the ordinary.

A couple of times my mother had caught me talking to him out loud or just looking up at him. She would ask: "Who are you talking to?" or "You talking to Mr Nobody again?" The name stuck and I would refer to him as that. My parents divorced in 1981, and my mother, two sisters and I left the Barbican in central London and moved across the river to Lewisham in south-east London, and I never saw Mr Nobody again.

Daniel McQueen, Whitstable, Kent, 2009

GEE-GEE AND MONKEY

My son had two invisible friends, "Gee-Gee and Monkey", and he was always talking to them and about them as soon as he could talk. We never found out if they were talking animals or people with strange names. We were on holiday when he was five and a half. The day before we were to return home, he said Gee-Gee and Monkey like living at the seaside so they are staying here. Apparently, they waved goodbye to us as we drove away and he never mentioned them for a whole year.

The following year, our destination was some miles further on. As we drove along the road about a quarter of a mile (400m) from our previous holiday, he suddenly waved and said: "Look, there's Gee-Gee and Monkey. They are still living here!" This was without any hint of where we were. This struck me as surprising, as a year is a very long time at that age.

Incidentally, he was an only child until he was four and a half; but I don't think that had any effect on the QCCs.

Peter Millie, by email, 2009

CINDY AND JOJO

When I was three to five years old, I had two QCCs called Cindy and Jojo, who always accompanied one another. Cindy was a girl a bit older than me and Jojo was a dog that followed her around. I recall that Cindy had long black hair and wore a floor-length red sequin dress, and Jojo was sandy-coloured – a bit like Dougal from the *Magic Roundabout*. One event that my mother recalls is that I was helping her to dust a bedroom one day. We finished working in the room and left, and as she closed the door behind us I started crying. When she asked me why I was crying, I told her she had shut Cindy and Jojo in the room – she had to open the door and let them into the hallway with us.

That was the first time my mum ever heard about Cindy and Jojo and she was quite shocked by what I told her, because about 10 years before I was born I had a cousin called Cindy who died when she was aged about five, and a couple of years before I was born my mum's dog Jojo died. The thing is, neither of my QCCs actually looked like my cousin or my mum's dog, yet they had used those two names out of all the names they could have used or I could have chosen. At such a young age I hadn't known about Cindy or Jojo existing in my family and so when I was older and learnt about my CCQs I was quite shocked.

Hayley Stevens, by email, 2009

PLINK-A-PLONK

I had an imaginary friend called Plink-a-Plonk when I was about four. It was of no specific sex, so presumably mainly female. It accompanied me during a stay in a holiday cabin near Dymchurch, Kent. I liked to talk about My Little Friend to my parents, but I don't remember that we played any specific games together. It was just a companion to be with. If I visualised it at all, I suppose it was something like me. I was an only child, and aware of a lack of siblings. It was a sort of practice friend and also part of an act I put on to amuse my parents, and myself.

The way to the beach was across a lane or small road, then along the top of a bank to some smelly wooden (and fly-infested) steps down to the sand. There was a pothole in the path along the bank and The Cat and The Dog (also imaginary) would always fall into this and I would call everybody to a halt while I lifted them out. I think my mother was a bit charmed with my imaginary friend, and my father took a more active interest and would ask "Is Plink-a-Plonk coming with us?" I suppose he had had an imaginary friend of his own at some time, though he never said.

Anne Hardwick, London, 2009

'LITTLE FEMALE BOTTOM'

When I was a small child growing up in Barcelona, my QCC was an extraordinarily fat woman in a bright floral dress with a big hat and a very small umbrella or parasol. She was blonde with long eyelashes and answered to the name of Culina (pronounced cool-eena, although the literal translation would be something like "little female bottom"). I can't remember what we used to talk about, although I do recall that she had a very soft voice and was slightly taller than me. She only appeared when I was outside the house. I don't recall much else about her, but it has been 32 years since I last saw her. When I was four, I suffered from Perthens disease, which effectively prevented me from walking for about three years until doctors managed to fit a steel bar to hold the head of the femur together. Culina would come to me before the disease, but not during or after it.

Francisco Morral-Cardoner, by email, 2009

DEAD QCCS

My daughter's two imaginary friends were called Soloney and Sparkle Woods, and they lived in the wooden playhouse at the bottom of the garden. Soloney was a 'proper' imaginary friend who used to come on holiday and trips out and things like that, but Sparkle Woods was 'real'. She used to distinguish between the two of them from a very young age (about two years old) and always said that Soloney was imaginary but was different from Sparkle Woods as she was a real person but I just couldn't see her. She is now seven and occasionally mentions Soloney, but Sparkle Woods has completely disappeared.

When I spoke to a neighbour about them, she told me an amusing story about her nephew who had two imaginary friends for years and years whom he talked

about constantly (Colin and Derek or something like that). One day when my neighbour asked about them, he said: "They are dead. They were hit by a bus," and never mentioned them again. Obviously his way of moving on. I never had imaginary friends myself, but my sister as a child was constantly followed by ants on motorbikes and skateboards.

Sam Stringer, by email, 2009

INVISIBLE PENGUIN

At 42, I no longer have any recollection of my own imaginary friend. At about the age of 18 months, until I was two, I believed that I had an invisible penguin friend, though not invisible to me, I assume. My mother tells me she used to have to leave a place at the table for it. She wasn't always able to sit right next to me on the sofa, as I required space between us for the penguin; and when she read bedtime stories she had to read them a second time for the penguin. She even had to tuck it into bed with me – although not every night.

There is a story of the time a woman sat next to my mother and me on a bus and I screamed that she was sitting on my penguin. The woman got up and looked for a toy penguin that she might have sat on, leaving my mother to explain in whispers that it "wasn't real".

Finally, around the time of my second birthday – my younger sister had just been born or was about to be born – I was given a knitted penguin toy. The hope, I think, was that I would bond with the toy and forget the imaginary one. Instead what happened was my invisible friend left, never to be heard of again, and I refused to accept the toy – often throwing it out of bed, and showed no interest in it whatsoever.

Steve Gardiner, London, 2009

FRIENDLY LION

I had a QCC that visited me every night as soon as my mother turned out my bedroom light. I was well under 10, but cannot remember my exact age or how long this went on. The QCC took the form of a lion, but one with human-like characteristics. It communicated with me, but whether verbally or telepathically I can't recall. I don't remember if it had a name. As soon as my mother closed the door, the lion would appear, take me from my bed and 'nurse' me on its knee in a human 'sitting-down' posture. Later it would return me to bed, and I would go to sleep. I suppose I should have been terrified, but I wasn't, although I can remem-

" My mother had to read my bedtime stories a second time for the penguin "

ber a sense of nervous anticipation as the light was turned off. My lion assured me of its friendliness and that it would always take care of me.

I never told my parents about this, even in later life. I regarded the experience as an intimate secret, which I felt my parents would dismiss as childish nonsense or fantasy. Nearly 60 years later, I still wonder what it was all about.

Henry Chester, Feltham, London 2009

MULTIPLE QCCS

LEGION OF CHAPS

Between the ages of seven and about nine, I had a legion of 'chaps', as I called them. Numbering at least 1,000, they were approximately 5in (13cm) tall and looked like very basic stick men. My chaps accompanied me everywhere I went (except to school); they had cars, tanks, aircraft and ships, all of which – I don't know why – were from World War I and the 1920s. Their aircraft would escort me if I was travelling anywhere by bus or train, flying slightly above and behind the vehicle in neat formations. When I went to the beach or local swimming pool, I would always have a flotilla of 'pocket' battleships sailing alongside me, crewed by my ever-attentive chaps.

They were always very busy around the house, patrolling the kitchen in their vehicles, and I recall them covering every table, shelf, or work surface with 'equipment' to do their various 'jobs' and 'maintenance'. My family found my chaps very amusing and imaginative, particularly my grandparents, who lived with us at the time. They gave me daily 'progress reports' on my chaps when I came home from school.

This was all in the mid-to-late 1970s. I'm pretty sure my chaps were influenced by a character in the *Beano* or *Dandy* comics who had an army of radio-controlled toy soldiers with tanks, aircraft, etc. Do any readers remember this?

Rhodri Lyndon Evans, Bridgend, South Wales, 2009

SUZIELAND

Ever since she could talk, my five-year-old daughter has had a lot of invisible friends – she calls them her "Suzies". The ones I know of are: Suzie, Big Big Up to the Sky Suzie, Little Suzie, Baby Suzie, Uncle Suzie and Mother Suzie. They can all fly, though she has never said whether they have wings or not. Big Big Up to the Sky Suzie is regularly ill and has died at least once and come back. She only mentioned Mother Suzie a few days ago when there was mention of another Baby Suzie. They all go to Suzieland at night. She has also said they sometimes go away over there, gesturing to the ceiling. Sometimes she'll tell them off for being naughty. I'm sure there are more of them than she lets on.

Steve Hon, by email, 2010

THE INVISIBLE GANG

I was a bright, solitary child blessed with a vivid imagination. I lived in a small village and there were few children my own age. I spent much of my free time alone, playing in the garden or the wild area round the back of our house.

My mother, a primary school teacher, has told me that she was aware that many children had invisible friends, but she was surprised that I seemed to have a multitude – at least a dozen! This group of quasi-corporeal companions seemed to be older children or possibly adults and all had slightly old-fashioned names such as Henry (I think he was my favourite), Peter and George.

Although my own memory of this time is now rather hazy (it was around 35 years ago) mother has recounted to me many times two stories which demonstrate clearly the strength of feeling and close connection I felt with my QCCs. On the first occasion, my brother, who is 18 months older than me, was already attending school, so I must have been about three years old. Mother had a habit of taking me to Debenhams in Peterborough for tea before collecting my brother, Julian, from school. The Debenhams coffee bar had a semi-circular serving counter, around which were placed high stools fixed to the floor. Mother and I sat on two of these stools, and we were joined by my gang of QCCs while we ate our toasted teacakes and drank tea. Two teenage girls then entered and proceeded to seat themselves *on top of* my friends, which prompted a hysterical outburst. "You're sitting on Henry! You're sitting on George!" I screamed. Mother was forced to remove me and my friends, leaving our teatime treat unfinished.

The second incident occurred when we were on holiday in Geneva, where we were staying in a rather grand hotel. Our family and my friends entered the lift, which was just big enough for us all, but just before the doors closed a couple of German guests slipped in too. Again I was inconsolable that my friends were being squashed, and as a result we were forced to take the stairs for the rest of our stay.

I don't remember when my QCCs stopped visiting me, but well into my teens I had other imaginary friends and pets, including two seagulls and a dragon.

I am now a professional musician, academic and teacher, and am currently conducting doctoral research at City University, London.
Rachel Hayward, by email, 2010

INVISIBLE FRIENDS... OR ENEMIES?

BUGGY

Although I did have a QCC called Sister when I was young, it is my daughter Charlotte's "friend" that I wish to tell you about. As soon as she was old enough to talk, she told us about her friend Buggy (my spelling). Buggy was not always around, but would tend to pop up from time to time. She never ate with us (I mean we never had to lay an extra place at the table) but would play with Charlotte or come out in the car with us. When Charlotte was about four, Buggy started to crop up more and more. I remembered my special imaginary friend and chatted to Charlotte about Buggy as though she were a real friend; I believe because of this my daughter felt comfortable speaking about Buggy. I would often hear her chatting in her room and pausing as though she were listening to another person.

One day, she came downstairs while I was preparing dinner and informed me that from now on Buggy would be living with us.

"OK darling," I said, "why is that"?

"Oh mummy, it's very sad, all of Buggy's family are dead, she has no one, so she is coming to live with us now."

"That's so sad."

"Yes, one day some soldiers came to Buggy's house and took all of Buggy's family away, but Buggy hid and they didn't find her, but her family were put in a big room and the air was bad and Buggy's family all died."

My daughter was four; she was not old enough to know about such things and we certainly never allowed her to view any programmes except CBBC!

About a week later, I was in my next-door neighbour's house having a cup of tea and told her about the conversation with Charlotte. When I related the soldier story, my neighbour told me that the old lady who had lived in our house before us was a Polish Jew called Charlotte, and she thought that her family had perished in the war in a concentration camp. Apparently, my daughter looked rather like the old lady – dark wavy hair and olive-coloured skin. Another Jewish neighbour later on told me that there is a Hebrew word that sounds like Buggy and means "someone who cares for others" – and later we found out that Polish Charlotte had been a midwife or community nurse. My daughter is now nine and Buggy is still about, but not as much as before.

I have witnessed some unexplained phenomena in our house over the past 11 years, which I always attribute to Buggy. Doors open by themselves and then, when I ask them to shut, they do! I often feel that I am not alone in a room. Just the other night, someone was holding my hand. And only recently, a tap was turned off for me – if it hadn't been, the floor would have been flooded. I never feel nervous or worried when such things occur, especially when they are so helpful.

Jo Alder, Clayhall, Essex, 2009

DAVID OF THE DRAINS

I'm from a large family, and we all had the usual round of imaginary friends – cats, ponies, dragons, talking dogs. For a while I even insisted my mum and dad left room for imaginary Rhubarb and Custard (from the 1970s cartoon) on the seat next to me! But my youngest sister had something a bit different. At the time, we were living on a farm and every day on our way up to the field to fetch down the geese (hey, it was the 1970s) we went by the small reservoir that served the village, a large storage tank covered over with grass which collected water from a natural spring, lime-rich from the chalky soil (the overflow formed spectacular stalactites).

It was here that my youngest sister met David, who was the sort of imaginary friend you don't want your little sister to have. David was a young boy, a little older than her, and he lived in the reservoir. He kept telling her to hide from us, and trying to get her to go down the drains to visit him. She told us that he looked ordinary, but he was often angry, or very sad. He wore a grey coat and heavy shoes, and made her feel "crackly". The drains were heavy, and the dangerous bits of the reservoir were tucked away, and anyway we didn't like David, or his suggestions.

After a bit of debate (and with some nervousness, in case she just laughed) my sister and I told our mum about David. She told us not to ask our little sister anything else about him, not to talk about him at all if possible, and also that we should not leave them alone together. We followed her advice, and made sure one of us was with "them" at all times, and after a while he came less and eventually started to avoid us. Years later, I asked Mum about this, wondering if there was any sort of hidden story going on. She remembered it distinctly, and described David as a "bad" imaginary friend, one that needed discouraging. Some imaginary friends, she said, are not good for the children who have them, and you have to help them get rid of them.
Jeremy Dennis, by email, 2010

AN OLD CHILD

When I was four or five, my parents turned the attic of our house in Virginia into a playroom for my sister and me. I vividly recall meeting a friend called Joey on the stairs up to the attic. He was definitely an adult, but seemed childish somehow. Now, I'd say he appeared brain-damaged. We would talk, but I can't remember about what. I don't think he appeared anywhere else. No one had to set a place for him at dinner, etc. I wasn't frightened of him, but he was creepy. He seems even creepier now, as I look back on that long, uncomprehending face, with the short blonde hair on top. It may not even have been blonde, but grey. An old child. I have wondered if he was a ghost. I never saw him after we moved from that house.
Debbie Pryor, by email, 2009

"HER NAME IS SALLY, AND SHE IS DEAD"

When I was a small child, I insisted to my parents that I had died in a fire, and all my life I have maintained a vivid image of this fire and have overcome a powerful fear of large fires, such as campfires or bonfires. I remember my flesh being seared and glass shattering, cutting into my arms and face. I can't imagine detail such as this being made up by a three-year-old, although I admit I can't remember what I was thinking or feeling as I thought of the memory. My mother says that I thought at the time that it had happened in this life, and I asked her repeatedly, "Don't you remember it? Remember that big fire?" I then told her about being burned and about the windows breaking and the glass cutting me. She asked me what happened next, and I shrugged my shoulders, sighing. "I died."

Throughout my life, whenever my mother has asked me about the fire, the same image has always leapt to my mind: I am in a red brick building, and I come into a room full of fire and smoke. I run toward the window, which shatters. I can feel my eyes burning, seared by the light and heat. This image has stayed with me all of these years and is still just as vivid today, at the age of 16.

Even at 16, I can remember being five or six and having a sense of loss. I had few friends at that age, and I can remember desperately longing for an imaginary friend named Sally. I would pretend that she was there, but was saddened knowing she wasn't really. When I was two or three, my mother recalls seeing me almost constantly talking. I would babble on and on about anything that leapt to my mind, seemingly to myself. I had a toy phone into which I would talk as well. However, when my mother asked me to whom I was speaking on the telephone, I replied, "Her name is Sally, she has long black hair, and she is dead." That was all I would say about her.

Greylyn Burk, Pleasureville, Kentucky, 2009

Write Your Way To A New Career!

Writers Bureau Celebrates Twenty-one Years of Helping New Writers

by Nick Daws

Hazel
McHaffie

Tim Skelton

When distance-learning pioneer Ernest Metcalfe founded The Writers Bureau in the late 1980s, he can hardly have dared hope that twenty-one years on it would be acknowledged as Britain's leading writing school. Yet so it proved, with thousands of Writers Bureau students seeing their work in print for the first time. And, for many of those who persevered with their writing, the dream of becoming a successful writer has turned into reality.

Students such as Tim Skelton. An engineer by profession, he had always harboured an ambition to write, and at the age of 40 signed up with The Writers Bureau. The decision changed his life: "My writing career took off exponentially. In 2005 I started appearing regularly in lifestyle and in-flight magazines. The following year I was commissioned by Bradt Travel Guides to write a guidebook to Luxembourg. And in the last year

"My writing career took off exponentially."

I've appeared in The Times and The Independent, and updated guidebooks for Fodor's, Thomas Cook, and the AA."

Another student who benefited was Hazel McHaffie. Hazel wanted to make her academic work in Medical Ethics more accessible to people, and decided to write the themes into novels. Following her Writers Bureau course, Hazel has had five novels published, and appeared at the Edinburgh International Book Festival in 2008. She also has her own website at www.hazelmchaffie.com.

Sometimes studying with The Writers Bureau takes students down new and unexpected paths. Patricia Holness originally enrolled on The Writers Bureau's Writing for Children course. However, she soon realised that what she was learning applied to other types of writing as well.

She is now a full-time writer, regularly selling short stories for both

children and adults. She also has a monthly column in Devon Life.

These are just a selection from the inspirational true stories from students of The Writers Bureau. There's no reason why YOU couldn't be their next success story. With a 15-day free trial and money-back guarantee, there is nothing to lose and potentially a whole new career to gain! So why not visit their website at www.writersbureau.com or call on Freephone 0800 856 2008 for more information?

WHY NOT BE A WRITER?

As a freelance writer, you can earn very good money in your spare time, writing the stories, articles, books, scripts etc that editors and publishers want. Millions of pounds are paid annually in fees and royalties. Earning your share can be fun, profitable and creatively most fulfilling.

To help you become a successful writer we offer you a first-class, home-study course from professional writers – with individual guidance from expert tutors and flexible tuition tailored to your own requirements. You are shown how to make the most of your abilities, where to find ideas, how to turn them into publishable writing and how to sell them. In short, we show you exactly how to become a published writer. **If you want writing success – this is the way to start!**

Whatever your writing ambitions, we can help you to achieve them. For we give you an effective, stimulating and most enjoyable creative writing course… appreciated by students and acclaimed by experts.

It's ideal for beginners. No previous experience or special background is required. You write and study at your own pace – you do not have to rush – as you have four years to complete your course. **Many others have been successful this way.** If they can do it – why can't you?

We are so confident that we can help you become a published writer that we give you a **full refund guarantee.** If you have not earned your course fees from published writing by the time you finish the course, we will refund them in full.

If you want to be a writer start by requesting a free copy of our prospectus 'Write and be Published'. Please call our freephone number or visit our website NOW.

COURSE FEATURES

♦ 30 FACT-PACKED MODULES
♦ 3 SPECIALIST HANDBOOKS
♦ 20 WRITTEN ASSIGNMENTS
♦ ADVISORY SERVICE
♦ TUTORIAL SUPPORT
♦ FLEXIBLE STUDY PROGRAMME
♦ STUDENT COMMUNITY AREA
♦ HOW TO PRESENT YOUR WORK
♦ HOW TO SELL YOUR WRITING
♦ 15 DAY TRIAL PERIOD
♦ FULL REFUND GUARANTEE

www.writersbureau.com

☎ FREEPHONE 24 HOURS

0800 856 2008

PLEASE QUOTE REF. AT1042

email: 10W1@writersbureau.com
Please include your name and address

4 *UFOs*

Unidentified Flying Objects are just that: things seen in the sky that we can't easily find a name or a cause for. Brilliant lights or fireballs that seem to display an almost conscious intelligence, weird-looking objects that don't resemble any known aircraft or, as some people have claimed, technologically advanced vessels supposedly piloted by 'aliens' from other worlds.

FLYING TRIANGLES

STAR WARS MILK FLOAT

Back in the summer of 1987 or 1988, while I was washing my car in front of our house (in Solihull) under a clear blue sky, I heard a weird noise that sounded like a cross between a helicopter and an electric milk float. It got louder and louder until, after what seemed like ages, a triangular craft came into view over the row of trees about half a dozen gardens down the road. Within seconds it was overhead. It was not elongated like Concorde, more of an equilateral triangle, and plain silver underneath without any markings. The back edge was completely straight and there was no sign of any emissions coming from it. It was fairly large and seemed to be flying at about twice the height of the large oak tree at the top of the drive. The nearest thing I've ever seen that looked like it is either a space shuttle or something out of *Star Wars*. It was travelling easily as fast as a jet fighter, and was gone in seconds. Was it some sort of secret plane? I've never heard of any other reports of a UFO making a racket like that. My mother heard it, and agreed it sounded weird, but didn't get out of the house in time to see it, and I never heard of any of the neighbours seeing or hearing it.

Jon Chidwick, Shirley, West Midlands, 2008

TRIANGLE SPOTTED

I was interested to read Jon Chidwick's report of a UFO sighting over Solihull, West Midlands, as I believe I saw the same object. I can't confirm the date, but 1987/88 sounds about right. I was in Handsworth, Birmingham, when I saw a triangular aircraft fly over my house. It was apparently higher than when Jon saw it; the distance between Solihull and Handsworth would account for that if the craft were climbing, and it was travelling more or less from the direction of Solihull.

The shape was the same equilateral triangle, with a straight back edge and no markings, though I registered mine as grey rather than silver. I also seem to remember a short 'fuselage' extending from the front end, with small, stubby stabiliser wings on it. I pointed it out to the person I was with, but she was occupied with a tangle of small children at the time, and has no memory of the incident. I have since come to think it was probably a secret military craft of some sort; I've seen pictures of Stealth aircraft that loosely resemble it. But I'm not investigating it too closely, as I prefer to have it remain a bit of a mystery.

Hunt Emerson, Handsworth, Birmingham, 2008

PYLON LIGHT SHOW

During September or early October 1996, I was riding from London to Bradford on my motorbike, a journey I made quite regularly at the time. It was about 10pm, and almost dark. North of Grantham, I traversed the power lines that run down from the power stations of Lincolnshire. Since I had been photographing workers repairing these lines a few months earlier, using helicopters to access the live lines, I glanced up along the line of pylons and was surprised to see a large glowing red object apparently among the power lines some miles to the north.

Continuing towards Newark, I was unable to see what the red object was, although I got occasional views of the pylons. Near Newark, the road curved and exited a small cutting, and to my right was a clear view of the power lines. Between two of the pylons was a glowing red shape, roughly oval and apparently connected to or tangled in the lines. Its height was as great as the distance between the highest and lowest lines on the pylons. I initially thought it might be a dirigible airship of the 'Goodyear' type, and wondered if the electricity could make helium glow red, but I almost immediately realised that it couldn't be anything of the sort. I rummaged around for my camera, stored in the bottom of

(I looked up, and the oval changed into a triangle of blue lights in formation...)

a bag on the motorbike, and when I next looked up, the oval had changed into a triangle of blue-white lights in a chevron formation as high as the pylons, which was moving south, silently along the line of the cables. The lights were very bright but small, similar to the effect from LEDs rather than conventional bulbs.

I was unable to tell whether there was a structure between the lights or whether they were merely flying in formation. They moved fairly slowly, passing pylons every few seconds, so I estimate a groundspeed of between 30 and 60mph (50-100km/h). I was certain this was not a conventional aircraft, and even if I had not seen the previous shape I would have immediately known that this was not flying in any conventional way.

After watching the lights for a few moments, I resumed searching for my camera, finally reaching it as the triangle came back towards me. I hadn't seen it turn around, but it was definitely the same object, simply reversed. It was still flying along the line of the power cables, the lowest lights just above the tops of the pylons.

As it passed the point where I had first seen it as an orange glow, it flipped over sideways – or at least that is how it appeared – and dropped into the slight railway cutting running east from Newark. I had finally got my camera out, and cursed myself for being too late to get a photo. Then I saw a green light moving fast towards me, very low down, and thought that I'd be able to get a picture of whatever this was, presumably some sort of companion object... I readied the camera, and as the green light passed low overhead I got a photo – of a Tornado Interceptor!

It was flying fast and extremely low, well below 1,000ft (300m), straight over the power lines and towards the centre of Newark – not at all conventional flying over a populated area at night. The green light had been the starboard navigation light. I was certain that the Tornado had been looking for what I'd been observing; it was obviously not flying any sort of 'training mission' or routine operation.

I considered contacting the MoD or the National Grid company at the time (I had the latter's PR contacts from earlier that year), but I presumed that all I would get for my troubles would be a denial, the usual "you tell us everything and we will tell you nothing", and that I might suffer consequences as a result of being on record. I decided to say nothing, and simply told friends about it when I arrived in Bradford, my destination, later that night.

I drew a diagram of what I had seen at the time to keep it accurate in my memory, and ever since I have been interested in reports of 'flying triangles', as this seems to tally with the second half of what I saw, although I'm interested to note that no one else seems to have reported the shape-changing feature which I observed.

Tony Taylor, by email, 2007

METALLIC VOICE

In the summer of 1992 I lived in Great Barr, Birmingham, and my parents had gone away on holiday. I asked my friend Stace to stay over, as I thought it would be fun having girly nights in with wine and videos. We were both about 25 at the time. My house overlooked a field and nature reserve so there were no buildings apart from the houses either side of us. I can't remember why, but we went out to the front lawn. Stace remembers it as the afternoon, but I think it was later. Our attention was suddenly drawn to a triangular object in the sky directly above us. It seemed metallic yet dark in appearance and at first we thought it was a hang glider, but it was stationary and seemed about 45ft (14m) above us. We stared at it for some time. I was a very amateur astronomer back then and ran in to get my telescope. As I set it up on the front lawn and adjusted the focus, the object moved swiftly to the side. I fixed the viewfinder on it again, but again it moved quickly out of shot. It was as if it didn't want to be examined close up. I couldn't focus on it at all. Then it moved extremely quickly to the right, changed to a cigar shape and flew off at an incredible speed.

About two days later, Stace and I mentioned the incident in general conversa-

tion and what we remembered more than anything was that it was speaking to us, like someone shouting over the wind, but the voice was metallic and inaudible. We remembered trying desperately to hear what it was saying, but couldn't understand the language.
Steph Slater, Ryde, Isle of Wight, 2009

STRANGE LIGHTS ON THE ROAD

DRIVING BLIND

It was a clear, late September night in 1999, and I had started off on my half-hour journey from my mother's house to mine at 9 o'clock. Driving as I had every week from Alyth, Perthshire, Scotland, to the city of Dundee. I relaxed, turned on Radio 4, waved goodbye to my mother and set off.

The road was quiet. I knew the route like the back of my hand and it was quite normal for me to make the journey almost on autopilot. You know that feeling when you drive somewhere and you're surprised you've arrived as you can't remember driving that far? This was a fairly common occurrence on these trips. But this night was different. I was about 20 minutes into the journey, listening to the drone of the radio, when I started to feel slightly odd.

Quickly, I sat straight up in my seat and looked around the car. Nothing in my headlights, nothing behind, as I sped along at a steady 60mph (100km/h). I listened intently to see if the car had started making any odd noises. Nothing. It occurred to me that the radio was off. I glanced at it, turned it up full; no noise. I cursed slightly and stared at the road ahead. Bloody radio's gone, I thought. The road at this part of the journey dropped downwards into a long left curve. And as I started my descent, something bizarre happened.

An incredibly vibrant flash of white light engulfed the car, brilliantly white. It wasn't a car coming in the other direction, or from a side street, or from behind. I wasn't blinded by the flash, and I noticed that the car clock had reset itself. Then, the next shock: about 15 seconds later the radio screamed at me, as I had left it on with the volume turned full up. I can only assume it was some sort of electrical strike, but with the sky being clear... well, who knows?
Gordon -- , by email, 2001

FIRE IN THE SKY

In the latter part of summer 2001, my wife and I were travelling to a camp near the Saskatchewan-Alberta border, where we were going to meet some friends. We had been driving for about four hours, and were nearing the end of our trip. We were travelling on one of the long, straight stretches of road which Saskatchewan is noted for. It was about 11pm and a clear night before moonrise, but in summer at this latitude (almost 53 degrees) there's generally a hint of the Sun's position below the horizon, so it shouldn't have been inky-dark.

It was, however, inky dark – the headlights were illuminating the road ahead, but seemed to be having less than their usual effect to the sides. Whether this is connected to the main phenomenon, I can't say, but it was somewhat unsettling. As the van rose out of a dip, we saw directly ahead, and slightly above our sightline, what can only be described as a ball of fire, equal in visual dimension to a fingernail at arm's length. It looked very much like the burn-off plume one sees at oil-refineries and at some oil well heads. We assumed initially that this is what it was, joking that right in the middle of the road is a duff place for an oil well.

Some three minutes later, at 60mph (100km/h), about 2.5 miles (4km), the object seemed no nearer, but remained directly ahead, at what seemed a comfortable distance, without any apparent movement either lateral or vertical. We again commented to each other on this, in the vein of "OK, just what is it, then?"

The ball held its apparent position for another two or three minutes, when the van again descended into a dip (Saskatchewan, contrary to legend, is not flat, it's slightly wrinkly). When we rose, there was no sign of the object. A bit less than 10 minutes of ruler-straight road later, we entered a town without any sign of anything which would produce such an effect; this would put us 6-8 miles (10-15km) from where it was last seen, and there wasn't a lot of cover on either side of the road. Once we passed through the town, the oppressive nature of the darkness also abated.

I didn't investigate the matter at all, because the short version of this story is, in essence, "nothing much happened" – but it was a curious effect which I thought your readers might find interesting. It certainly fits Mr Fort's thesis of something having sport with us monkeys.

Dirck de Lint, Saskatchewan, Canada, 2003

M11 SPOTLIGHT

On 15 June 2007, my sister and I were driving from Leicester to visit our parents in Rayne near Braintree, Essex. At about 11:40pm we were travelling towards Stanst-

❝ We saw what can only be described as a ball of fire in the middle of the road ahead ❞

ed on the M11, near Audley End. The roads were fairly clear and although there had been heavy rain throughout the day the sky was mostly clear by this time. Sitting in the front passenger seat, I had a very good view of the road. I noticed a stationary, vertical, bright green beam of light about 20ft (6m) in front of us. The beam was coming down from the sky – I could see it up as far as windscreen would allow – and it hit the ground like a stage spotlight. As we were travelling at the speed limit, it all happened very fast. The car drove through the beam and I turned round to see that it was still visible behind us.

What was doubly strange was that my sister, who was driving, hadn't noticed it. Although it was late, I don't think I was tired and imagined it, as I am a night owl and rarely go to bed before 1am. We discussed what the light might have been. Duxford Air Museum was very close, as was Stansted airport; however, the late hour made it unlikely that it was an aircraft from Duxford, and although I could see a plane in the distance preparing to land at Stansted, I couldn't see any other aircraft in the sky at the time. The area of the M11 on which we were travelling has many 'Works Unit Only' signs and in the surrounding area there are several country lanes that don't appear on any maps, along which one passes several secluded copses of trees that reveal glimpses of radar and other technical equipment. The area also includes local airbases and military bases. My sister also considered the idea that a new form of motorway monitoring was being tested. Can readers offer any explanation?
Chante Sayers, Walsall, West Midlands, 2007

THE THIRD KIND?

TINFOIL GIANT

A friend and I had an unusual experience in June 2003 in West Sussex. The time was approximately 10pm; almost dark, but with some twilight remaining.

We were coming back from another friend's house along a section of country road we have driven individually many times before. My friend was driving and I sat in the passenger seat. We slowed for a tight left-hand bend in the road and as we turned it, driving at this point at about 20mph (32km/h), the headlights caught someone moving amongst the trees on the outside of the bend. I was about to say "Did you see that?" but my friend had already confirmed he had (with an expletive I'd best not write here). We only caught a brief glance of the 'person', but it was one of the most bizarre things I've ever seen, for two reasons: first and foremost, the person's size, which was staggering and, indeed, what initially made us catch our breath. The figure was at least 8ft (2.4m) tall, and whilst from our brief observation it was hard to make an accurate estimate, he was clearly larger than he should have been, perpectivewise.

It was all too quick to notice any particular facial features; he was virtually facing us, but looking slightly down as the lights shone on him, and seemed to be stepping sideways over something in the undergrowth, as his right leg was moving upwards and sideways. The other very unusual aspect was that the head-lights reflected a large glare off his clothing, which seemed to be shiny, almost like foil.

It all happened so fast, but there was no doubt what we'd seen was very strange. My friend and I confirmed to each other what we had both witnessed and, after a couple of moments of indecision, he reversed back to the bend and pointed the headlights into the trees approximately where we had seen the figure. All appeared normal. I even got out of the car and called (to my friend's fervent objection; I'd had some Dutch courage that night, but he was sober!), but no one seemed to be moving about in the woods and there was no trace of anything. We talked excitedly about it on the way home, but it got forgotten as these things do.

I don't personally believe in extraterrestrials, so for my own part I've ruled out anything like that, and being a fairly practically-minded person I've come up with various explanations, such as kids mucking about. But the problem of

size keeps coming back – I even checked the Internet the following week to see if 8ft-plus people were more common than I'd thought, rationalising that it was some weirdo in a foil suit. It certainly wasn't any kind of model, because it was definitely animated. I'm still puzzling over it.

Name withheld, by email, 2003

THE MAN FROM THE SKY

In 1977, my family and I were living on a smallholding next to Beccles Common in Suffolk. One bright, sunny morning in February or March, I heard my twin daughters, Wanda and Rosemarie, aged three-and-a-half, crying and calling me. They had been playing outside near the stable block. As I rushed out of the back porch door, one of the twins ran towards the house in a very disturbed state.

"Mummy, mummy, we've just seen a man jump from an aeroplane!"

"Where is he?"

"Walking up our drive."

By now her sister had reached me. Both were crying as I bustled them through the house. The other twin told the same story as her sister, adding that the man frightened her very much, and that he was tall with yellow hair. I washed their faces and when they had calmed down I questioned them again. They couldn't give a satisfactory description of the "aeroplane", except to say that it was wide. It must have been very quiet; otherwise I would have heard it. Just then, I heard the grating sound made by our side gate, when it is either being opened or shut. I ran out to investigate, but there was no one visible. I looked right round the house and even glanced in the cattle barns.

A few days later, we went shopping in town. I took the pushchair, as it was a long way for the twins to walk, so if they felt tired they could have a ride. On the way back, we came through the little iron gate leading from the Avenue and I glanced up the path to our house in the distance. It was unusually quiet, and there weren't even any golfers, though most mornings one or two were play-ing (part of the Common was used as a golf course). We crossed over the path leading to the golf house and started walking across the grass to join the track leading home.

When I looked up the path again, I saw a man about 800 yards (730m) away, behaving oddly. He flopped about, then straightened up and started walking towards us. I noticed what looked like a long streak of lightning in the sky above the point where he had been falling about. This quickly disappeared and then I saw a little white circle, perfectly round, which moved very fast and was soon out of sight. The twins seemed full of energy and were running ahead, but as the strange man approached they turned tail, scampered back to me, and got into the pushchair. "That's the man in the aeroplane," they exclaimed.

He was over 6ft (1.8m) tall and dressed in blue-grey protective clothing, like a boiler suit, tight at the ankles and wrists, and apparently of a lightweight material, like nylon. His boots seemed to be made from the same material, and he had grey gauntlet gloves. He had earphones on and as we drew level I could hear a sound similar to white noise from an untuned radio. Then I heard quite a loud foreign voice coming through the static. The strangest feature of all was his pinky-red eyes. He was staring into the middle distance all the time and didn't look our way once. After he passed, I turned round for another look and noticed his magnificent shoulder-length hair, which shone a fantastic golden-red in the morning sunlight.

We had now reached the top end of the track, roughly the spot where I had seen the man falling about. To our right, a herd of cows appeared to be going berserk, running round and round the field in a most disturbed fashion. I looked back again and found that the man had vanished. There were only a few sparse bushes, so where had he gone? I turned the pushchair round and retraced our steps all the way down to the car park, but there was no sign of the man anywhere.

A few days later, the twins and I were collecting firewood on the Common. I glanced towards a golf green and saw what appeared to be a very small, dark grey caravan standing on two little legs. It was egg-shaped and had one wide window in the front, as far as I could tell. The land at that spot was very marshy, which would have made it extremely difficult to drive across, and I couldn't see any tracks. The twins caught up with me and pulled my arm saying, "There's the aeroplane, mum." I told them it was a caravan, but they insisted it was the aeroplane they had seen earlier. Surprisingly, they wanted to have a closer look, but I dissuaded them as it was very muddy where the "caravan" was standing. We came to a small wooded area and through the trees I saw a very tall man dressed in a similar fashion to the one we had seen a few days earlier. I couldn't see his face as he was turned away from us. Although it was a bright morning, it was rather dark among the trees and he was in shadow.

Maureen Gaines, Lowestoft, Suffolk, 2007

5

The unnatural world

The great outdoors, from rolling hills and forests to the high seas, is often where we go to forget our everyday cares and commune with nature. But strange things can happen there; the ancient woods and streams often appear to be the haunts of trickster-like spirits or the Green Man; and the secrets of the oceans can sometimes turn deadly, as in the case of a rare killer wave.

SPIRITS OF NATURE

WOODLAND EXCLUSION

I have lived all my life in Mountfield, a small village in East Sussex surrounded by ancient woodland. Until comparatively recently, the village was populated mostly by families who have lived there for generations. As small children after WWII, we were all aware that there were certain areas of woodland best avoided towards nightfall and others well known as blessed places where solace could be found in time of trouble.

One wood, known as Castle Wood because of the remains of ancient earthworks, is an area known for atmosphere. I walk it regularly and spend some time on the earthwork meditating, but on one occasion, in early October 1998, something very curious happened.

It was a perfectly still, glorious autumn afternoon. I entered the woodland and immediately felt a heightened awareness. As I approached the main wood up a rutted cart track, the branches of the trees began to move, though I could feel no breeze at all. I slowed my pace, but the wind in the trees became very strong, and as I reached the edge of the earthworks, branches on either side of the path came down and barred my way. Inside the wood, I could just see a flock of large black birds, either rooks or crows, flapping around wildly, though they made no cawing noise.

I was brought up to acknowledge and respect the existence of earth spirits and elementals, and, though I was mystified and a little alarmed, I stood my ground and sent a psychic message in greeting to whatever was there, and I appreciated that I was not welcome that day. As I walked back down the track, the wind died down. At the bottom of the track I turned and looked back, and where I had just walked, brambles which had been in the hedgerow had fallen across the path, making it impossible for anyone else to walk into the wood.

On the way home, I called on the village tree warden and told him what had happened. He said that he too had not been 'allowed' into the woods for about three weeks. We were later informed that the Water Board was at that time proposing to make a road right through the wood to a reservoir that supplies Hastings with water. The surveyors encountered such obstacles, difficulties and local opposition that they abandoned the plan and our peaceful, gentle woodland remains untouched but for occasional coppicing.

Jacqueline L Spriggs, Mountfield, East Sussex, 2001

TRICKSTER SPIRITS

In 1996 or 1997, my fossil-collecting took me to a remote valley near Hay-on-Wye on the Welsh border. I followed a public right-of-way that ran parallel to a stream in the valley below. The path is little used, but occasionally you encounter visiting walkers. I know the owner of the surrounding land and have his permission to go there any time to collect fossils.

The path turns up a side valley after about three quarters of a mile (1.2km) and eventually crosses a stream. It then heads steeply uphill to open ground. Just as the path turns into the side valley, another short path leads down to the stream. I followed this for a few yards until I came to an outcrop of rock, the target of my journey. The main path ran about 20-25ft (6-8m) above this outcrop. There were a few large rocks nearby and I decided to set about these with my hammer, conscious of the stream babbling away in the background.

I immediately began to feel uncomfortable and lonely, and had a feeling of being watched, but I carried on. I was relieved to hear the sound of children playing, which seemed to come from the open ground across the side valley and beyond the trees. The sound appeared to be almost out of earshot. As I worked I expected to see a troupe of children appear, perhaps led by an adult or two, but the sounds disappeared and I felt another wave of loneliness sweep over me.

" I saw an enormous face made up of foliage, like a Green Man carving "

There was a thud to my left and I looked to see a stone the size of a walnut roll down the bank. I had no doubt that this missile had been thrown or dropped from a height and was certain that someone was playing a trick on me. I could not see the path directly above me and in an instant I grabbed my tools and rucksack and ran up to investigate. There was no one to be seen. If the missile had come through the trees, it would have struck some foliage and I would have heard it earlier, so I concluded that it was dropped from a height.

Somewhat unnerved, I beat a hasty retreat back up the path the way I had originally come, hoping that I might catch up with the culprits, but I met no one. All this happened in early summer as there was no thick undergrowth as yet, although the trees were in leaf.

Roderick B Williams, Brecon, Powys, 2000

GREEN MAN ENCOUNTER

One summer afternoon in 2007 I was returning from central London and my train had spent a few too many minutes idling at the platform in New Malden station. Lost in thought, I had been looking out of the window at nothing in particular when I suddenly saw something that made me gasp out loud. At the far end of the London-bound platform is a thick bank of trees and shrubs behind a fence. I was astonished to see what appeared to be an enormous face made up of the surrounding foliage looming out at the opposite platform and looking very similar to the typical appearance of the 'Green Man', as seen in church carvings. The face was about 5ft (1.5m) in diameter and about 7ft (2m) or so from the ground.

I was amazed how perfect the face seemed to be – though at the same time I knew it was just my brain demonstrating its knack for face recognition in random patterns. I probably gazed in wonder for 20-odd seconds before the most shocking thing happened.

Suddenly, and with tremendous velocity, the entire face withdrew backwards into the vegetation, which caused the surrounding bushes and trees to sway violently. Most strikingly of all, a branch that must have been under the 'face' swung upwards with immense force – as if a huge weight had been lifted from it – before smacking into the surrounding greenery and, I suppose, reassuming its original position. This whole motion took about a second and the face had completely disappeared! I could accept that a fox or even a human might have been sitting on the branches and had jumped off, causing them to bounce back into position, but this would not easily account for the very distinct retraction of the face, as if it were wrenched backwards into a tunnel.

The face in no way looked constructed or man-made and seemed to consist of a natural, though utterly remarkable, arrangement. The features of the thing were clear to see and I was particularly struck by the grinning mouth and star-ing eyes. Quite how the verdant visage was sucked backwards I have no idea. I have often wondered how, or indeed why, anyone would have achieved this bizarre effect for bored South West Trains passengers. The train drew away and I sat back in my chair feeling strangely unnerved. On all of my subsequent jour-neys through the station I have never seen anything like this again.

Nick Skerten, Kingston upon Thames, London, 2009

CHTHONIC HEARTBEAT

About three years ago (2001), my wife and I were walking in Wakerley Woods in Northamptonshire. It was a calm, sunny day and we were walking off the path in the shade of pine trees when my wife, who was about 10 metres (32ft) in front of me, stopped dead in her tracks. After a moment she turned and said "Can you hear that?" She appeared a little puzzled and also just a tiny bit spooked. I stopped, listened, but couldn't hear anything. She insisted I listen again but I could still hear nothing. However, she was adamant there was a sound and described it as being very low, so much so as to be almost better apprehended as a sensation. I found that I was able to 'tune in' to a dull throb, best described as a kind of chthonic heartbeat.

It was rhythmical and sensed in a rather unpleasantly visceral way; when you tuned in to it you had the sense of it being so massively dispersed that you were almost part of it. We were completely unable to determine what might be causing it. There are fairly large roads in the area but this would not account for the periodicity of the effect; nor did it seem that this could be the source as there was no traffic noise audible. There was the definite sensation that whatever was producing the vibration was massive, as it seemed to pervade the earth and the air. I lived in the area at the time and noticed no reports of anomalous seismic activity.

Pete Wilson, by email, 2004

STRANGENESS AT SEA

THE KILLER WAVE

When I saw the killer wave from the bridge of the *Cape Horn*, I took it for a natural peril; it was only much later that I realised that I might be one of the very few people to have observed a rare marine phenomenon – a monster seiche wave – at close quarters... and survived.

The *Cape Horn* was the standard 'three island' ship of the period. When I joined her in 1930 she was almost a new ship. The man in charge, Captain ES Wilkie, had commanded the last active square-rigged ship on the British register. He and I were the only sailing ship men aboard, and for this reason he would talk to me occasionally.

The incident happened during a Force 9 or 10 gale in the Pacific, sometime between April and June 1935. We were about 10 or 12 days out of a Canadian or US west coast port taking sawn lumber to Shanghai. It was blowing hard with 25 feet (7.6m) seas running and the distance from crest to crest exceeded the ship's length (425ft/130m). The phosphorescence given off by the breaking seas provided plenty of light to see by as I made my way over the deck-load towards the bridge.

It was 4am and my wheel. Ahead and to port one could see for a couple of miles, but the horizon was not clearly defined. The starboard window of the wheelhouse was constantly drenched by heavy spray and useless for observation. The temperature was around zero. I had the helm hard-a-starboard continually, but from time to time eased the wheel a few spokes, then slammed it down again. (It was a common seaman's belief that if modern steering gear were held hard-over too long, a bubble of air would form within the cylinder or tubes and prevent movement of the rudder.) In a full gale I was taking no chances.

About 4:30am, I noticed a change in the regular run of the seas ahead. A larger wave was forming, to judge from the gaps of blue water between the crests. The Chief Mate, Mr McKenzie, had the watch and I drew his attention to it. "Here's a 'ninth wave' bearing down, Mister." He examined it with the glasses, took a bearing from the ship's compass, checked the ship's head, then moved back to the corner window.

A 'ninth wave' is a common expression, meaning a single wave larger than the others. As I kept my eyes on it, it slowly increased in size. Hoping the Mate would increase the engine revolutions to face up to this new threat, I said: "She's nearly five points off and won't answer." He remained silent. Later, I added: "It's not just one big wave, there are others behind it just as big. I can see their crests breaking here and there." His left hand moved towards the engine telegraph, hesitated and drew back.

By this time the wave had become so huge that I knew it would capsize the ship. No increase in speed would save us now. I was puzzled by the slowness of the advance of the sea; we seemed to be drifting together. Then I noticed that what I had initially taken for wave crests were actually widely spaced geysers, dancing on the upper surface. These geysers – or whatever they were – were rising to a height of about 20 feet (6m) and dropping to half that before rising again, sometimes curving against the wind. The upper surface of the sea appeared flat and endless, stretching towards the unseen horizon. By 'flat' I mean there was no defined wave motion; the surface boiled gently in whorls, exactly like the water filling a lock of the Panama Canal.

I knew beyond question that I was a dead man, but the idea didn't seem to worry me unduly. Rather, there was an absence of feeling. Suddenly I was shocked back to the present. I could plainly hear the thumping and rattling of the rocker arms of the main engine and the noise of the big exhaust in the funnel. Then, like the slamming of a watertight door, the wind dropped from a full gale to a calm. I knew what was happening; the height of the sea had cut off the wind making a temporary lee for the ship. Glancing at the compass, I saw with surprise and delight that the ship's head was coming up to windward. In fits and starts it moved in the right direction. I talked to her: "C'mon my sweet beauty, get up there. Hurry 'fore the bastard wind comes back. Do it for me lover..." stuff

like that, but meaning every whispered word.

The bows were only about 30 feet (9m) off the far end of the 'sea' when she rammed it. Then all hell broke loose. I felt the shock as the fo'c's'le head went in and the deck-load for'ard tore loose. There was another crunching thud beneath my feet as the sea demolished the lower bridge rail. I thought: "There's the lifeboats gone for a burton."

Just then, and with incredible speed, the whole face of the wave altered. A curtain of water rose from the sea and enclosed it. Where the existing face was deep and flat, this curtain appeared to be made of joined vertical columns about three feet (90cm) in diameter, uniform and crested, and sloping at the same angle as the great wave behind it. They looked exactly like huge steel pistons coated with oil. The crest passed the wheelhouse windows downwards in about three seconds.

I gripped the wheel harder. The for'ard windows were struck by a sea that I fully expected to demolish the whole front of the structure. This was strange; it acted like water but didn't have the character of water with force behind it... no shattering explosion of glass, no rendering of woodwork... just a heavy thump. In that instant – as if a switch had been pressed – the three front windows turned pure white. This, again, was strange; there was none of the movements you'd expect from water on glass... no splayed runnels... no small bubbles... just the purest white I have ever seen, as if they had turned into three blocks of ice. In the blink of an eye it was gone, and you could see out of them again.

Then the big wave was gone. I looked for the Mate, but he was outside. As the vessel listed heavily to port, I saw a normally big sea pass by us as the water drained from the bridge. The Old Man arrived, much to my relief, and immediately rang the telegraph. He was barefooted in soaked pyjamas and his uniform cap, shivering, for the wind had returned. He had words with the Mate (beyond my hearing), who departed at great speed. Captain Wilkie glanced briefly at the compass and said: "All right Craig. What really happened?"

His question relieved me. It meant the Mate had not seen me alter course to windward without orders. If anything had happened to anyone down below, the sea would get the blame, not me. I answered: "She wouldn't answer her helm, sir; not enough anyway. It was the biggest sea I've ever seen. I've seen some big'uns off the Horn, but nothing like this." He nodded towards the binnacle: "Keep her at that while I dry off. If you want me, stamp on the deck." After I struck the four bells at the end of the watch, I wanted a good look at the lower bridge. The stan-

((*Just then, and with incredible speed, the whole face of the great wave altered*))

chions on the fore part remained, but all the woodwork except the capping rail had gone. The boats were in perfect order, canvas covers intact. The afterdeck was untouched. I could hardly believe it, after taking onboard such a heavy sea.

Part of the deck-load was floating alongside still attached by a few wires; elsewhere the stacks of timber were intact but in disarray. The fo'c's'le had been flooded to the level of the upper tier of bunks, but this was quite normal in this run in any sort of weather. Nobody made any more comments about it than usual; it seemed as if nobody but the Mate and me had seen what we went through. He never spoke about it afterwards – we never hit it off well, anyway – and neither did I.

I am left with my memory of those critical minutes, like a stretch of film with neither beginning nor end. Contrary to usual storm conditions, visibility was excellent. Wherever one looked, the air was charged with phosphorescence, and the water was alive with it. The prevailing colour of the solid water was a dark blue, with the breaking crests and 'geysers' showing a normal white. When the great wave had passed, the colour of the seas changed back to grey. The sky was gradually becoming lighter in colour, except directly over the ship, where it had assumed an arrowhead formation (the point facing the wind and the two sides clearly defined). The course of the enormous wave was directly towards the ship's bow, yet the wind was on our quarter throughout. It made no leeway until the wind stopped and the ship reached to wind'ard and hit it. The wave appeared independent of the rest of the sea, while the 'geysers' seemed like a great pumping system, raising and lowering the water level within it. If there was any gas involved, it was imperceptible; there was no smell, and the oil lamp lighting the compass card burned steadily through the whole incident.

So what was it? Where did it come from – and where did it go after it left us? Are there 'holes' in the sea as there are said to be 'black holes' in space? I've often wondered. My own conclusion is that it was hollow – a gigantic bubble.

Gavin Craig, 1980

WEIRD MISTS

THE HANGING BLANKET OF DARTMOOR

In May 1994, my wife and I had a caravan holiday near Chagford on the edge of Dartmoor. We return to the same large farm field every year. The caravan is in a completely isolated 'blind' corner, with large hedges or banks about seven to nine feet (2-2.7m) high. The nearest building, Lower Shapley farmhouse, is 200 yards (180m) away at the top of our field, and beyond that is a lane leading to a no-through road onto the moors. There are no other caravans, campers or dwellings nearby.

It was a clear, dry night, with little breeze and a moon brightly seen between a fair amount of cloud. Sometime between 2am and 4am, answering my usual nightly call of nature, I stepped out of the caravan and was confronted by a white, vertical, oblong blanket, phosphorescent, but giving off no light. It was clear of the ground, about 10 to 15ft (3-4.5m) long and 4 to 5 ft (1.2-1.5m) high. On the grass between it and me there were 'scatterings' (as if there had been a light snow fall) of similar white phosphorescent material. Whilst the blanket was 'solid', completely hiding the hedge about 20ft (6m) behind it, the surrounding hedge, bank below and landscape over it were clear of any mist. The grass could be seen through the ground 'dusting'. There was no other white stuff to be seen in the vicinity.

On my return after about two minutes, I warned my wife, whom I had disturbed as I left and who also wished to go out, that she should prepare for a shock. I didn't tell her what I had seen, as I wanted her to be an independent witness. She confirmed what I had seen, so the phenomenon had lasted at least (say) five minutes. We lay and talked about it, but sadly didn't think of going back out, taking a photograph or even looking out to see if it had moved or disappeared. I suppose we were in a state of shock, but we were not in any way fearful.

There was nothing to be seen early the next day. Later recollections led me to believe that the top edge of the blanket was quite well defined, but not straight or level – though my wife believes it was straight and level. All was still, and the Moon appeared briefly from time to time between the clouds. I think the caravan shadow was missing when the Moon shone. The Moon couldn't have cast a tree shadow near the ground dusting area. The dusting appeared to be in horseshoe patterns, facing predominantly in the same leftward direction.

I discussed the matter with the farmer and his parents, who could offer no explanation. The Meteorological Office was also "unable to help". I am 69 and my wife is 75 and teetotal.

Norman James, Epsom, Surrey, 1995

ANOTHER ODD MIST?

Concerning 'The Hanging Blanket of Dartmoor': about two years ago (1993) I saw an object that was similar but not identical.

Part of my work involves a night inspection of some private land off a dead-end track beyond a gate. I unlocked the gate and returned to the car to drive through, but as I started to move off I noticed an object some 30ft (9m) beyond the gate. It was uneven, roughly butterfly-shaped, white, solid, flat and feature-less with sharply defined edges about 3ft (90cm) high by 4ft (1.2m) wide and 4ft from the ground at its lowest point. There was no light emanating from the object itself; it appeared as a white object does at night and was completely still. As I watched, the object slowly faded away, not from any one point, but evenly all over until it was completely gone. I drove through where it had been and there was nothing there at all. Unlike the Dartmoor phenomenon there was no 'snow".

I suspect an optical illusion, as the object was vertical and square to my view. I have never seen anything like it before or since. I would be interested to know if any readers know what the object could have been. In passing, I have carried out these inspections weekly for many years and have twice seen bright lights in the sky resembling a shower of stars surrounded by a silver glowing cloud with a comet-like tail travelling very fast from horizon to horizon. I have always attributed these to space debris.

Mr G Lester, Milton Keynes, 1995

6 *Ugly Rumours*

Urban legends are those far-fetched sounding stories (often with a cautionary twist) that usually reach us via a 'friend of a friend' (and, these days, the Internet). Although the source of these tales can never be traced, people persist in believing them to be true. Here are some classic examples in which schoolkids from across Britain got themselves into a panic over an imminent skinhead invasion!

BARBARIAN INVASIONS

SEVENTIES SKINHEAD PANICS

One day – I think in the spring of 1973, when I was nearly 13 – I arrived at school, Rivington Road Secondary, St Helens, Merseyside, to find the place awash with rumours of an impending skinhead invasion. Apparently, gangs of skinheads had been ambushing other teenagers and, so the story went, slashing them with razors. The classic line that the 'skins' were said to use was: "Does your mother sew? Well, get her to sew this!" (Slash!)

The tales increased all through the week, to include physical (but not sexual) assaults with umbrellas and milk bottles. By Thursday, anxious parents were meeting their offspring from school – this was in the days when most people walked or took buses to school, rather than being ferried about in cars. By Friday morning, the school was in a state of near-hysteria. We had been told 'the skins' rang up the targeted school five minutes before they came, and then up to 1,000 of them would descend, razors at the ready.

On Friday afternoon, we girls had needlework in a classroom opposite one of the deputy head-teacher's rooms. Horror of horrors, at about ten to four, a telephone was heard ringing in her room. We all stopped work, went completely silent, and exchanged terrified looks. Then one of the two deputy teachers walked calmly into the classroom and announced in measured tones that there was absolutely no truth in the skinhead rumour. By the following Monday, we were all back to discussing T-Rex, Gary Glitter and David Cassidy, rumours forgotten.

Funnily enough, later that year I moved to a different school, also in St Helens, and met people from other schools in the town. Every one of them had heard the skinhead stories and in some schools the eldest boys organised the closing of the school gates at break and lunchtimes and patrolled the school perimeters.

To this day I wonder, now and then, where this tale came from. As I recall, there wasn't a problem with skinheads in St Helens – not one that I was aware of anyway – and I doubt there were 1,000 skinheads in the whole of Merseyside. We were all very frightened and all accepted the stories as true. It didn't occur to me to wonder how up to 1,000 skinheads descending on a school could be ignored by local people and the police, but there you are.

Why though, if parents had heard the tales, did the teaching staff apparently not know about them and why did it take until Friday afternoon to officially deny them? And why were the skinheads chosen as the aggressors, out of all the various gangs and groups? I'd love to know if similar tales circulated anywhere else, or if it was confined to St Helens.

Lois Stock, Haverhill, Suffolk, 1994

In 1973 I was a second-year student at the now defunct Glamorgan College of Education, which used to overlook the seaside town of Barry, several miles west of Cardiff in Wales. One day, late in the afternoon, a rumour spread among the students that 200 skinheads were arriving by train from Brighton, intent on attacking the college. About 100 of us armed ourselves with cricket bats, chair legs and whatever else we could find, and ventured out towards the town to meet the expected onslaught. Nothing happened, and after a wait of some hours we dispersed.

I heard no more of the skinheads. It was believed by many of us that they had got wind of our preparedness and had fled the area. At the time I, too, thought we had achieved a great feat of arms against a dangerous enemy, but I soon began to wonder: no one had encountered a skinhead face-to-face, and there was never any follow-up evidence that there had been any kind of invasion of the town.

Viv Hobbs, Blackwood, Gwent, 1994

((A rumour spread that 200 skinheads were arriving from Brighton *))*

In 1970 or 1971, when I was a pupil at a very 'respectable' school in Merseyside, a rumour began to circulate about an impending attack by a gang of marauding truants from a notorious inner-city school. Eventually the rumour-mongers announced a specific date for the attack and several of us arrived at school that day carrying 'offensive weapons'. I brought a length of rusty metal, which I had found in the garden shed. To this day, I have no idea what I intended to do with it in the event of being attacked. The staff at the school took the rumour seriously enough to keep us indoors at lunchtime and (after some soul-searching) to allow us to leave early. Needless to say, the threatened assault never took place.

My younger brother remembers that the same rumour circulated around his school in another suburb of Liverpool. He also remembers a story about a youth being attacked by skinheads on his birthday, and having the words "Happy Birthday" carved on his body. The rumour about the marauding gang had racial overtones since most of the pupils at the school in question were black.
Kevin Mahoney, Sheffield, South Yorkshire, 1994

For a short while in the early 1970s, rumours of massed gangs of skinheads circulated at Bramley Broad Lane School in Leeds. It was said they inserted razor blades into bars of soap.
Eddy Jenkinson, Eindhoven, Holland, 1994

An account by ex-Harrovian Simon Sebag Montefiore alleging an actual skin-head offensive on Harrow public school in the late 1970s appeared in the *Evening Standard* on 12 October 1995.

Apparently, after much tension in the town between pupils and skins, it was one day announced that "the skins are attacking the school: hundreds of them! It's a skinhead army!" Montefiore continues: "We laughed, but I ran out to see what was literally a solid phalanx of giant skinheads, probably at least 70 of them, running along the high street... wielding spanners a foot long." He then maintains that "as far as the eye could see there were skinheads beating up boys and masters," and it is at this point that the account sounds too much like fiction.

The cult book *Boot Boys* by 'Richard Allen' (James Moffatt) was a bestseller in the early 1970s and it could be that much consternation was fuelled by it, including the St Helens scare and Montefiore's boastful narrative. Defined as: "The savage story of Britain's newest teenage cult of violence", *Boot Boys* centred on the anti-social exploits of Joe Hawkins, whom Allen described as "the epitome of society's menace". The skinhead stereotype can be seen as one form of a protean figure in contemporary folklore whose exaggerated anti-social tendencies are based on social or racial prejudice and glamorised depictions in pulp literature and films.

Alistair Moffatt, London, 1995

THE CHELSEA SMILERS

A panic similar to "The Great Skinhead Invasion" of 1973 swept through the large secondary school in south-east London where I worked in 1987. It was said that a gang of Chelsea Football Club supporters called "The Chelsea Smilers" would arrive in the area in a blue van with a smiley face painted on the side and accost children as they went home from school. "The Chelsea Smilers" would apparently ask the victim if they supported Chelsea. If the answer was negative they would slash the face of the victim with a knife (or razor) causing a smile-like wound to the face. According to one informant, it seems that if the victim did support Chelsea the Smilers would first slightly cut the victim's wrist and then their own and perform some kind of 'blood brothers' ceremony.

Children spoke of attacks happening at neighbouring schools and over a few days tension increased as rumour spread that the Smilers were "heading our

way". By the end of the week, groups of children were in near hysteria over the imminent attack. Apparently, the blue van was "seen" parked near the school. Parents expressed concern and only an official denial by the deputy head teacher over the school's Tannoy system seemed to calm things down. He pointed out in a masterly display of logic, which the children could not fault, that there was no reason on earth why the Smilers, if they did exist, which they didn't, would come all the way to south-east London when there were plenty of people to slash in their own part of London. All rumour and panic ended by the following week.
Malcolm Stewart, London, 1994

One morning in 1987, I arrived at my school in London to hear strong rumours of an imminent attack by "The Chelsea Smilers". The members of this gang were said to drive around in blue vans and attack people with, of all things, credit cards. Their method was to slash each corner of their victim's mouth with a credit card, thus leaving the unfortunate person with a permanent 'smile' on their face. Stories began to circulate about how somebody or other knew someone who had heard of a school where this gruesome event had occurred.

Towards the end of the week, we were told in assembly that the school had made enquiries with the police, who then assured the school that they had never heard of the Chelsea Smilers, that this rumour was rife in many schools throughout London, and that there really was nothing to worry about. As with the Skinhead Scare, by Monday the whole issue had more or less died out.
Mr R Pohl, London, 1994

LINGERING LEGENDS
The urban legends about mass skinhead attacks on schoolchildren are still percolating through the global meme-scape. At the millennial New Year (1999/2000), I attended a rave called 'The Gathering', held in the Takaka mountains near Nelson in the South Island of New Zealand, at which rumours quickly circulated that gangs of skinheads had planted caches of weapons in the woods months before in preparation for their own unique millennial celebrations at the expense of the innocent ravers. Needless to say, this mild hysteria was completely unfounded, with the only casualties from the weekend being E-freaks winched off the hilltop with hypothermia after forgetting that their urban clubbing garb was rather inadequate for withstanding the sub-alpine elements.

Although pretty weak by the sensational standards of most mass hysteria outbreaks, the story did reveal some interesting psychosocial subtexts. The threat of destructive, pre-determined chaos was definitely in keeping with the millennial end-times paranoia, whilst the divisions between hippie/rave and skinhead cultures were much in evidence. Most of the ravers were middle-class kids from the North Island. The West Coast of the South Island, not far from where the event was staged and where the skinheads were said to be based, is nationally demonised as a provincial, 'white trash' backwater.

The rumour also illustrates New Zealand's perennial inferiority complex in relation to its colonial roots. A popular version of this 'cultural cringe' states that due to our relative geographical isolation from the rest of the world, social, cultural, and artistic trends from Europe and America eventually trickle down here about 10 years after their northern hemisphere peaks, which accounts for the fact that an urban legend from 1970s England is still doing the rounds down under almost 30 years later.

Dean Ballinger, Hamilton, New Zealand, 2002

Regarding the rumours of invading skinhead armies: in 2001, the Anti-Nazi League (a branch of the Socialist Workers Party) warned of a planned National Front March through the centre of Aberdeen, and a big anti-Nazi demonstration was organised. On the day, no neo-Nazi march happened, although the ANL claimed that National Front leaflets were distributed in some housing estates on the outskirts of the city. The National Front has very little support north of the border. Apparently, this kind of thing happens quite often. Cynics note that the SWP get a lot of publicity at these "counter demonstrations" and lots of copies of the *Socialist Worker* get sold.

Ian Sanders, Dalmellington, Ayrshire, 2002

A Startling Memory Feat That YOU Can Do!

How I learned the secret in one evening. It has helped me every day."

When my old friend Richard Faulkner invited me to a dinner party at his house, I little thought it would be the direct means of doubling my salary in less than two years. Yet it was, and here is the way it all came about.

Towards the end of the evening things began to drag a bit as they often at parties. Finally someone suggested the old idea of having everyone do a 'party-piece'. Some sang, others forced weird sounds out of the

piano, recited, told stories and so on.

Then it came to Peter Brown's turn. He said he had a simple 'trick' which he hoped we would like. First he asked to be blindfolded. Those present were to call out 25 random numbers of three figures each, such as 161, 249, and so on. He asked me to list the numbers in order as they were called.

Peter then astounded everyone by repeating the entire list of 25 numbers backwards and forwards. Then he asked people to request numbers by their position in the list, such as the eighth number called, the fourth number and so on. Instantly he repeated back the correct number in the positions called. He did this with the entire list – over and over again without making a single mistake.

Then Peter asked someone to

shuffle a deck of cards and call them out in order. Still blindfolded he instantly named the cards in their order backwards and forwards.

You may well imagine our amazement at Peter's remarkable memory feat.

"There was really nothing to it – simply a memory feat"

On the way home that evening I asked Peter Brown how it was done. He said there was really nothing to it — simply a memory feat. Anyone could develop a good memory, he said, by following a few simple rules. And then he told me exactly how to do it.

What Peter said I took to heart. In one evening I made remarkable strides towards improving my memory. In just a few days I learned to do exactly what he had done.

"I can instantly recall anything I want to remember"

I was fast acquiring that mental grasp and alertness I had so often admired in men who were spoken of as "brilliant" and "geniuses".

Then I noticed a marked improvement in my writing and conversational powers. What's more my salary has increased-dramatically.

These are only a few of the hundreds of ways I have profited by my trained memory. Now I find it easy to recall everything I read. I can recall in

detail almost at will. I rarely make a mistake.

What Peter told me that eventful evening was this: "Send for details of Dr. Bruno Furst's Memory Course." I did. That was my first step in learning to do all the remarkable things I have told you about. In fact, I was so impressed that I got permission to publish Dr. Furst's Course myself.

BOB HEAP

We, the publishers, have printed full details of Dr. Furst's unique memory training method in a free information pack. For your free copy, either phone **0800 298 7070** free, post the coupon below, visit our website at **www.firstclassmemory.com** or send an e-mail (see coupon) **TODAY.**

7

Ghostly goings-on

Ghostly apparitions continue to be reported from all over the world, and not just from stately homes and historic castles. It would seem that hauntings are just as likely to occur in everyday settings such as modern council houses, and that they can happen in the workplace as well as the home – as our collection of chilling tales of haunted hospitals demonstrates.

SPECTRES IN THE HOME

AN ANGRY GHOST

Following my divorce, our two-year-old twins and I were obliged to go into rented accommodation. Having settled the girls at the local playgroup and started my self-employed new career in the Lincolnshire village, I was loath to go far and couldn't believe my luck when a 19th-century farmworker's cottage came up for rent next to the church. I could afford the rent and, although a little isolated, it was in a lovely position and clean and tidy.

We moved in on a cold April day in 1991. I turned the heating up full and lit the fire in the sitting room as the place had quite a chill. I then set about unpacking in the kitchen looking out onto the beautiful west end of the church and graveyard. I could hear the girls chattering away to themselves and exploring the rooms. Eventually they joined me in the kitchen.

"Do you like our new house?" I asked, keen to get their approval.

They looked at one another, made a grave face and said very quietly: "We like the house, but we don't like the lady on the stairs".

The hair on the back of my neck stood up. "What lady? There is no lady here, just us – this is our house now."

They looked unconvinced. "No, there is a lady, in a long brown dress with long brown hair pulled over her face, and she's angry, she's very angry, she doesn't want us here!"

I could see they were getting upset and so decided not to question them any further; I assumed they were unnerved by the change of surroundings and thought 'the lady' would go away.

But she didn't. Night after night they talked about her, where she was in the house, what she was doing and saying, and how she was getting more and more angry. I saw nothing, but several times when I went into a room I got the feeling someone had just left… also a fleeting smell of pipe tobacco smoke… strange for a lady.

One night I had a friend visit. She needed to use the upstairs bathroom and I gave her directions. I couldn't believe how quickly she returned, nor how pale she was. She said nothing to me until we left the house but then she told me she walked into a cold damp mist on the upstairs landing that took her breath away.

The bedroom light switch was over near the door, so every time I went to bed, it was a quick glance round the room, switch off the light, dive into bed and pull the covers over my head, and hope the girls didn't call for me in the night. One night, I had just performed this routine when I heard a rustling noise followed by a huge bang. My heart was pounding so much I thought it would explode, but I knew I had to get out of bed and switch the light on. I found a mirror had come off the wall and slid down behind the dressing table. I laughed with relief until some kind soul the next day told me that ghosts hate mirrors.

In a vain attempt to catch the girls out, I questioned them separately to see if the lady was a twin imaginary friend, but they always had exactly the same story – where she was and what she said. After four months in the cottage, I couldn't stand it any longer and decided to forfeit the remaining three months' rent and move to a modern property nearer the centre of the village. I was apprehensive that the lady would come with us… but she didn't, and the twins never mentioned her again.

For weeks, I tried to fathom the mystery. I asked the locals and did research on the area. No one had experienced anything unusual in the cottage before; however, I did discover it was built on the site of the old monastic priory.

Di Ablewhite, Long Bennington, Nottinghamshire, 2010

THE OLD COUPLE

When I was young, I lived with my parents and brother and sister in a small four-

" There's a lady in a long dress... She's very angry, she doesn't want us here "

bedroom council house called "Freeways" in Cheverly, near Newbury in Berkshire. About 23 years ago, when I was five, we spent a few days with my granddad around the first anniversary of grandma's passing away. Not long after our return, mum ran into an old friend, who said she had called round; an old lady had answered our front door and said there was no Sue or Pete (my mum and dad) living at that address.

Mum then questioned our neighbours, who had been feeding our animals while we were away, and asked if they had seen or heard anything. They said that a few times there had been an empty milk bottle on the front doorstep, and once they had found the front door open, but as nothing appeared to have been moved or taken, they just assumed they had forgotten to lock it. Then a few people said they had seen a caravan parked in our drive and others had seen an elderly couple going in and out of the house. The funny thing was that only half the street had seen anything. My parents were really worried and called the police, but as nothing had happened to us directly, they were unable to do anything.

Then one Sunday evening, as we were sitting in the front room watching *Antiques Roadshow* on television, mum noticed a very strong smell of bleach; she felt it burning the inside of her nose. The rest of us couldn't smell anything. Later, I remember feeling really cold sitting next to an open log fire and then a coathanger hanging on the bird cage that was suspended from the ceiling started to swing really violently, which made our bird go mad. This is all I can remember of that night.

Not long after, as my sister was getting out of the bath, she heard some very heavy breathing and dragging feet coming towards the bathroom. The rest of the family was in the garden. Scared, she ran out of the bathroom onto the landing and collided with someone or something and heard it fall against the wall, but she didn't stop to look back. My parents didn't find anything apart from what looked like a pattern on the carpet of something dragging its feet.

As for the elderly couple, nothing was found out about them and they were never seen again. To this day, the families that move into that house don't seem to live there for longer than a year – or so I've been told. Our local newspaper found out about our haunting. It has now become a well-known ghost story for the locality.

Victoria Price, by email, 2007

THE FACE IN THE PLASTER

In 1993, my family and I were living in an old house in Dewlish, Dorset. The house had an annex occupied by our elder daughter. It served as a self-contained flat with its own bedroom, lounge and bathroom. One day she mentioned feeling a 'presence' in there, combined with a distinctive smell – not unpleasant, but one that she was unable to describe as she had never experienced anything like it before. At first we dismissed this as just a figment of a teenager's wild imagination; but then she asked my wife if she'd been cleaning in her bedroom. When my wife said she hadn't, my daughter said that was strange, because some items on her dressing table had definitely been moved around – notably a razor blade that she kept to sharpen her eyebrow pencil.

We started to take her more seriously after this and our anxiety increased considerably when she said that one night, to make sure that she wasn't imagining things, she had placed the razor blade into a powder compact. The next morning she found the blade back on her dressing table.

One day she came rushing out of her room, as white as a sheet, saying that she had felt the 'presence' very strongly and the curtains in her room had suddenly billowed, despite the fact that her windows were closed. We immediately went in to check, but everything appeared to be normal.

My daughter said that sometimes, during the night, she felt as if someone were standing by her bed looking down at her. She felt quite calm because this 'person' wasn't giving off any threatening or aggressive vibes. It just seemed happy to stand and observe her.

There was another peculiar development when we decided to have her flat redecorated. The men employed to do the job came and asked us if we knew about the trapdoor they had uncovered under the carpet in the lounge. We didn't. Underneath were steps down into a brick-lined cellar, on one side of which was a tunnel leading off in the direction of the village church and cemetery across from our house.

Perhaps we were being over-cautious, but none of us felt inclined to explore further. We asked people in the village and at the church if they had heard of anything strange about our house. Some of the old-timers told us that the house 'had a history', but they wouldn't elaborate however hard we pressed.

The workmen peeled off a number of layers of old wallpaper in the lounge in preparation for re-decorating. After removing the final layer of paper on one wall, they exposed a sketch of a man's face drawn on the plaster. He had piercing deep-set eyes, and an expression of utter despair. When they showed it to us, our daughter said: "That's him. He's giving off the same vibes. I'm certain that's him."

Due to its condition, the plaster had to be completely removed. Once the 'face' had been destroyed, my daughter never again felt the 'presence' or experienced the smell she had talked about. She said that the flat had taken on a completely different atmosphere.

Martin Baynes, Oliva, Valencia, Spain, 2006

ELUSIVE LAUGHTER

One winter afternoon in about 2001, I was busy in the lounge when I heard a young girl's giggles. I smiled to myself. There's nothing sweeter than hearing my children's laughter. I carried on with what I was doing. The giggles started again. Curious, I crept into the hallway and poked my head around the corner, hoping to have the last laugh and make my girls jump. To my surprise there was no one there, yet I could still hear faint giggles.

I went upstairs to see where my daughters (aged nine and seven) were, thinking they were probably playing a trick on me. When I looked in their room, one was asleep; the other was engrossed in a book. I asked my daughter what she had been laughing at but she said that she hadn't been laughing. I thought it a little strange, but shrugged it off.

Days later, my husband mentioned hearing children's laughter in the hallway, but when he looked for the girls they weren't there. A shiver ran down my spine and goosebumps covered my arms as I remembered the giggles I had heard a few days previously. His words made me feel relieved I wasn't imagining things.

A few weeks later, before going to bed in the early hours, I went upstairs to the bathroom. As I got to the door, I noticed my daughter wearing a long white nightie, her hair trailing half way down her back. I remember wondering why she was wearing one of those long petticoats to bed. They were only to be worn under her St David's Day costume. She stood with her back towards me just inside her bedroom. I thought she might have been sleepwalking and turned to tell her to get back into bed because it was late.

Before I had a chance to say anything, I watched the young girl fade into the darkness of the bedroom. I stood silently in shock for a few seconds, before checking on my two daughters, who were sleeping soundly in bed.

On a different night in the same week, I checked on my children before I went to bed. There in the doorway of my daughters' bedroom stood the young girl again, just as before. She wore the same nightdress, but this time her long dark hair flowed beneath a frilly cap. In her right hand she held an old-fashioned lamp, the shape of a gravy boat, which held a single lit candle.

I held my breath and stood as still as stone as I watched her take several steps into the room. Halfway across the floor, she began to fade and disappeared into the darkness once more.

I often wonder who she was and why she'd visited that night. Was she the young child who I'd heard giggling in my hallway? The house, incidentally, dates from the 1940s or 50s, if that has any bearing on the phenomena.

Lisa Plowman, Upper Church Village, Mid Glamorgan, 2009

GHOST DOG

In 1983, my brother Peter and I and a friend, Rod, had just moved into a share household in the Sydney suburb of Enmore. Peter and I were in a small upstairs room that we had chosen for a sound studio. We were discussing the positioning of our gear when from inside the room (almost in one of the walls) we both heard the distinct sound of a dog panting. There was no dog in the room.

A few weeks later, I was home and alone, and just about to come out of the upstairs bathroom when I heard the sound of a dog running up the stairs and along the corridor. It stopped outside the bathroom door. At that time, I had quite a fear of dogs, so I waited a short while to see if it was going to leave. I gradually opened the door and there was nothing there. I cautiously checked the house. All the doors and windows were closed and there was no sign of any dog.

A few weeks later, Peter had been home alone for most of the morning. He was just about to go to work and grabbed his keys and bag from the dining room table. He walked along the corridor towards the front door, past a makeshift cupboard under the stairs. From inside this cupboard he heard the scratching and clawing of what sounded like a medium-sized dog. It was a kind of frantic scratching and freaked him out so much that he turned round and left by the back door, up the side alley, and over a locked gate. He told the story that evening.

About a month after this, Rod met a new girl, Kim. We were having an introductory meal and retired to the lounge. The mood was calm and mellow. We were burning a few candles and having another glass of cheap student wine. None of us was at all drunk. We were chatting, listening to music, facing inwards. Kim was facing the door to the corridor. There was a lull in the conversation broken by Kim, who said, "I didn't know you guys had a dog".

Peter said, "That's because we don't!"

"But I just saw one!"

All the doors downstairs were closed. Kim said that she had just seen a small black and white spaniel-like dog walk past the bottom of the stairs. No one had mentioned anything about our phantom dog to Kim.

Steph Miller, Sydney, Australia, 2009

THE MONK, THE SOLDIER AND THE WITCHES

In 1999, my mum bought a 19th-century house in Ludlow, Shropshire, built over the old city walls. As soon as she moved in, she and my grandmother noticed strange things happening: objects that changed position, slamming doors, taps that turned on by themselves. They managed to ignore the phenomena, until my mum woke up one day and saw what appeared to be a mediæval monk in the corner of her room. At first, she thought she must still be dreaming, but the monk was still there after she blinked. He stared at her for a while, and then vanished completely. She tried to be rational about the experience, but couldn't help finding it unsettling.

A few nights after her first encounter with the monk, she woke up again shivering in the middle of the night. She said that the room was icy cold. When she opened her eyes, she saw a figure hovering over her in the attire of a World War I soldier. She was so terrified that she jumped out of bed and ran out of the house, still in her dressing gown. From that moment on, she decided she wouldn't spend

" She saw what appeared to be a mediaeval monk in the corner of her room "

another night on her own in the house, and called an exorcist. She was told that the house was haunted by two different entities: the monk was protecting her, but the soldier had malevolent intentions. As well as these two different entities, there were poltergeist-like phenomena apparently connected to some mortal remains buried under the back door – the most sinister spot of the house. These, at least according to the exorcist, were related to witchcraft ceremonies conducted outside of the city walls. My mum ended up selling the house.

Toby R, Bristol, 2010

HAUNTED HOSPITALS

HOSPITAL GHOSTS

In 1977, I was a 27-year-old staff nurse working nights at a community hospital for the care of the elderly in north-east Wales. It had been built around 1902 as an isolation centre for infectious diseases and had a gloomy atmosphere with droopy curtains and ancient iron beds. The hospital was demolished in 2004.

I was the youngest member of staff and had worked at the hospital just nine months. One dry autumn night in 1977, at 1am, I walked into a darkened ward housing 12 sleeping patients and saw a man standing at the bottom end of one of the beds. He was a good 6ft (1.8m) tall, with an upright authoritative bearing. He had grey hair and was wearing a uniform of thick, black material, including a double-breasted jacket glinting with large silver buttons. Was he a soldier, or perhaps a sea captain? He looked solid enough. I remember his skin, rough in the dull window light. I viewed him sideways on for just a few seconds, but long enough to recognise him if I ever saw him again.

Shocked, I walked quickly away and scurried into the kitchen, where staff members were sitting, and told them in detail what I had just witnessed. To my great relief, they said the man often 'visited' and that patients frequently reported a uniformed soldier stationed during the night at the end of the bed. The staff, too, had eyeballed the military spectre in the same area of the ward. He'd come and go. It wasn't a rare event! They said there used to be a tall man in the very bed I had identified.

That hospital was ridden with ghosts. One time, we nurses went for our rest period in an old dining room outside of the main building. We were trying to catnap and I couldn't sleep because I could hear children playing, laughing and yelling, but there were no children anywhere nearby. I told the staff and the others said that this was often heard.

Another day, as I rested in the staff office with my eyes shut, something touched my face. It felt like a hand. I flinched at the clammy cold touch and opened my eyes, but nobody was in sight. One night I noticed some curtains move, and I mentioned it to the ward sister. "Oh, there's a ghost following me," she said. "It's my friend." She then addressed it: "Go on, get away." Another time, the nurses were talking about a particular patient during a night shift and all of a sudden a portrait of that person, a Christmas photograph, came flying off the wall and smashed behind a chair.

Jane Murray (not her real name), by email, 2008

ZIMMER ZELDA

Having read of Jane Murray's experiences of hospital ghosts, I feel moved to recount one of my own. In spring 1994, I started working nightshifts for a nursing agency at Donisthorpe Hall, an old people's home in north Leeds, looking after a retired textiles worker who lived alone in an otherwise empty ward owing to behavioural issues. One night, while my patient was sound asleep, I repaired to the adjacent day room for a cigarette (still permissible in those days). Suddenly, the extractor fan switched on. It had no automatic controls, just a mains switch and an on-switch, which also opened the shutters covering the fan blades and took a good thumb-push to operate.

I thought little of it until it happened again three nights later as I sat only feet away. There was no one else on the ward apart from my patient. I didn't mention it at the time, but not long afterwards, between 3 and 4am, I became aware of the sound of a zimmer frame clattering down the ward corridor – no footsteps, just the zimmer. This started happening night after night and eventually I told one of the regular staff, who disclosed that the ward was haunted by a lady called Zelda who used a zimmer, wore orthotic slippers (hence no footsteps) and didn't like smoking! She had been irascible and difficult, and had once appeared to the (very psychic) staff nurse, who promptly told the shade that seeing as Zelda didn't like her when she was alive she could p*** off now she was dead!

Zelda's visits to her old ward continued throughout my six months there. One night, I awoke from my rest period nap to find the hairs on the back of my neck standing up and the feeling I wasn't alone. I went to the staff rest area, which overlooked my ward, only to be asked why I was there when the patient was awake and standing in the bay window. In fact, he was sound asleep!

Other regulars told of a thick mist which descended on the convalescent ward every night, but was only visible to anyone on the ward looking out, and how when the hospital was being built – on the site of an old Quaker burial ground – some workers had fled the site in terror after a man dressed in old-fashioned Puritan garb had appeared, glowering down into their trench. They never went back.

Old folk's homes and hospitals usually abound with ghosts, but one built over an old cemetery seems the work of a Stephen King fan. And my patient? He would try winding me up with talk of "the spirits of the dead" and slept soundly through it all.

John Coates, Leeds, West Yorkshire, 2009

HORROR HOSPITAL

I work in a special needs hospital where weird things happen regularly. We often say that the hospital is haunted, and no one really likes to do night shifts there. There are monitors in the children's rooms so that we can hear them crying even if we're not anywhere near them. On many occasions, we have heard sighs and cries coming from empty rooms, and one of the older children regularly talks to a woman who isn't there at all.

Recently I was doing a morning shift when another nurse and I heard screams and bumps coming from a room we thought was empty at the time. Worried about the girl who usually occupies that room (and who we believed had been taken out for a walk), we opened the door and discovered that there was nobody there. We had to report the incident to the nurse in chief. She told us that she had the feeling that something was going to happen, as the previous night the atmosphere had been very agitated. Apparently a portrait had fallen off the wall of the same room for no apparent reason – the broken glass had almost hit the girl who slept in the bed. The portrait was of a boy who used to sleep in the room before and had who died exactly a year before the incident.

Although I was scared, I had to continue doing my shift. While changing the nappies of two children, I heard the door of the bathroom shutting behind me, and the click of the lock. I tried to open it but it seemed that somebody had locked it from outside. I still can't explain who might have done it, as neither my colleagues nor any of the children would have played a practical joke about something like that. My colleagues finally arrived and opened the door for us. By this time, all I wanted was to finish my shift and go home.
Lucy L, Ireland, 2010

THE PHANTOM BEHIND
When I was working in a Staffordshire hospital I was told several ghost stories by the actual witnesses. One ward had a central nurses' station where staff could sit for the all-important brew while safely observing all comings and goings. In the corner of this ward was a bedspace whose bed had been removed so that excess equipment could be stored there. Wheelchairs, walking frames, dismantled beds and odd furniture had been ingeniously stacked up to totally fill the space and the curtain had then been drawn around it: there was absolutely no room for anyone to move inside the curtain.

Well, in the dead of night, a nurse saw the curtain lift and bulge outward, exactly as if moved by a nurse's behind as she bent over the bed! The nurse rubbed her eyes, looked again and nudged her mate with a 'Do you see what I see?" Her mate certainly did and both girls watched the behind move busily around the bed – which wasn't there, remember!

They watched, spellbound, for a couple of minutes as the movement continued on around the bed to the other side. Eventually they tiptoed over and pulled the curtain back – nothing but a pile of scrap, and nowhere for anyone to hide or get past them!
Carla R, by email, 2002

GHOSTS OF THE UNDERGROUND

PUSHY SPECTRE

I am a police officer with the British Transport Police, working on the London Underground. One night some years ago, I had to go to King's Cross station after the last trains had run and the station had been closed to all but the night staff and engineering workers. As I went into the booking hall, I noticed that two of the 'exit barriers' were flipping open of their own accord quite violently. Having completed what I had to do, I walked past the memorial clock in the booking hall above the ticket machines and noticed that it was dedicated to those who died in the fire on 18 November 1987. I paid little heed to this until a colleague pointed out that it happened to be the eighth anniversary of the fire.

About a year after this, I had to go to Tottenham Court Road station, again at night when it was closed. To get to the lower part of the station requires travelling down a fairly long escalator. Again, after completing my particular errand, I left. As I went back up the escalator, I was holding onto the handrail when I was shoved violently from behind, causing me to stumble forward and lose my grip on the handrail. I turned around to remonstrate with whoever had done this, but found myself alone, yet with a sore spot between my shoulder blades. This did unnerve me.

Barry Harding, by email, 2002

HEADLESS PASSENGER

Once, when visiting London in 1991, I had a very singular experience at Tottenham Court Road tube station. I'd tried my hand at busking, with limited success; the sheer volume of people, the noise and a creeping sense of claustrophobia had got the better of me. I was on my way back to Brighton, where I lived at the time, which involved getting to Victoria station. As I approached the tube exit, everything appeared to go into slow motion. I attributed this to the general feeling of unreality I get in tube stations – of being disengaged from my surroundings. This was heightened by a sense of all city sound receding suddenly. The noise of traffic and bustling crowds was suddenly replaced by one sound: high heels, click-clacking down the exit steps towards me. I looked to my right, and there, amidst the crowd, was a woman in a purple chiffon dress. She was quite tall, appeared to be in a hurry… and headless.

At the time, I was preoccupied with getting out of there, back to the relative tranquillity of Brighton. Later, on the train back to the coast, I tried to remember the headless woman. I got the strong impression that she was of the 1940s, in her late-thirties, well dressed. I remembered the sound of her heels most clearly, and was impressed by the way nothing else seemed to exist in that moment. Why was she headless? Of course I'll never know – perhaps she was one of the many Londoners who'd sought refuge during the Blitz; or perhaps she was still on her way to a secret 'assignation', her presence unknown to all but me at that moment.
Niall Stone, Tregarth, Gwynedd, 2008

8 Paranormal powers

Scientists remain sceptical, but many people believe they possess unusual powers beyond those of the five senses. Some seem to be able to catch glimpses of the future, often through dreams, while others appear to be able to move objects without physically touching them. And then there are the 'SLIders' - those who, often unwittingly, cause 'Street Lamp Interference'.

SEEING INTO THE FUTURE

9/11 PREVIEW

For those who experience them, precognitive dreams are proof of the paranormal, something beyond consensus reality. Of course, they can be explained away as coincidence; but JW Dunne in *An Experiment with Time* (1927) set up criteria to handle that possibility in evaluating many apparent precogs. Some of these were also described in *Fate* magazine many years ago, in an article describing reported dream premonitions of the *Titanic* disaster. So why haven't there been any precognitive dreams reported for 9/11?

There was at least one, my own, and probably many others. Of course, planes flying into buildings, even two at once, could be called coincidence. But my dream was more cryptic than that and memorably strange. The scene was a Manhattan apartment. The wall of one room was painted with a mural of the Manhattan skyline. Two men stood in front, and one of them pointed at the wall a gun with a wide, aluminium-coloured barrel. The other man raised a hand with index finger extended, then dropped it sharply while saying "fire". The first man did so and part of the mural was erased. The same sequence was repeated, and another part of the picture erased. This was about two years before the attacks, and unusual enough to stick in my mind until they happened.

Maybe that was just coincidence, but there's more. One day in 2003, I was reading the paper in a Denver coffee shop in a bank building while two men were installing a metal roll-up divider to be closed after hours and separate the store area from the lobby. They were driving a pair of bolts into the floor to hold the catch-plate, and one of them warned that the air gun would make a loud noise, of which he would warn patrons of the coffee shop by saying "fire". This happened, and something prompted me to remember the dream, and then, check the date on the newspaper. It was September 11.

What are the odds of all that? Broad enough (like one in a quadrillion) to fit the parameters of probability that mathematicians tell us can account for many amazing incidents? Or was the reason "queerer than we can suppose?"
Richard Porter, Denver, Colorado, 2009

PRECOGNITIVE TALENT

I seem to have a precognitive talent. I often know who is calling when the phone rings and sometimes know exactly what they want. I often dream something quite random and the next day it comes true. For instance, I once dreamed that my family had won a hoover. The next day I woke to find a piece of junk mail telling us that we had won a hoover. Once I heard the phone ring very early in the morning and sat straight up in bed on the first ring, something I would never usually do. I knew instinctively that the call was to tell my family that my beloved grandmother had passed away. Unfortunately, it was true.
Amy Harrison, Bishop Auckland, Co. Durham, 2009

THE GREEN BLANKET

When I still lived with my parents in the north of England, our local airport was about a 40-minute drive away. My parents had been on holiday and I was due to collect them from the airport the following day. That night, I had the most awful dream, with a strong feeling that something terrible was going to happen the next day. In my dream there was a body on the ground covered with a green blanket.

The next day, I drove to the airport to collect my parents as arranged, all the way feeling increasingly nervous. By the time I got there, I was in quite a state and once I'd found my parents my father decided he would drive us home. When we were some 10 minutes from the airport, the traffic began to slow. I noticed a build-up of traffic on the opposite side of the road. As we passed the end of the

" I had a very vivid dream that my family was burying my grandmother "

jam we could see there had been a motorbike accident. On the ground next to the bike lay a body covered in the paramedics' green blanket. I told my parents, who thought I'd lost the plot, but considering the state I was in when I met them at the airport I think they gradually came to believe me.

Suzy -- , London, 2009

DREAM OF A RING

In 2008, I had a very vivid dream that my family was burying my grandmother and my uncle, her younger son, took her wedding ring. I saw this as symbolic of his greedy nature and I told my best friend and my mother about how silly it was. About six weeks later, my mother telephoned to say that my grandmother had been found dead. The funeral arrangements were quickly made as my father (whose mother she was) had a holiday in Scotland planned. It was agreed that my father should handle the funeral directors (because my side of the family are atheists and don't like to get involved with Catholic ceremonies). On the day of the funeral, it transpired that my uncle had gone behind our backs to the funeral directors and requested that my grandmother's wedding ring be taken and given to his wife as she had apparently promised it before passing away. The first we knew of this was when my father had to sign for it before driving to the church.

There are a few things that make this ring business a bit odd. In 17 years of widowhood, my grandmother had never removed the ring, and she died without a legal will. Furthermore, as I am her closest female descendent, it would have come to me, not a daughter-in-law she had hardly met (as my uncle met, married and lived with her in Malaysia). I have to hope that eventually the part of my dream where I united the ring with my grandmother's body may yet come true.

Cez Connolly, by email, 2009

FURNACE PAINTING

I have a close friend, M, who lived around the corner from me from the age of six. We pretty much grew up in each other's houses. I had always been fascinated by her grandfather's paintings that adorned the walls of almost every room in the house. Her grandfather had been an Austrian painter of some note during the 1920s and 1930s, but had been somewhat overlooked in the postwar period. He favoured rather grim industrial scenes in his work, though he also painted impressive still lifes and portraits.

In my twenties I returned to visit M's parents. Her father was busily preparing for a major exhibition of the grandfather's work, the first in my lifetime.

I was very excited about it, and particularly asked after my favourite painting, a dark scene of a man feeding a furnace, surrounded by steam and water. M's father looked at me with some astonishment, and replied that no such painting existed. I was very taken aback as my memory of it was clear as day. Not two days later M herself phoned me, and during the course of the conversation mentioned having exactly the same discussion with her father. We agreed that he must have missed a painting in the cataloguing process.

M's father returned from the exhibition slightly perturbed. The painting does, indeed, exist. It had been in a private collection overseas, and had never been reproduced or exhibited since it was originally bought. There was simply no way either M or myself could have seen it.

Kate Brett, Exeter, South Australia, 2003

CHIP PAN FIRE FORETOLD

My husband and I were enjoying a quiet cup of coffee early one Friday evening. Suddenly I thought I could smell smoke. I rushed out to the kitchen and it seemed to be full of smoke. I could no longer smell it and the 'smoke' vanished very quickly. When I told my husband he didn't believe me.

The following day was my son's birthday and we were taking him to Blackpool to see the lights as a treat. Just before we left the house I noticed a smell of burning. When I went out to the kitchen the chip pan was smoking. If I hadn't

noticed the smell there would have been a fire whilst we were out. Somebody was warning me the previous day. Whoever they were I thank them.
Pamela Nowell, Upton, Wirral, 2008

NEIGHBOUR'S GOODBYE

During the late 1990s, I used to live in a block of 44 flats in Malaga, Spain. The 44 families shared three lifts, so it was very common to meet other neighbours while waiting for the lift.

One night, I dreamed I met one of the neighbours in the entrance to the block. He was a kind, elderly gentleman who I hadn't seen in a few days. In my dream I asked him how he was. He explained to me that he had been very ill and had needed to stay at home for a while, but that today he was finally feeling much better and had decided to go for a walk.

The following morning I left my flat, as usual, and froze as soon as I entered the lift. There was a note stuck in the mirror informing the community that this elderly gentleman had passed away the night before – just before I dreamed of him.
MJ, Bristol, 2010

STREET LAMP INTERFERENCE

WINKING OUT

I have experienced SLI – Street Lamp Interference – on several occasions. One time in college I was walking across campus to meet my girlfriend when three street lamps went out one after the other as I walked past. When I got to my girl-friend's, I told her about this but her reaction was scornful. We then went into the living room to watch some TV, but all four bulbs in the room blew as soon as she turned on the switch. She's going out with someone else now.

A more useful variant on the phenomenon is Pedestrian Crossing Interference (PCI), or even Traffic Light Interference (TLI), although obviously you have to be a bit more responsible about them. If you get PCI going, you'll never have to wait for that little green man again; he'll see you coming and ease your way.
Jim Mannix, by email, 2000

For 15 years now I have been the recipient of a strange sort of attention from above – streetlights go out over my head with astonishing regularity. Since I started keeping actual track of the numbers, I have visually spotted 78 in the last six years. I estimate the total to be close to 200. Several friends have only witnessed it while in my presence, in the car or on foot.

On one occasion I got quite aggravated and demanded out loud that some proof be forthcoming. Three more streetlights then self-extinguished before I had gone another three miles! I have made inquiries with the municipal agency in charge of streetlights, who stated that they do not cycle on and off regularly (the theory always proposed by the sceptical). If everyone saw as many go out as I do, practically all of them would be out!

Leo Scarpelli, Olympia, Washington State, 2000

On 17 September 2000, as I walked home down a busy main road, three lights winked out just as I passed under each one. I didn't think anything about the first one cutting out, but the second going as I walked under it caught my attention. Not long after I passed by, it lit up again, and for the several minutes it was in sight it didn't cut out. The third light, on the other side of the road, went as I got parallel with it.

David Patrick, by email, 2000

I was a teenager living in a small Yorkshire village, and there were many occasions when street lights would go out as I approached them; usually at a distance of about 10 yards (9m). The phenomenon would usually occur when I was alone, although several times when accompanied, my companions also witnessed the event. Most found this interesting, yet none were ever frightened – but rather intrigued. My various employments have taken me to every part of the British Isles and on uncountable occasions I have experienced streetlights going out as I approached. There were many times when I knew it was going to happen.

One time when I was driving home in the early hours of the morning along the M62, a whole row of motorway lights suddenly went out as I approached at 70mph (112km/h). I must admit that was a bit scary. On another occasion, as I pulled into a pub car park on the A19 near York, the illuminated pub sign went out. I sat in my car for about five minutes waiting to see what would hap-

pen. Nothing did until I got out of the car, when the sign lit up again.

I just took the phenomenon for granted. Although such events are now quite rare – happening only about once a year – I am still intrigued and mystified why I appear to have this ability.

Michael Barwell, by email, 2009

Since 1992, I have noticed my ability to disrupt several types of city lighting by simply walking or driving slowly by them. This doesn't happen with every light, but a small, consistent percentage continue to go out. In 1999, I began videotaping these events. I discovered that these types of lighting are routinely equipped with photo-sensitive cells that respond to changing light, going on and off automatically. Once I've disrupted them, they don't simply go off, but begin to cycle on and off in intervals of a minute or more. For all practical purposes, they are broken and must be replaced.

All this is on videotape. I can do this in any city because the lights used are universal as far as I can tell.

Janusz Kozikowski, by email, 2009

SLIDERS

The mystery of Street Lamp Interference (SLI) remains unexplained, but with more than 200 cases on record we can at least define the problem. It happens spontaneously, generally (though not invariably) when the subject is in an unusual state of mind (anxious, happy, angry, relaxed – you name it!). Since a physical action is involved – the operation of the switch – some physical force is required: but this seems to come from the mind of the subject, which is something that conventional science would rather not contemplate. No SLIder can do it to order, but a few have on occasion deliberately caused it to occur.

Many SLIders also affect other appliances, ranging from digital watches to supermarket checkouts, domestic lights to railway crossings. Some do it rarely, some over a limited period then never again, others periodically over many years, even a lifetime. Why this power is directed specifically at street lamps is another intriguing aspect of the enigma.

For more about this phenomenon, see my new book *Sliders* (Anomalist Books, San Antonio & New York, 2010).

Hilary Evans, London, 2010

❝ I saw it was the exact same time on the clock that I'd decided to kill my boyfriend ❞

PSYCHOKINESIS

CONQUERING TIME

When my father was young, he could never wear a wristwatch because as soon as he put it on, it stopped. If someone else put the same watch on, it worked. When I was two years old, I wouldn't stay in my bedroom at night and used to vault out of my cot and run downstairs. One night, I was extremely disturbed and wouldn't stay in the room, so my parents made the living room safe for me and went to bed, absolutely exhausted. I was found the following morning, peacefully asleep and every clock in the house had stopped at 2.30am. They weren't electric clocks, so a power cut couldn't account for it.

Around Easter 1999, I was waiting for my (now ex-) boyfriend to arrive. He was late. I was very angry. He eventually turned up, then left after a while. Later on, I was talking to my mother and she noticed that the carriage clock on the mantelpiece had stopped. When I looked at it, I realised that it was the exact same time on the clock that I had decided to kill my boyfriend. My mother asked me to start the clock again, so I did – without touching the clock at all.

My father has a theory: A clock is a device that can communicate with another dimension (albeit crudely). After all, it measures something that we don't under-

stand, something which it is argued may not even exist; and yet it measures it to a high degree of accuracy that rules our lives completely.
Gillian Neuhauser, by email, 1999

THE BOLT

During the 1980s, I lived alone in an old three-storey house in a storm-battered fishing village on the rugged coast of north-east England. In common with many properties in the village, my house had no back door. A sturdy wooden four-panel front door gave access into a flagged courtyard around which other houses were tightly grouped. Because of the sloping ground, the windows in the back of my house overlooked the rooftops of buildings at the rear.

For a few years in the 1980s I held an unsatisfactory job in adult education in a nearby town. One day was so unpleasant that I announced dramatically: "I'm going to pretend that today never happened. I'm going to pretend I never even left home this morning." On arriving home, I inserted the Yale key in the lock. Although the key turned, the door wouldn't open. A neighbour used a ladder to gain access through a bedroom window. He found the front door firmly bolted.

So the question is, how had I managed to leave home that morning? As there was no back door and the downstairs windows were locked, I could only have unbolted the front door in order to get out. It is highly unlikely that, during the day, someone brought a ladder, climbed in the bedroom window, bolted the front door, and then left by the window and ladder. They would have been seen by some of the numerous neighbours. Nothing was disturbed in the house. Had my wish to have remained at home caused the bolt to slide across? Was this an example of psychokinesis?
Gloria Wilson, Yorkshire, 2004

THE WAY OF ZEN

When I was young in the early 1950s, I used to watch my father move a needle that he would float on the surface tension in a half glass of water. Getting the darn needle to float was hard enough for me, but then he'd stand back across the room and call that he was going to make it spin clockwise or counter-clockwise. And he would. He could start it in one direction, stop it and start it going the other direction. I never managed more than a slight bob that just made the needle sink to the bottom. My father always told me that the way to do it was by "not-trying" – a wonderfully Zen explanation from someone who had most probably never heard of, much less studied, Zen practice or thought.
Marilyn Zavitz, Toronto, Canada, 2005

9

Strange sounds

From the entrancing songs of the Sirens luring sailors to their deaths, to the wail of the Banshee announcing an impending death, the world of sounds has always had its spooky side. From phantom choirs, screaming spirits and voices from nowhere to a veritable symphony of mysterious taps, bangs, ticks, rattles and clicks, we present a selection of aural oddities from our files.

DISEMBODIED VOICES

SCREAMING SPIRIT

In 1986, I was 16 years old and living in the seaside town of Wollongong in New South Wales, Australia. I was dating a young lass who lived six to nine miles (10–15 km) away, about halfway up the escarpment of Mount Keira. I would ride my pushbike to her house about three times a week to hang out and hopefully steal a kiss or two. Beside Mount Keira is a smaller mountain known locally as Devil's Mountain. From the Mount Keira lookout, on a clear day, you could see three large sixes cleared in the bushland of Devil's Mountain. These were said to be the work of Satanists, designed to provide a place for their rituals.

One midweek evening around 9pm, I started for home. The return ride was always easier, being downhill most of the way. I had travelled a few streets and was just nearing the crest of my first hill when, from behind and above me in the darkness, I heard a spine-tingling, unnatural scream that sounded neither human nor animal. As I thundered downhill, I did my best to turn and look up to see where and what was tailing me. It sounded close to my shoulders. I could see nothing but was struck with fear and pedalled for my life.

Some miles further on, I heard the wailing night spirit again. I turned and peered into the darkness, as it seemed close enough to swoop down and claw at my head; but once again I could see nothing. Terrified, I soldiered on until I had reached my own street and was climbing the hill steadily in low gear. Just as I mounted the crest and was tearing down the other side, the scream returned and followed me down the hill, but departed as I reached the bottom. I threw my bike on the grass and bolted up the stairs, closing the front door quickly behind me. I made my way to the bathroom to relieve myself. As I looked up from splashing water on my face, I peered out of the little window that opened onto the backyard and heard the screech again. I promptly retreated to my bedroom and hid under the covers.

Chris Lethbridge, by email, 2009

HEAVENLY CHOIR PRACTICE

When I was about 15 (around 1989) I went away with a youth group, of which I was a member, to a Bible camp at a showground in the east of England. The girl I had been sharing a tent with had been taken into hospital suddenly so I was staying there alone. It was late summer and very warm. One morning, I was woken by the Sun coming through the thin canvas of the tent. As I awoke, I became aware of some exquisite choral singing, getting steadily louder. I assumed that this was some choir practice going on in one of the halls and lay back to listen. The singing was awesome. It was very simple, consisting of only three or four words and cyclical, going round and round and round...

Eventually, I sat up and put my head outside the tent and abruptly the singing stopped. I estimate it was only around seven or eight o'clock in the morning and there was no one around except for a couple of my mates, four or five tents away, having a cup of tea and talking softly so as not to wake anyone. I called over to them and asked if they'd heard any choirs singing and they said no, looking very puzzled. Sure that I'd imagined it, I lay down in my tent again. As soon as I closed my eyes again the singing began – so many voices, joyful, soaring and pure. I got up and put my head out again – nothing but quiet!

Later in the day, one of the pastors approached me and said that one of the boys had told him I'd heard singing in my tent and told me I'd heard angels singing in a very matter-of-fact kind of way. I was stunned. I can't explain what happened and I don't believe someone played a trick on me. Whilst not really a follower of the traditional Christian church anymore, I've found this very comforting, and if proof were needed, suggestive of something else beyond our lives. It's also left me with a strange tendency for bursting into spontaneous tears

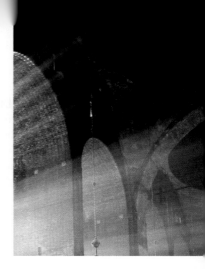

As I awoke, I became aware of some exquisite choral singing, getting louder

against my will when I hear certain kinds of choral singing...
Portia --, by email, 2003

BAND PRACTICE CHATTERERS

I was in a band for a while a couple of years ago, and we used to practise in a large room on the top floor of an old woollen mill in Bradford. As we were all young, the novelty of sheer volume had not yet worn off, so we used to practise obscenely loudly.

While playing, I would often hear the sound of a loud, but very indistinct, conversation over the music. Concerned about upsetting the neighbours, I would sometimes call a halt to the music, only to hear the voices hush as the music stopped, or sometimes slightly after. Other members of the band began to notice the 'chat', to my great relief, as I was beginning to doubt my sanity. There were no people nearby to make the noise, as the room was quite isolated in an otherwise disused building complex.

The other strange aspect is that the 'chat' wasn't there all the time, but only occasionally, usually around 6pm. Sometimes, when the noise was at its most noticeable, there would be a strong and unmistakable scent of pipe tobacco. I had initially put this down to overload on my amplifier, but on one occasion I actually did destroy the output stage of my amp and the burning smell that generated was quite different.
Daniel B Wood, by email, 2004

MYSTERY MOBILE CALL

We'd stayed overnight for New Year at some close friends' place, a semi-detached villa that's been in one of the couple's family for years. We got back to the house at about 3am after leaving a party. I awoke before my friends and went downstairs to make a coffee. I had been pottering about for about 45 minutes before they both came down to seek hangover remedies.

On entering the kitchen, my friends asked me who I had been speaking to on my mobile phone at 5am and why had I walked up and down their landing whilst making the call, disturbing them as they were trying to sleep. Now there was no one else apart from us in the house; their children were with family overnight and their other relatives who own the adjoining house were away for New Year, so there would be no noise to carry through the building from next door.

Being a bit groggy still, I explained that I hadn't got out of bed until 45mins before they did, and I hadn't received or made any calls on my mobile as I had left it in their lounge when we had got back from the party.

I asked if they had been able to hear what 'I' had apparently been saying, but they both said that it had been indistinct; their landing is quite long and their door had been closed. They both assured me that the voice had become louder and then quieter, as if somebody was walking towards and then away from their door. They even heard the tread of floorboards.

Now I know that we had celebrated New Year with a few drinks, but we were not exceptionally drunk and I most certainly wasn't in a state where I could not remember what I was doing. I was also on a different floor to them, so wouldn't have any reason to go up to their room. I had to show my friends the received and dialled numbers on my phone before they believed that I had not drunkenly got up when they thought I had.

I myself did not hear anything and I asked if it could have been noise from outside the house that they had heard, but they were adamant that it was a different sound to what they would recognise as passers-by or noise from the adjoining house (one of them even went next door to check, and there had been no one there).

My friends are both rational adults, parents to two children and firm sceptics. They laughed and joked about it, although my female friend became a bit distressed later as all the theories we could think of to explain the 'voice' they had heard were dashed.

TheQuixote, by email, 2004

KNOCK, KNOCK - WHO'S THERE?

THE BLACK SHADOW

It was around 1970 or 1971, and I was about 12-13 years old. Our family, in rural Northwest Ohio, consisted of two parents and five boys (with me the third oldest), and had not long ago moved to a newly-built house two lots down from our old one. Some construction details remained to be finished.

A few years earlier, as a smaller child, I had been terrified every night of monsters when going to bed, pulling the covers up over my head and trying not to move so they couldn't see me or tell I was there. It wasn't helped by the fact that, in the old house, the door to the attic was right at the foot of my top bunk bed. But by the time of this account, such childish fears were no longer an influence.

On this particular (school) night, I went to bed in my room, the last of two upstairs on the right side of the hallway. Drifting off to sleep with the door closed (others were still awake downstairs), I was awakened by a loud, normal-sounding knocking on the bedroom door, as if someone was requesting entrance to see me. But going to the door, no one was there.

Thinking I was mistaken, I went back to bed. This time, I wasn't even drifting off when the knocking came again, a very normal 'let-me-in-I-want-to-see-you' knock, maybe five raps on the door. Opening it again, I found no one there. Having older brothers fond of playing jokes on younger siblings, I also checked the next couple of rooms, the closet, and under the bed, thinking maybe one of them was hiding and having a little fun at my expense. But no one was in evidence anywhere I checked.

Well, by now, being suspicious of brothers' potential pranks, I walked downstairs and asked who wanted me. No one, brothers or parents, indicated they had come up to see me in my bedroom. Not satisfied with the answers, but getting no information, I shut my door and went back to bed, determined not to be caught 'sleeping' again.

I lay awake, waiting for the knock I was sure was coming (I didn't trust my older brothers as far as I could throw them). Sure enough, shortly the very normal-sounding knocking sounded clearly, and clearly it was coming from the door. But when I went to open it again, no one was there, and no one was nearby in a position to hide after knocking on the door.

Enough was enough. I left the door ajar, and lay awake, waiting to catch the dastardly brother so intent on spoiling my sleep. And very soon after that, the knocking sounded again. Except this time, awake, I could clearly see a black shape or shadow hitting itself against the door's hallway side. It wasn't recognisable as anything – not an animal, not an object – just a velvety black shape. The knocking stopped, and it was gone. It hadn't gone 'away' in any direction – it was just gone.

I might not have been scared of monsters anymore, but I was a little 'tweaked' by what I saw. I checked around for a bird, an animal, a bat – anything that could have gotten in the house and banged against my door. I didn't find anything that night, or the next day, and neither did anyone else. It sure wasn't my brothers or my parents. I can't call it a ghost, but what it was, I never found out, and I spent more than a few uneasy nights in the room until the immediacy of the experience faded. The incident never repeated itself.

T Miller, by email, 2001

HIDE AND SEEK

When I was about 12 -13 years old I lived with my family in an old Victorian house in Withington, Manchester. With some school friends we had experimented with table- tilting in our front cellar, with some success, but each of us accused the others of cheating.

Some time later I began to hear knocking sounds from the attic, which at one time would have been the servants' bedrooms. It sounded as if the furniture was being sharply rapped by someone's knuckles and was quite loud. I would go and investigate, not being scared at that time by such things. As soon as I entered the room and switched on the light, the knocking would stop, and there was never anything to see. It would then start up in a different room with the same results, and it became a sort of game of hide and seek, but without the finding!

The sounds were sporadic and sometimes did not happen for weeks. My stepmother refused to go into the cellar to fetch coal after she swore something pinched her bottom ascending the steps one night. My father thought this hilarious, but I remember she was very upset at the time. Eventually the knockings just stopped. Other members of the family heard them, and my aunt and stepmother said we had caused them by "mucking about" calling up spirits.

Brian Ellwood, by email, 2001

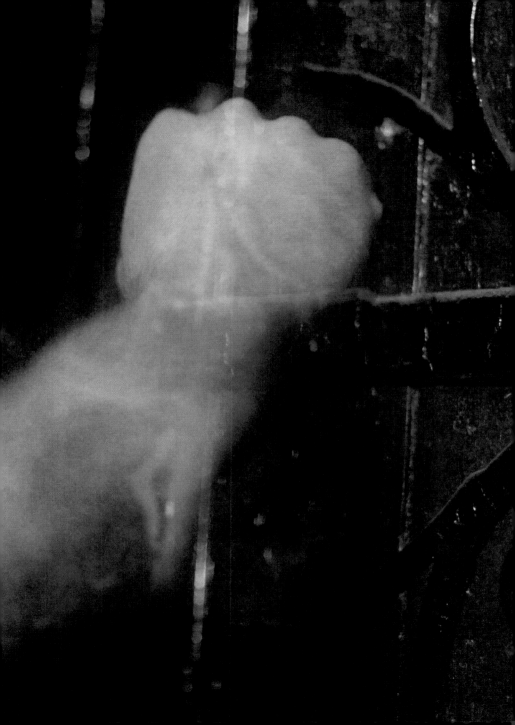

TAPPING, TICKING AND CLICKING

TICKED OFF

Since childhood, I have experienced an unusual phenomenon – a rapping or ticking noise that seems inexplicable in that it has no fixed speed, loudness or point of origin. It is mobile and in many ways random; it does, however, nearly always seem to sound as if it is coming from a point within the wall. I can only recall one occasion when it did not, when, in front of two friends, it moved from a wall to under the floorboards and then died away.

The noise itself was stronger and more akin to a tapping when I was younger. Now I'm in my late twenties, and it sounds more like a loud clock ticking. It possesses no obvious pattern, regularity or duration, and I have not been in possession of one constant electrical item from childhood until now, and certainly not one that can 'throw' the sounds of its internal mechanisms. One of the more unusual aspects of it is that it appears to lose me temporarily when I move house. I have moved about eight times in the past 10 years and it has ended up taking about a fortnight to start up (catch up?) again. When I made the biggest move – from Wales to England – it took approximately two years to occur. Hence this letter, because the other day it started again.

I also seem to have some level of interaction with it. One night, annoyed at its particular speed and audibility, I punched the wall where it was. It proceeded to move about a foot to the right and start again. This process was repeated several more times that night. It is not really frightening and for years I haven't questioned it; it was just there. It only occurs when I am at home and, as far as I know, has not been noticed by anyone in my absence.

It has manifested in front of witnesses, though in general it is loath to do so. It seems to be louder at night; this may be because it is more audible in the quieter environment. I have awoken to hear it ticking merrily away in a far corner of a room and then awoken again later with it still doing so, but from a point to my left. Such behaviour seems to me to preclude the most obvious explanations.
Martin Einon, Montpelier, Bristol, 1998

PHANTOM CLOCK?

I grew up listening to a very similar phenomenon to that of Martin Einon. I would hear a noise almost identical to the "tick-tock" of a clock, except that it had a

" The sound was rhythmic and perfectly timed, sounding just like a clock "

tendency to slow down on occasion after being audible for a minute or two.

As with Mr Einon's sound, it was heard mostly at night, but in my case I could never pinpoint its location. Our house had no clocks that audibly ticked and the fuse box was ruled out as it didn't appear to make any noise. My sister also heard the sound during the time we had to share the room, convincing me that I wasn't just 'hearing things'. (We joked about a ghost with a watch.)

Since then, I've lived in that room several times on and off and have never heard it again. I don't think I heard it since the extensive building work my father carried out some years ago.

Causes I suspected at the time included insects, 'clicking' bats, electrical transformer and nearby high-tension power lines. Whatever the cause, the sound was rhythmic and perfectly timed, sounding just like a clock. It would rise and fall in volume but was always only just on the edge of hearing.

Simon Robbins, Ottawa, Ontario, 1999

THE TICKING

From the age of about 14, I began hearing a sound that seems identical to that reported by Simon Robbins. It sounded mechanical, like a fast ticking, tended to slow before it stopped, and to shift location from near the walls to the centre of the room. I and my brother and sister (who was a lot younger) all heard it separately and together, and like Mr Robbins we also used to joke that it was 'a ghost with a stop-watch'!

Although mysterious, the sound never seemed spooky, but my sister was frightened when she first heard it – she ran downstairs crying that there was 'a rattlesnake' in her bedroom. We assumed this was a bad dream until I also heard the sound in her room, and reassured her that it was only 'the Ticking'. We lived in an old cottage with no central heating and no obvious source for the sound.

Many years later, with my own young children, I heard 'the Ticking' again – in an old cottage, as before. My son used to hear it quite loudly; to me it was fainter, but absolutely recognisable. My husband doesn't remember hearing it at all. As always, if one of us mentioned it, it would stop immediately – but often resumed after a few moments. It usually occurred in the afternoons or early evening, when the house was quiet.

However, it isn't confined to old buildings, nor even to buildings at all. I have occasionally heard it even in our present house, a 1920s semi, and most remarkably in an outdoor location, on the shores on Lyn y Fan Fach, a lake near the Brecon Beacons. This was a still summer's dusk. Both my children heard it as well. It may be significant that just before it started, I had been thinking of a friend of ours who'd recently been killed in a tragic accident; I was imagining how much she would have loved this lake. So maybe there's a 'ghostly' aspect after all.

That was 19 years ago; my children are now 29 and 30, but they still remember the phenomenon vividly. Until now, we believed it was some weird happening unique to our family – it's a relief to discover that others have heard it too! Personally, it seems linked in my life to times of unhappiness and trauma, though it was strangely reassuring to hear it at the time.

Hilary Llewellyn-Williams, Llanelli, Carmarthenshire, 1999

NOISES OFF

Around the late 1980s, when I was in my mid-30s, I lived for a while in a pleasant rented, furnished, 19th-century cottage on the outskirts of the picturesque Surrey village of Pirbright with my wife Val (now deceased). We sometimes read books of mutual interest together, with me reading out loud. One evening, we'd been enjoying Michael Bentine's paranormally flavoured autobiography *The Door Marked Summer*, which talked (amongst other things) about his and his father's experiments with spirit "table rapping".

At around midnight, we settled into our double bed upstairs and were soon both deeply asleep. Then something woke me. I glanced at the electric clock on the bedside table to my left. It was 2am. The room was dark and still. I could hear a faint but distinct sound, seemingly coming from the parcel shelf in the old, small built-in wardrobe in the left corner of the room. At first I thought it was the scratching of a rodent's claws. I fancied that a mouse or rat had somehow gained entry. Moments later, it resolved itself into the sound wood makes when being slowly twisted or crushed. It was only just audible – which made it seem all the more threatening in the heavy silence.

I pondered on this for a few seconds, feeling increasingly uneasy as I stared in the direction of the wardrobe – and the next moment, from the opposite side of the room, where an old wooden chest of drawers stood against the wall, an ear-shattering KRRRAKKK! of splitting wood rent the air. It was so loud and unexpected my heart nearly stopped. Val woke in an instant and sat up, screaming "OhmyGod! What is it?" I reached down my side of the bed and, when I eventually fumbled the light on, the room looked completely normal. The sound in the wardrobe had ceased. All that could be heard now was our frantic breathing, Val's frightened whimpers – and my curses.

It took me a minute to regain my composure and venture out of bed to the old chest of drawers. I carefully dragged it away from the wall, to discover that the slightly warped plywood back panel had a split running from top to bottom. We couldn't say whether that split had already been there – we'd never previously checked its overall condition – and closer examination in the light of day yielded no further clues. (We asked our landlord about it some days later, but he didn't know whether it had been there previously.) There was also nothing untoward to be found in the wardrobe.

The following night – against all the odds, you'd think – it happened again. There was no precursory sound from the wardrobe, but I awoke a few seconds before hearing the same crack of splitting wood, though much less ferocious, from the chest of drawers. It struck me as being a rather half-hearted attempt this time. Val stirred, but didn't come fully awake. Without bothering to turn on the light, I muttered into my pillow words to the effect of: "All right, you've made your point, thank you," speaking to the 'spirit' – as I imagined Michael Bentine would have done in this situation – and went back to sleep. That was the last of it.

Did we charge our environment with our own psychic energy, causing the wood to split? Or was a visiting spirit giving us a spectacular example of "table-rapping" in action, as if to underline the reality of the phenomenon we'd been reading about?

Bob Kingsley, Banwell, Somerset, 2008

Now you see it...

We expect the world to be a solid, predictable sort of place in which things are either there, or they're not. In fact, puddles and drips of water can appear from nowhere, while precious objects can vanish without trace and reappear just as mysteriously. Are the pixies behind it? And, if we ask them nicely, might they be kind enough to give us back our missing stuff?

WEIRD WATER

MYSTERY SPILLS

In the early hours of 25 June 1998, I was woken by a loud crackling noise. It seemed to be coming from the side of the bed where the electric clock radio was. I discovered that the noise was indeed coming from the clock. The cloth on which it was standing on the bedside cabinet was soaked with water, which had entered the clock, creating the crackling sound. The carpet beneath the cabinet was also saturated. I don't have a glass of water at night, nor is there a radiator, only an electric storage heater. There were no roof leaks or damp walls; in fact, the night was warm and dry. The cloth on the cabinet was so wet through that I had to wring it out and I soaked up the moisture on the carpet below with lots of newspaper. I dried out the clock on the heater and it began to work again. I am completely baffled.

Elaine Dobson, Rotherham, South Yorkshire, 1998

On 8 March 2006, we discovered a patch of water on an inside windowsill (the window is between two rooms, not on an outside wall). It was as if a glass of water had been spilt. There were no drips or splashes and the wall, ceiling and top of the frame were all completely dry. I mopped it up, and have kept an eye on it since, but it has not returned. We have no idea where it originated.

Pam Thornton, Llandegla, Clwyd, 2006

At 1pm on 17 May 2006, I stepped out my back door to find a sizeable patch of water on the paving at the rear of my house where, moments earlier, I had noticed nothing unusual. May was an unusually wet month in the UK, and although there were grey clouds in the sky that day, no amount of rain could have produced this water which was splashed around in an area approximately 5ft (1.5m) by 3ft (90cm). There must have been about three or four pints worth which, from the splash pattern, could only have fallen from the air.

Moments later, I found I was having a nosebleed, something that hasn't happened to me for years. The water was unusual enough for me to photograph it – but not so pictorially interesting to prevent me from later erasing the picture. I cannot definitely say that the appearance of the water and my nosebleed were connected, but it is intriguing to correlate them.

Jerry Glover, by email, 2006

PHANTOM DRIPS

I wonder whether any other readers have experienced what I can only describe as a 'phantom drip'. Several times recently I have entered a room (not always the same one) at home, only to have my attention caught by what appears to be a drip from the door jamb. I also 'hear' a sound as it would be due to hit the floor. Inspection of the floor reveals no wet patch, nor any other evidence that the drip ever existed! My wife also claims to have seen it, but is less clear about the sound.

Ian Lawes, Brighton, East Sussex, 1996

My husband and I have been experiencing the 'phantom drip' for about a year now, and have had more than a dozen events in all, in both our bathroom and kitchen. You might think these are obvious places for just such a drip, but in each case there is no evidence at all of condensation or the slightest moisture anywhere in the ceiling to account for it. The drip is ice cold, and usually manages to land squarely on top of the head, leaving behind a patch of coldness that can only be described as water without the wetness. On one occasion while standing in our kitchen feeding the cat, both the cat and I watched 'something' drip from the ceiling (although I didn't see it emerge) and land on the tiled floor about 4in

" Three or four times a year, a single large drop of water will hit my bald patch "

(10cm) from the cat's head with a loud spat. I inspected the whole area for the wet mark a drip like this should have made, but found absolutely nothing.
Helen Harling, Bristol, Avon, 1997

Three or four times a year, always in my own home, a single large drop will hit my bald patch. I am a tall man and when this happens I immediately reach up to feel the ceiling. There is never a hint of moisture there.
Viv Hobbs, Blackwood, Gwent, 1999

My family have experienced the 'phantom drip', in our present house and in our last one. It fell in a steady procession, in various shades of blue, continually beside our old front door, where only the eldest girl could see it, and would dodge around an outstretched hand. In our present home it falls from the ceiling in the kitchen, looking like cloudy egg white. Ectoplasm?
  My husband Graham, a hard-headed science-teaching sceptic, was amazed to see it time after time, often climbing up to feel the ceiling or grovelling on the floor after it, to no avail. One day, in broad daylight, I happened to be looking his way when a very large blob landed with an audible *splat!* on his balding pate. He gasped in shock and slapped his hand on his head, but found nothing: the ceiling was dry. I saw and heard it and Graham heard and felt it: it was deathly cold, he said. We're at a loss. What the, er, devil is it?
Carla R, by email, 2001

LOST AND FOUND

A TELEPORTED TALE

In 1968, when I was 16, I was in the habit of reading in bed, and was halfway through a second reading of a superb book by Eric Frank Russell, whose title I can no longer remember, but whose theme was – appropriately enough for these paranoid days — a lone man's struggle to reveal the truth about a US government's cover-up of a failed, or never really attempted, space mission to Mars. I put the book down on my bedside table one night and went to sleep.

The next night the book was nowhere to be found. My parents disclaimed any knowledge of moving it, as did my younger sister. I took the room apart, checked drawers, desk and dismantled the bed. The book was quite definitely not in that room. Over the next few months I gradually gave up hope of ever seeing it again, but one night about six months after its disappearance, I slid my hand between the bedframe and the mattress and felt the distinctive shape of a paperback. It was the book, in a place which had been searched months earlier and which in any case had seen numerous changes of bed linen over the intervening time. The book had disappeared and had returned.

I recall that 1968 was the year in which policemen in Essex chased fiery crosses for miles, an event widely reported at the time; there were also numerous UFO sightings in the news about then. It was against this background that my book went and came back. I think it returned about the time the Apollo 8 astronauts returned from their circumnavigation of the Moon. Many eyes and minds were turned skywards and outwards in those days and I got it into my head that my book had been abducted by mischievous aliens who read it, passed it on to their friends and eventually returned it. Total nonsense, of course, but the idea that my bedroom might be some kind of sub-space transportation focus (*Star Trek* and *2001* were looming large at the time too) made going to sleep a pretty nerve-racking experience for a while: if a book could go, why not me?

I finished reading the book and it eventually disappeared permanently by the more conventional method of being lent to someone who never returned it. I would be interested to hear if anyone else has experienced such cavalier and inexplicable treatment of their libraries. I would also be interested to hear from anyone who could provide me with the title of the book from the brief thematic synopsis above. Eric Frank Russell was a superbly witty and wry writer of excel-

lent science fiction. Whoever abducted the book had good taste.
Tony Purcell, Chelmsford, Essex, 1997

POPCORN SURPRISE

I want to tell you about what is, to date, my only brush with the unexplained – an experience as trivial as it is astounding. I can't prove a word of it, of course, but your readers may agree that no one would bother making up a tale so peculiar.

At around the age of nine or so, I found a jar of dried corn kernels, and one Saturday afternoon in 1980 I attempted to make popcorn by placing these kernels onto a teaspoon and sticking this into the grate of a gas fire. My parents had gone out, otherwise I wouldn't have attempted such a dangerous venture. It got me little further than producing two singed corn kernels, and heating the spoon to such a degree that I burnt my hand. I flung the spoon down, and as I did so, heard my father's car in the driveway. As the car doors slammed, all my attention was devoted to finding and concealing the evidence. The spoon and one of the singed corn kernels were easily located and disposed of, but the other burnt kernel eluded me. I searched high and low, not just on that occasion, but for several days thereafter, but never found it.

Several months later, I went into a joke shop with a friend, where we purchased, amongst other items, a pair of fake cigarettes. These were simply white plastic tubes with a red painted end, and if you blew on them, a small cloud of flour or talcum powder was emitted to give the impression of smoke. We walked along the street puffing on our 'cigarettes' until I noticed an awkward lump in the mouth-end of my own. I asked my friend if there was something similar in his cigarette, but he said not. I pushed this hard, intractable lump, eventually squeezing it out of the end of the cigarette, where it revealed itself to be a corn kernel, singed at one end. Have any readers ever found a singed corn kernel in the end of a fake cigarette, I wonder, or was this some strange example of my sins finding me out?
Matt Baylis, London, 2010

RECOVERED TIME

My cousin Jessica's godmother gave her a pretty gold wristwatch with a dainty chain strap for her birthday. She wore it constantly and often stopped to admire it. One night, after a visit to the cinema, she slipped away to a patch of waste ground behind the picture house for a few stolen kisses with her boyfriend. I waited for them at the local chip shop, but when they didn't turn up I went searching for them and found them on their hands and knees among the weeds looking for her watch. As it was rapidly getting dark, I suggested we come back and look in daylight. We searched in vain the next morning. No watch had been handed in at the cinema or the local police station.

Five years later, Jessica was engaged to another young man. She had been to the bingo (the cinema had been converted) with some friends and had arranged to meet her fiancé afterwards. The ardour of passionate young love led them to seek out a quiet spot for a kissing session in the same patch of waste ground where the watch had been lost.

Jessica stumbled over a Cadbury's Roses carton, picked it up to make sure it was empty and to her utter amazement found her watch inside. There was no doubt it was the same watch. After five years of British weather it was miraculously undamaged and when she wound it up it kept perfect time. Had it really lain there unnoticed all these years? And why, of all the people in the world, had the finder been the original owner?

Alexandria Martin, Aldershot, Hampshire, 1996

THE MISSING CHARM

One Saturday in May 2005, a friend and I took the bus to the 'Witchfest' at Fairfield Halls in Croydon, Surrey. While perusing the general paraphernalia and jewellery on sale, a themed charm bracelet in silver caught my eye, and I treated myself to it. Arriving home that night, again by bus, I placed the bracelet safely in a ceramic dish on a table to one side of one of my two sofas. There it remained until the following Saturday, when my friends Sheila and Paul came round for the evening. I hadn't worn the bracelet during this time, as the six charms were not yet soldered on (although the jump rings by which the charms were attached were fully closed and quite robust). During the evening, I showed the bracelet to Sheila, who commented that she particularly liked the cat-on-a-broomstick charm. Afterwards, I put it back in the dish on the table next to the sofa (that I was sitting on). The sofa Sheila and Paul were sitting on was at right angles to mine, about 4ft (1.2m) away, on the same side as the table with the dish on it.

There it stayed until the next day, when I decided I'd like another look at it with the intention of removing the charms and replacing them in a more pleasing arrangement. I'd already removed several of them when I realised that

there were now only five, and the missing one was the cat on the broomstick. Of course, my first thought was that it had fallen off, but it wasn't in the dish or on the floor. Even though the jump ring was fully closed, it could have caught on something, I reasoned, and was probably to be found on the second sofa, (which is actually a sofa bed), where Sheila and Paul had been sitting. I had a thorough look, and in spite of the fact a throw was covering it, and therefore it was impossible for anything to have slipped down the sides or the back of the seat cushions, I removed the throw and checked anyway – no sign of it.

I then pulled the bed out: still no sign of it. I moved the sofa away from the wall it backed onto and even removed the cushion covers, but still no luck. I carried on searching, even in places I knew it wasn't likely to be, and eventually gave up. It had seemingly just disappeared into thin air; but logically, I thought, perhaps it had come off and caught on Sheila's clothing, and then fallen off when they were on their way home. Yes, that must be what happened, I concluded, even though it wouldn't be that easy to open a fully closed jump ring without the aid of pliers, and not one of the three of us there that evening noticed it fall off the bracelet, or indeed catch on anyone's clothing. Sheila later confirmed that she hadn't seen it since that night.

In time, I replaced the missing charm with a duplicate from the same company and collected a few more besides. Then, one Saturday evening in May 2007, I drove to see my mother in Crawley, Sussex. I arrived back home at about 10.00 – 10.30pm. As I opened the car door, the key and fob slipped from my hand and dropped to the garage floor. There is no electricity supply to my garage, and I couldn't see a thing when I looked down to find it. Fortunately, I reached down and put my hand straight on it, and as I picked it up, noticed something directly underneath, faintly glinting in the sparse light provided by the car park beyond. I picked up the mystery object and took it to the front of the garage where the lamplight was stronger and, after a few seconds of initial bewilderment, realised I was looking at my long-lost charm!

The jump ring was not in evidence. It was late at night, I was on my own and had just found an item that had reappeared as strangely as it had disappeared. At no point had the charm or the bracelet ever been anywhere near my garage, and Sheila and Paul don't have a key to it; besides which, they aren't given to such pranks. I don't think it could've been there all that time; it looked a bit scuffed, but not as much as you might expect had it been driven over and trodden on for two years – and surely I would've noticed it before? Even odder

> ❝ *The ring could have been anywhere —talk about a needle in a haystack!* ❞

that I should drop my key precisely over the charm and then discover it in pitch blackness, when I'd used my car numerous times in daylight during the two years it had been missing. It's almost as if our friends from the hidden realms had engineered it that way.

Sue Gardner, Sutton, Surrey, 2008

JUST ASK

PIXIE POWER

From time to time, *Fortean Times* has carried letters from people who have successfully asked the pixies to find lost objects for them.

Here's a photo (above) of a heavy mediæval silver ring that I often wear. A few months ago, while putting out hay for my sheep, it slipped off my finger. It could have been anywhere, in deep straw, in a farm shed 40ft (12m) long and 35ft (11m) wide. My partner and I searched long and hard for it, but eventually we gave up. Just before Christmas, however, we went back to the job armed with a powerful metal detector. In the interim, much straw and hay had been put out, and hundreds of sheep had trampled through the shed. Talk about a needle in a haystack!

We went over the whole building, unearthing several rummy agricultural bits of metal buried deep in the earth floor – but the ring was not among them. Eventually I cried in desperation: "Pixies, please help me!" Instantly – literally instantly – the headphones buzzed. The detector coil was right over a pile of hay-dust I'd scanned several times already. I scrabbled in the dust, and the ring fell out.

This is not the first time I've appealed to the pixies since reading about other people's experiences, nor the first time they've helped. In fact, they haven't failed me yet. But this result was so immediate, so striking, so utterly obliging, that I fell to wondering how to repay these charming little elementals. I could put a small ad in the *Daily Telegraph*, I suppose, like those one often sees thanking St Jude for services rendered. I suspect that pixies don't read the *Telegraph*, but they might read *Fortean Times*, so a letter to you seemed somehow more appropriate.

Thank you pixies. How on earth do you do it?

Ali Barnes, Poundstock, Cornwall, 2009

SUCCESSFUL APPEAL

One day in February 2008, I was rather stressed out because I had a radio interview the following day about some books I'd published, and one of the main titles I wanted to take along was missing. I looked everywhere I could think of, without success. I began musing about other things in my life that have gone missing over the years. I remembered reading in letters in *FT* from people claiming to have found missing items by politely requesting aloud for their return from the gremlins or whatever entities had taken them. So, not really expecting any success, I said aloud: "According to *Fortean Times*, this should work. Would the elves, færies, gremlins, gnomes, or whatever took my book please return it in time for my interview tomorrow." The idea immediately popped into my mind that the book was in an old, antique humpback trunk full of comic books in my front parlour. I went and looked – and there it was !

Alan Lance Andersen, Roland, Iowa, 2008

PIXILATED REMOTE

I recently bought a new laptop computer (Dell XPS M1530), which came with a rather nifty remote control which plugs into a slot on the right-hand side of the machine. Two weeks ago, the remote suddenly disappeared. I turned my flat inside-out trying to find it, but to no avail. After a week of searching, I gave up and tried the tactic of asking out loud for it to be returned, as various people writing to *FT* said this gave positive results. I didn't really hold my breath! Tonight I switched on the laptop and was amazed to find the remote inserted back in its slot in the laptop. My hair stood on end!

Danny Cogdon, by email, 2009

THANKS TO ST ANTHONY

I first noticed my wallet was missing on a Tuesday and couldn't clearly place its whereabouts since the preceding Saturday. So started the seemingly endless round of phone calls to pubs, police, and friends. No one had seen it, and so started the second round to banks, post-offices, utility companies and so on. I'd had the wallet over 20 years and with its long, heavy metal chain, which attached to any belt, it had seemed impervious to loss or theft. By the end of the week I'd pretty much given up hope, while my kittens looked on sagely and I wondered whether they could have stashed it somewhere with the rest of the treasures and trinkets that had mysteriously vanished since they came to stay.

My new *FT* plopped through the letterbox and I was reminded of the story about directly petitioning some saint or other for the return of lost items. Picking a historical dictionary off the shelf, I quickly located Saint Anthony and, with a mixture of embarrassment and nervousness, loudly announced to my front room: "Please Saint Anthony, can I have my wallet back, it's really important." I then walked to the kitchen to put the kettle on.

When I returned to the front room, the wallet was sitting on the floor in plain view. It sat, openly, between two piles of books I stare at every day. The chain trailed on the ground and I must have practically been standing on it when looking at the book of saints. For added incredulity, it was inches from where my flatmate sits every night and was in front of a mirror, so also giving its reflection. Could it have been sitting there for nearly a week in plain view?

The cats were sleeping in different rooms and while they *could* have stolen it, its return would have required a nigh-on impossible mix of stealth and timing. Is it any more ludicrous to entertain the possibility of spiritual intervention than super-intelligent (and possibly belligerent) cats? Well, perhaps; but it had happened exactly as other *FT* readers had testified it would, and among the few Catholic friends I have it seems common knowledge that this will work.

Saint Anthony has been described as the Billy Graham of his day; but his strident zeal was apparently tempered with mercy. I hope it was that sense of mercy that remedied my situation.

Tim Weinberg, Brighton, East Sussex, 2010

11 *Night terrors*

There are few things as terrifying as waking up in the small hours and sensing a strange presence in your bedroom... especially if you then find that it has glowing red eyes, gives off an aura of pure evil and is sitting on your chest! Many of these disconcerting experiences are down to sleep paralysis or waking dreams... but what if some of these nightmares are something more solid?

WAKING DREAMS?

GOTHIC NIGHT TERROR

One night, when I was about 16, I awoke at about 1am after sleeping for an hour. I found I couldn't move properly; there was a tightness in my chest and I had no power over my arms or legs, although I could move my head. Then I became aware of something sitting on my chest, facing me, looking at me. There was very little light in the room, just enough to make out the shape that was pressing on top of me. From what I could make out, it was some kind of animal, like a monkey in shape, brown and hairy. In my terror, I was distinctly aware that the thing was alive; I had the impression it had been waiting for me to wake up.

The next two minutes or so are among the most terrifying I have experienced. The thing just sat there exuding a very evil aura, growling and making a mouth-clearing sound. As I tried to move, it moved closer to my face. It had a malevolent face with red eyes, somewhat monkey-like only more demonic – very much like the creature in Henry Fuseli's painting *The Nightmare*, except that mine was closer to an animal than his chubby, ogreish thing with its pensive, amused expression. What Fuseli captured very well in relation to what I was seeing was the creature's semi-visibility, the colour of the skin, and the eyes.

The thing must have 'known' that I was awake because then it started to speak to me, in English. I don't recall exactly what it said, only that it was decidedly unfriendly. It was cruel and taunting and it wanted me to know how pathetic it held me to be. It knew I was powerless at that time and relished my helplessness. It spoke mockingly in a rasping, inhuman voice that was horrible to hear.

I managed to speak, asking it, somewhat absurdly, what it was and what it was doing, but when it started to speak I was unable to respond except in whimpers as it was restricting my ability to breathe properly. Part of me wanted to continue the experience, but the sense of its malevolence coupled with my helplessness and uncertainty over what was going to happen next was just too much. It wanted to see me harmed, that I knew, so I made a huge effort to recover my power of movement, breathing and speech so as to keep it away from my neck and face. As I did, forcing myself to overcome the awful force this thing was having, it slowly melted away, taking about a minute to vanish. All trace of it was finally banished when I switched on the light beside me.

The whole experience had lasted no more than five minutes. With the thing gone, I lay there trying to make sense of what I'd experienced. I am positive it was not a dream. Yet, was it something from my own mind and personality, something I had manifested or imagined, or something separate from my consciousness, separate even from ordinary reality? If someone had entered my room when the experience was underway, would they have seen and heard it too? When later I found a small picture of Fuseli's *The Nightmare* in a magazine, I instantly knew this is what had happened to me. I retained this picture for years afterwards so as not to forget and as 'proof' that such things are possible…

To put perspective on my state of mind at the time, I was due to travel to London the next morning for an interview and was feeling very stressed about the prospect, as I also was about my first serious relationship with a girl. These pressures certainly contributed to producing the thing, perhaps somehow 'nourishing' it into becoming manifest. Fuseli was recovering from an unhappy love affair and a portrait of the woman was discovered on the reverse of the canvas of *The Nightmare*. I consider this to have been an important aspect of the circumstances of the painting's creation.

Jerry Glover, by email, 2006

RED-EYED SPIRIT

When I was 10 years old, I awoke one night in my bedroom at around 3am. I decided to get up and use the loo. I was fully awake and definitely not dreaming

❝ *It had a malevolent face with red eyes, monkey-like and demonic* ❞

at the time. Being young, I always found getting up in the middle of the night rather creepy and really didn't like venturing out of my bedroom. It was not that I felt that there was anything malevolent or supernatural lurking, I really just did not like walking around the house in the dark.

Upon leaving the bathroom, I thought that I would seek some reassurance from my parents, just to ease my fears a little bit. I just wanted them to tell me that there was nothing to be scared of, and to go back to sleep. However, when I opened the door of their dark bedroom something caught my eye underneath the dressing table, which was positioned directly below the window that looked straight onto where I was standing. This table had an arch on the underside for a chair to slide in.

When I looked, I saw something extremely weird that I cannot explain to this day – it's even hard to try and put it into words. It was a spirit of some sort, crouched in the arch of the dressing table and it was glowing white. It had its arms wrapped around its legs. Its body was facing to the right, whilst its head was turned facing me. This 'thing' was looking directly at me and had glowing red eyes, which looked demonic; this is what captured my attention in the first place. What scared me most about it was the fact that it looked human; this might sound ridiculous, but it looked the spitting image of my mum, only really angry and malevolent.

I looked at this spirit for around 10 seconds, but it seemed like much longer. It did not move at all. I could not believe what I was seeing. I thought to myself, what is my mum doing under there? However, I quickly realised that it wasn't her. She was lying fast asleep in bed. I felt as if the fiery red eyes were staring into my soul as the thing continued to stare at me. Coming to my senses quickly, I screamed at full volume, waking my parents, and then ran to switch on the light.

As soon as I turned on the light, whatever was there had disappeared. I was frantic and told my parents what had happened. They dismissed it as me being half asleep and still dreaming, but I know for a fact that I wasn't. I fully recall everything that I had done prior to visiting the room (walking through the living room and hall and going to the bathroom) and was awake for 5-10 minutes before the incident.

Since this happened to me, nobody else in my house has seen anything of the same nature. I have never seen the thing again, thankfully, as it really scared me – and does now, even thinking about it! Nonetheless, since seeing this spirit I have been curious as to what it actually was. I am not convinced that it was a ghost due to the fact that it looked the double of my very-much-alive mum and the fact that its eyes were glowing red.

In the past few months I have been more eager than ever to find out what this was and came across a book that discussed elementals. This seemed like the most plausible explanation, as what I read coincided with my experience of the crouching and the glowing eyes. I also read that these spirits are only really found outdoors in natural settings, but my encounter happened in the bedroom of a bog-standard four in a blockhouse in the suburbs of Glasgow.

Laura-Anne Leddie, by email, 2010

THE FLY

I had an extremely vivid hypnopompic dream around June 1997. I was a fashion student in London, living in a hall of residence. My room had two windows, and during the afternoon and evening, the sun blazed in. One afternoon, I fell asleep on my bed for a couple of hours, and was awoken by the light as it moved across the room and fell upon me. But this was not the usual dozy woken state I was used to. Instead, I became aware of my surroundings; I even remember that my eyes were open, and my conscious mind was working as normal.

I then saw an enormous fly, about six inches (15cm) long, buzzing around the room. It was a black, lumpy mass, with stiff bristles sprouting from its body, and small clear wings on its back. It reminded me of the strange, misshapen creatures of Bosch or Breughel.

The thought suddenly came to me that this thing was going to land on my face, and that my body was completely paralysed. My limbs felt like dead objects, all power of movement denied me. A terror seized me, although no worse than I had experienced in childhood nightmares. After only a few seconds, my conscious mind asserted itself and I began to think as if I were awake and lucid as normal. I said to myself: "What are you doing? This is just a lucid dream, the fly is nothing, and the paralysis is just that which your brain exerts upon your body as part of your normal sleep pattern." The fly immediately disappeared and movement was restored.

While I realise that this was all just a strange manifestation of my mind, the reality of it has remained with me ever since as a reminder of the strange powers the mind can exert upon us.

Esma Pearcey, by email, 2008

THE APPLE HAG

Falling asleep one night, I had a hypnagogic vision of a hag. She leaned right up to my face and breathed: "Remember me". The vision was accompanied by a great deal of fear. On waking, I stumbled to the bathroom and found four apple stalks, all the same length, lined up on the sink. There were no apples in the house at the time. I then went to the kitchen, where I found all four gas taps on the oven turned on. It must have happened the moment I walked in, as there was no smell of gas.

Shaun Petrie, by email, 2008

BEDROOM VISITORS

THEY CAME BY NIGHT

I'd like to relate two instances of unwelcome bedroom visitors. The first was when I was about eight and sleeping in the bedroom of a bungalow belonging to family friends. I awoke to see a strange phosphorescent creature standing near the bed, something like a child's drawing of a skeleton, but just in outline without bones or other details. The closest comparison I can think of is the pin-man drawing in *The Saint* books, which I was then too young to have read. Its head was oval, not round, and as far as I can remember, it had eyes but no other features. As I watched, paralysed with fright, it began to jump up and down as if on springs. At this point, I screamed the place down and adults came running to see what was going on, assuming I'd had a nightmare. To this day, I'm sure I hadn't, and of course they found nothing, but I was always nervous of sleeping in that room again.

The second incident happened in 2004 in the back bedroom of the house here in Derby where I lived till quite recently. In the small hours, I awoke as I heard and felt something trying to jump onto the bed. "Get off!" I shouted, thinking it was one of our cats escaped from the kitchen. I gave it a push, then suddenly realised it was much bigger and heavier than any cat. It fell off the bed, then had another go, and I could hear its claws scratching at the bedclothes and wooden bed-frame. I saw something resembling a small bear with a long nose and very thick curly fur. It also had long claws, which it dug into my hand quite painfully. Years ago, there was a cartoon character called 'Flook' in a daily newspaper, and my mystery visitor rather resembled a malevolent version of it. On hearing my description, my daughter said it sounded like an anteater with an afro, which summed it up very well.

I was paralysed with fright at some point during the encounter, but I also remember pushing the thing off the bed and hearing it thud onto the floor. After the third successful attempt to dislodge it, I came to my senses and put the light on. There was nothing there, of course, and later investigation proved both our cats to be still shut in the kitchen. However – and here comes the interesting bit – in the morning I found I had some hefty scratches on my right hand and several fingernails were broken, with one jagged bit of nail twisted round, sticking into my skin. So – was there really something there and did it scratch me, or did I hit the edge of the bed or side of the dressing table first (and if so, why?), then dream up the creature to explain it? I suffer from migraine, but didn't have it on this occasion.

Years earlier, another daughter saw an apparition (which seemed to be the ghost of an old gardener) in the same bedroom, but her visitor seemed quite benevolent. The house was built on a former market garden.

Brenda Ray, Mickleover, Derby, 2008

BESTIAL GROAN

About 15 years ago, I was staying over at an old friend's flat above his small shop in Oxhey Village, Hertfordshire. We spent the evening as we usually did back

then, drinking a few beers and listening to music from his rather vast collection. Around 1am, we decided to crash out, and settled down in our separate beds in the same room, listening to the gentle strains of Nick Drake in candlelight.

Several tracks into the CD, the suitably crepuscular strains of his song 'Black Eyed Dog' began. As the track progressed, a dark atmosphere seemed to fill the room, and as it reached the lyric "black eyed dog came to my door" the music began to slow down, as if being played on vinyl with a finger impeding the rotation, and over what I guess must have been a few seconds ground to what I can only describe as a demonic halt. Now, we are all familiar with scratched CDs: they judder and skip, not grind to a halt as in this case. The moment the music stopped, the air inside the room became thick, rather like peering through a fog or being underwater. This may sound unbelievable, but the candles began to flicker as if starved of oxygen, and from below the upstairs room we were in came the most unearthly and truly hideous sound I have ever heard – and believe me, working as a professional musician and sound engineer for many years, I've heard some pretty grim frequencies! Imagine the grating of something very heavy being dragged across concrete, coupled with the scraping of fingernails on a blackboard, and what for some reason suggested to me a hippopotamus in agonised death throes. Whatever it was, it was a hideously bestial groan that I can only describe as 'not of this world'.

This 'night terror', both of us fully conscious, lasted perhaps 10 seconds. The strange indoor miasma cleared, and the stereo remained silent. Needless to say, we were both somewhat freaked, indeed it is one of the very few times in my life, being an atheist, I have actually crossed myself and experienced some 'fear of God'. I stress that we were both relatively sober, not overly tired, and shared the same experience. Was the iconic Black Dog evoking some troubled suicidal spirit present in the house?

To this day, both of us still find the entire incident inexplicable, but it was not without precedent as far as the location is concerned. My friend, while living there for several years with his girlfriend, experienced several other ghostly apparitions and poltergeist-like activity, including a workman being physically pushed from a stepladder across the room. His mother, a Christian, was so concerned that she called a priest to exorcise the place, after which all activity seemingly stopped. My friend no longer lives above the shop, but continues to run it as a business with no further disturbance.

Jules Landau, by email, 2009

❝ I could the make out the thing's bald head, skeletal teeth, and hooked nose ❞

NIGHT VISITOR

Here is a painting (above) of a creature I saw one night in September 1996 when my friend Neil and I were sharing a room in a Guildford hotel the night before a friend's wedding.

During the night, I saw the face of another friend who was unable to attend the wedding, so close that he was almost on top of me. The image was clear and real against a brilliant white background. I remember thinking or saying to him, "Rob, what are you doing?"

When I opened my eyes, the room was black apart from a crack of light from the street lamp outside the curtains. I noticed someone at the end of my bed. At first I thought Neil, who has a medical condition, was having an attack and crawling towards me for help – but he was still asleep.

The figure appeared to be light grey all over; it was either kneeling or very short – about 4ft (1.2m) high. It seemed to be carrying some kind of light or instrument in its left hand. Its right arm seemed lumpy in comparison with the rest of the body. I could make out a bald head, skeletal teeth and a hooked nose; its eyes were in shadow.

The oddest thing of all was that another disembodied human arm seemed to be reaching over its right shoulder and pointing frantically at my friend's bed. It seemed to be looking for something; as it turned towards Neil's bed, I decided that it was time for action. But as soon as my foot moved towards the floor, the creature receded into the mirror on the far wall like the image on a TV screen shrinking to a white dot. It was as if it had been recalled as soon as my wakefulness had been noticed. I was fascinated rather than frightened by the peculiar events.

Paul Carey, South Ockenden, Essex, 1998

SHADOW DANCER

I was staying at my friend Tom's place in Brighton, part of an old Georgian building which had once been a hotel. The apartment was on the ground floor in what used to be the dining area. My friend's landlady was away and so we decided to take over her massive double bed, which certainly beat the crappy sofa I was sleeping on and Tom's mattress on the floor. He had previously joked that the apartment was haunted, but I just put this down to his overactive imagination.

So, off to bed we went – the super-duper-deluxe-high-level-comfort bed. Later that night, I was awakened by Tom shaking me. Before he even said anything I noticed how incredibly cold the room had become and that I was covered in goose-bumps. Tom then said: "It's here – the ghost!" I collected my senses and stared out across the mammoth bed to the corner of the room, now illuminated by moonlight except for a 'blacker-than-black' three-dimensional 'shadow' of what appeared to be a young girl dancing. I remember thinking how amazing this was at the time and, surprisingly, I felt little fear. I said to Tom, "Am I really seeing what I think I'm seeing?" and he replied, "Yeah, it looks like it's dancing."

We both stared at the thing for what must have been at least a minute, totally absorbed by the strange, black, shadow-like quality of the entity. Then, suddenly, it started to move closer towards the bed, at which point I began to panic. "I don't think I can stay in here tonight," I declared, before running out of the room, closely followed by Tom. We decided to spend the rest of the weekend back in his room. Even this didn't entirely help; while we didn't see the entity again, there were various further incidents such as objects like ashtrays suddenly dropping off shelves and occasional strange giggling noises.

Christopher Davies, Stockholm, 2010

12 The Twilight zone

When we've gathered together the ghost stories and catalogued the crypto-creatures, we're still left with a large pile of bizarre tales that simply resist easy categorisation: strange hooded figures seen on a lonely road; a mirror that reflects back someone else's face; weird lights hovering round a television, or an everyday scene frozen into slow-motion: welcome to the Twilight Zone...

ON THE ROAD

SPOOKY CYCLIST

In 2003, I was visiting my brother in the Scottish Highlands. One night at about 7pm, we drove to a friend's house, with Stuart driving and me in the passenger seat. The journey took us along many winding, dark, deserted roads often flanked by tall trees. As we were making our way along the B9512 near Kingussie, I noticed a tall figure on the left-hand side of the road that seemed to be human, and appeared to be illuminated by a great number of Christmas tree-style lights. My initial feeling was that it was a humorously decorated mannequin advertising a nearby business. I laughed and asked Stuart what it was, but he had no idea, and in fact sounded a little disturbed. As we got closer, I saw that the figure had its back to us, was seated on a bicycle, and was completely still and perfectly balanced despite being 'mid-cycle'. I got quite a shiver as we went by, and the strange sight stuck in my mind throughout our visit to the friend.

On the homeward journey, I asked Stuart to slow down as we approached the spot of the earlier sighting so that we could discover what the figure was advertising, or his general purpose. As we approached, my stomach sank as I realised the figure was now on the opposite side of the road! "He" seemed to be wearing a luminous green workman's tunic, though in truth I had such shivers (I couldn't say why really, other than the strangeness of the scene) that I couldn't bear to look for too long. My brother was nonplussed, and we were both quite unnerved by the figure. I would be delighted to hear from anyone who knows of any similar sightings in the area, and perhaps their origins.

Scott Taylor, Bristol, 2005

BIZARRE CAR

When I was about seven years old, my mother would pick my father up after work from our local railway station in Bracknell, Berkshire, at about 8pm. One night when we were driving to the station, there was a car driving in front of us, moving at about 30mph (48km/h), without any lights on and, from what we could see, nobody driving. I can remember my mum saying, "What is this idiot doing?" That was weird, but what was weirder was that in an instant the car was no longer in front of us but was parked at the side of the road. It did not slow down or pull over – it was as if it had never even been moving. It was almost as if we had missed a few seconds in time. "Wasn't that car in front of us just now?" I asked my mother. "Yes it was," she said, looking shocked. When I asked more questions, she said that we must have imagined it. The whole thing was very strange.

SW, Sydney, Australia, 2005

THE HOLY COMPANY

Late one night, about 20 years ago, I was driving to the small village in the mountains of Asturias, in the north west of Spain, where some of my family live. The small narrow road forces you to drive slowly, especially when it's dark, so I was being particularly careful. I saw something shining by the trees, quite close to the road, and quickly realised it was a fire. With a shiver, I noticed that there were several hooded figures standing around the flames, all of them dressed in dark colours. Feeling superstitious, I didn't want to stare at them, so I kept driving as fast as I possibly could, forgetting my previous caution.

I arrived at the village feeling rather nervous, although I didn't want to admit it. I've heard many old tales about the Holy Company – a procession of souls in torment that wander around rural areas and are considered to be a harbinger of death. The following morning we found out that there had been a car crash on that very road the day before. I can't say for sure that it happened at exactly on the same spot I'd seen the hooded figures, but I found it deeply disturbing.

AD, Asturias, Spain, 2010

(With a shiver, I noticed that there were several hooded figures standing there)

NOCTURNAL ILLUSION

I am a musician so I am used to late nights (and strange happenings!). For several nights in 2004, my colleagues and I returned from Maidstone in Kent along the M25 westbound towards Gatwick. After passing Clackett Lane service station, the road turns slowly right up a long hill. As we reached about three-quarters of the way up the hill in the battered old Transit, a man ran across the road in front of us from the central reservation. As I was in the passenger seat, I could see him run directly at us. I shouted at the driver, but he had seen nothing – there was no thump and we continued up the hill, with me in a cold sweat.

On the next trip and subsequent trip I watched carefully and saw the same phenomenon again and again but was slowly able to piece together the apparition. Close to the top of the hill a triangular road sign had been left in the central reservation facing eastbound traffic, so there was no reflective side facing us. The 'man' was in fact the shadow of this sign thrown by the headlights of oncoming cars on the other carriageway and its movement was caused by the motion of these lights. I have often wondered if this is the reason for the large number of accidents at Clackett Lane!

Richard Barden, by email, 2006

WHACKY WHITE VANS

In June 2000, I was driving into my nearest town which is about 40 miles (64km) away, when I had to yield at an intersection to let a brand new, white, window van go by. Through the passenger window I could see a mesh grill behind the seat and apart from the front windows the rest of the windows were tinted black. In the front sat the driver and passenger who could have been twins, as both had on white shirts with red ties and both had dark hair in a brush cut. Both wore the same type of sunglasses and looked neither left nor right as they passed by the intersection.

The van had no names or logos on it, nor did it have a licence plate; certainly nothing too strange about that, but this white van was followed by nine more evenly spaced, identical vans. Not only did the vans look like clones but so did the passengers and drivers. I had the impression I was watching a film in a loop, and there was a funny feeling in the air, as the air feels just before a thunderstorm, only the sky was perfectly clear and dry. I couldn't see the next van until it was there and past me. I live on the rural prairies and believe me you can see 20 or 30 miles (32-48km) in any direction at any given time and I couldn't see those vans until they were almost on top of me. They drove down an old dirt road and I lost sight of them.

In the small town where I live, one brand new van with strangers in it would be the subject of conversation and interest, let alone 10 of them. However, when I mentioned the incident and made a few inquiries, I drew a blank. It appears that I was the only one who saw them. There have been a lot of strange aerial sightings here, and crop circles have appeared in a very remote area, so we have our share of 'strangeness'.

Ruth Summersides, Saskatchewan, Canada, 2001

Around noon on 1 October 2003, I was sitting at a traffic light in the left-turn lane waiting for the green arrow. I was first in line and there was a lot of lunchtime traffic flowing in both directions across the intersection in front of me. I was staring straight ahead, but I kept an eye on the traffic flowing from left to right as I waited for the left-turn signal. I noticed a white SUV crossing the intersection at about 30-40mph (48-64km/h) – and then it 'jumped back' about 10ft (3m) and went across again.

I didn't see it jump back, it was just going across – then it was going across again. It definitely wasn't two different cars of the same type. There was a continuous line of traffic moving across at the time. The scene simply repeated itself. Had I blinked, changed the radio station, looked away or up at the light and then back at the traffic, I would have missed it.

It seemed as if a dimension overlapped or possibly a time warp occurred. It

didn't feel like *déjà vu* – but that's exactly what it was, only in the physical. It reminded me of the scene in the first *Matrix* movie when the cat walks across the doorway, and then repeats itself – the glitch in the Matrix.
Anna Webb, Cincinnati, Ohio, 2004

In 1990, when I was about 10, I was walking down the street past my friend's house. Ahead of me, a white van pulled into the driveway of a house. I remember the sound of the engine, then the engine stopping. As I walked past the house, I saw four people get out, walk inside and shut the door. I continued walking and I heard the sound of an engine behind me. I looked backward and saw the *same* white van pulling into the *same* driveway. It pulled up, and the *same* four people got out, walked inside, and shut the door. You could say this was all just a matter of delayed cognition – though I don't know how, as it was all from a different perspective.
Ryan Egesdahl, Houston, Texas, 2004

MIRROR, MIRROR...

HAUNTED MIRROR

My friend Anna was working as an English teacher in Budapest between 1992 and 1994. She had a flat in an oldish (perhaps 1930s) apartment block. The furniture, apparently, looked like it had been there since the place was built – all very solid wooden stuff. In her dining room, there was a large antique mirror, and it was this that was the spooky thing. Anna swears blind that at certain times of the day, usually between 2 and 4 in the afternoon, anyone looking in it would see not just themselves, but a group of six or seven soldiers in the room with them! The soldiers were wearing, according to her, "First World War-type uniforms" and had old rifles. The mirror always showed the same thing: The men were relaxing around a table, eating and chatting, while one of them looked anxiously out of the window. And that was it.

Sadly, the mirror got broken by a visitor to the flat who got freaked out by what he saw. Bugger.
Paul Gallantry, by email, 2004

WOMAN IN THE MIRROR
When I was about 17, my mates and I did a Ouija session for a laugh. It may be that what followed was directly caused by this, or possibly just prompted by our very spooked state of mind.

Two of us had identical dreams the following night! We thought this to be a curious enough phenomenon, but the real twist was the content. Both of us dreamed that we woke up in the night, sat up in bed and looked in the mirror on the wall directly opposite the bed (which my mate really had in his room, but I didn't).

In the mirror, each of us saw our own face, and standing behind, as if looking over my shoulder into the mirror, a woman dressed in an exquisite silk kimono, but with a horribly burned face.

In reality, it would have been impossible for anyone to stand behind us like this, with each of us sitting up in bed – a bed with its head against the wall in the usual way.

The next morning I took all mirrors out of my room. After that I was rather uneasy about mirrors in bedrooms for about 10 years.
Seversm, 2004

TOILET TERROR
We often used to go to a Thameside pub in Windsor called the Donkey House. It was originally called the Kings Arms, and had been there for, well, donkey's years. When we were children, my sister and I used to go there with our father for a lemonade after fishing trips. The pub is still there, but the name and management have changed.

One day in 2005, my sister Lesley and I had been shopping and wandering about the town and needed a drink. It was a normal Saturday afternoon in late spring and throngs of tourists were beginning to arrive.

We sat inside, to the left of the long dark bar and away from the people eating, as we were smoking. We ordered a couple of pints of cider and, as usual, I needed to use the bathroom – it's a combination of my sister making me laugh and a weak bladder. As it was my round, I said I'd pop to the ladies first, then get the drinks in; so I rushed to the loo.

It was up a steep, narrow staircase at the opposite end of the bar. I went up the stairs, through a door, up another smaller set of steps that had a huge mirror

overhanging them, through another fire door and into the loo. There were three or four cubicles. It was a really normal looking set-up, if a little out of date, pinkish and floral. All the doors were closed so I had to push them to see if they were locked or not, but it soon became evident that I was the only person in there.

In the cubicle I was still laughing a little – laughing out loud in fact! All of a sudden I felt the need to stop, as if someone didn't approve of my laughter, or I'd subconsciously been scolded. The atmosphere changed instantly – it felt electrified. My skin bristled, and I felt disturbed. I can only describe the feeling as being like the fear you might experience when faced with a huge growling dog or a crazed, drunken lunatic. I was shaking with adrenalin, experiencing confusing smells and images, and a sense of primal fear.

I had to get out, fast. I fumbled with the lock, tore open the cubicle, still rearranging my clothes. I didn't dare stay to wash my hands. I grabbed the door handle – and came face to face with the full-length mirror hanging over the steps. My face. But it didn't look like me. The face was terrified; there was confusion and a blur of movement behind me. I flew down the steps. There was another door to contend with, then the last furlong back to safety. My feet didn't touch the ground; if I'd fallen I wouldn't have felt any pain. I was in the midst of fight or flight and I was fleeing for my life.

I smashed through the last door and into the bar, back to the warmth and the light and the living. People turned to see what the commotion was. I rushed to the bar and steadied myself. My sister called out, and when I failed to answer her she came over, looking perplexed.

"Christ, what's the problem with you? You look AWFUL!"

"I don't know what just happened," I said, clearly shaken.

The barman came over. He'd sussed out the situation.

"You alright love? Same again? You look like you've seen a ghost".

"I – er, I don't know what just happened – upstairs," I said. My mouth was dry, my face was white. I looked into the mirror behind the bar and saw wide, staring frightened eyes.

"Oh, upstairs, the toilets. Yes, sorry about that. Are you alright?"

Then he went on: "Listen, next time you need the loo, use the disabled one down here. You don't have to go upstairs again. We've lost a few customers due to that, upstairs, in the ladies. Sorry about that. Want a brandy?"

My sister wanted the whole story, but I really didn't know what to tell her, apart from what I have described here. So we badgered the barman to tell us more. Some women had seen a man upstairs, others had felt the presence of a young woman and child. But that wasn't all.

The staff had regularly seen a man sitting in the farthest corner, after last orders were called, only to look over again to see that no one was there. This apparition had also appeared after the door was locked and the staff were cleaning up. During cashing up one night, a pint of beer had been thrown across the bar, and other 'happenings' had been reported by staff.

I haven't been back. But I bet the new management have relocated the ladies.
Ann Shenton, Windsor, 2010

STRANGE VISIONS

KELVINGROVE TIME SLIP

During 1985–6, I was a post-graduate student of marketing at Strathclyde University. A couple of nights a week, I'd stay over at a friend's flat in Kerseland Street in the West End. If the weather was good, I'd often walk from Cathedral Street (just up from Queen Street Station) all the way out along Dumbarton Road to the West End. This provided plenty of time for (mainly prosaic) reflection... sometimes accompanied by a specially prepared Walkman soundtrack.

One particular evening – I have no recollection of the time of year but suspect it was before the clocks went back, or after they went forward again, so early autumn or late spring – I was walking past Kelvingrove Art Gallery and Museum, heading west towards the bridge over the River Kelvin (grid reference NS 86368213). I believe I saw, for a split second, this view as it would have been in the late 19th century: horse-drawn carriages, lots of people on foot, men in top hats, women in bustles, parasols or umbrellas. Strangely, despite my interest in architecture, it was the movement and the people that struck me most. I have little or no memory of the buildings or whether the scene was markedly different from how it looked in 1985. I'm not sure if I was actually there or seeing it at one remove, as if on film. As quickly as this moving image appeared it vanished, leaving me slightly breathless, slightly chilled and puzzled.

Was it simply the remembrance of a photo I'd once seen? I may have been reflecting on my own family: I've done occasional bits of genealogy and knew that my great grandfather was born in Great George Street, also in the West End, and he and his family must have walked where I was walking now. Or had I caught a glimpse of the past? Was it my memory, or a sort of shared memory? I have no idea. I'm not prone to visions or delusions. I'm profoundly unmystical, although that is not to say I'm not fascinated by what happened that evening. I've never experienced anything similar since then.

Anna Kelvin, (not her real name), Glasgow, 2008

STILL LIFE

On Saturday, 9 June, my wife and I were first out of St Joseph's parish church in Worksop (Nottinghamshire) because we were in a terrific rush. Mass started at 6pm and finished at 7, but my wife, a nurse, starts work at 8. In the intervening hour, we have to cook and eat, take the dogs for a walk, get changed and (in her case) drive to work.

It was hot and oppressive. In our haste, we failed to acknowledge various friends (who, on reflection, were staring at us dumbly), but no problem, we would see them the following week. It struck me that everyone was a bit, well, slow... or was it me who was in such a rush? We got into the car, I fired up, and turned into Wessex Road to do a U-turn in the mouth of the road. Halfway through my 'U', some fellow turned up and stopped at the junction. I waited for him to move on. And waited... and waited. Why didn't he move? No one was coming, the road was clear. I looked at him. He was frozen with his mouth open. Everyone else was frozen too!

A man with a black Labrador stood ramrod straight; his dog, also frozen, had a stick clamped in its jaws. Everyone and everything was motionless – except my wife and me. I just whipped round everything and drove away. "What's up with people?" my wife remarked. "They'd move fast enough if they had to be at work in half an hour." I looked in my mirror and everyone was moving again.

It was uncomfortably hot – and quiet. I don't even recall birds singing – nothing – it all seemed kind of muffled, distant. I'm not claiming that time stood still – but I do know that for well over a minute everyone in the vicinity looked as if they'd been deep frozen, then snapped out of it and carried on with whatever they were doing. I had this horrible sensation that only I knew what was going on; as if a 'freeze ray' had beamed down on everyone, but missed me. I'm glad my wife commented, as this showed it wasn't a 'solus' hallucination,

heatstroke, or whatever; it's never happened before.
Jack Romano, Worksop, Nottinghamshire, 2008

ALTERNATIVE BIRMINGHAM

I live in Birmingham and often cross St Phillip's Churchyard as I return from shopping in the city centre. This churchyard has largely had its tombstones removed. It is a pleasant open space with paths and benches and plenty of grass. Loads of youths congregate there to chat each other up, snog on the few remaining tombstones, dance and generally hang out. Colloquially it is known as Pigeon Park.

About two years ago, I was crossing the churchyard when something strange happened. It was drizzling and I had my umbrella up. There weren't that many people about, as it was a miserable Friday afternoon too early for the Goths and Emos to have got back from school and changed into their other uniform. I stopped and put my umbrella down in the centre of the space to see if my bus was about to appear and I'd need to run for it – but I was confronted by an entirely different view to the one I was expecting. I presumed that I'd somehow veered off in the wrong direction, so stopped and turned round through 360 degrees. But no, all the railings in Colmore Row were missing as – more importantly – were the bus stops! These are very noticeable, being of the bus shelter type, and fill up the whole length of this side of the churchyard. I was not amused. This meant a trek across several streets to get to the nearest 103 bus stop. By checking 'landmarks' such as an idiosyncratic shoe shop, I was now totally convinced that I was not simply looking in the wrong direction.

The whole scenario was both strange and also terribly prosaic. I was just cross. Then I realised that my hearing was a bit peculiar – exactly as if I'd got my fingers in my ears. This was no flickering illusion, however, as I stomped about a bit, undecided as to which direction to go in. I set back off towards Colmore Row in order to pick up my bus around Margaret Street, but as I emerged through the corner gateway my ears 'cleared' and everything was back in place: railings, bus stops etc.

What actually happened I've no idea. I sometimes think I slipped into an alternative version of Birmingham (I know, it doesn't bear thinking about, does it?) for about four or five minutes. My watch was working and I had no impression of having lost (or gained) any time. No one in the other place looked any different; there was no trace of being in the past or the future. It seemed just like a different 'now' in some way. I've known this place for years and my alternative version was in no way like any of the other stages I've observed. So this suggests that I wasn't slipping into a remembered vision of the place. Reflecting on the experience on my way home on the bus, I did feel that while I was in 'the place where the bus stops were absent", things were going a bit 'slowly' – as well as being hushed in some way.

I often cross this space – on my way to the same bus stop – and avoid walking over a section of slabs where the experience seemed to start as I have found it makes me feel lightheaded and giddy.

I do wonder if the 'sonic devices' used to disperse large congregations of young people might play some part in this. I'm far too old to hear them but perhaps, as rumoured, the council has installed them around St Phillips and somehow I'm picking up on them and getting my brain scrambled. I'd be really intrigued to know if any other Birmingham folk have had a similar experience.
Mary Worrall, by email, 2008

WEIRD LIGHTS

THE BLUE LIGHT
I was living in Delaware, near Newark, when in the late fall of 1996 I was putting clothes away in my son's room. It was between 8-9 pm, and as I walked to his dresser I saw a light outside his window near the house...

It was near the base of the house to the bottom left, out of my immediate viewing range. It grew in size and sounded like arc-welding or some kind of electrical discharge. It was very bright, blue-white, and noisy. I was taken by surprise, and knew that our propane tank was on that side of the house, so I left the room quickly and yelled at my son to get out of the tub. I was afraid that the house might be on fire. I went back into my son's room to get his robe, and noticed that the light and noise was gone. I grabbed a flashlight and went outside to inspect the damage. There wasn't any!

My father used to weld, so I know that kind of light means high temperatures. There were dry leaves lying in the vicinity of the light show, but none were singed or even disturbed. The light was right against our house, but the brick and siding had no marks on them. The propane tank, just a few feet away, also bore no evidence of any arcing, burning or other electrical damage.

It was a clear night, no clouds, no storm activity. I thought about ball-lightning, but there was absolutely no evidence that anything had happened. I called the propane company out the next morning and they told me that the tank was not leaking or damaged in any way. The whole event lasted probably 5-10 seconds and has eluded any explanation. I wasn't dreaming, or on any kind of drugs or medication, and I hadn't been drinking either. Has this ever happened to anyone else?

Mike Philips, by email, 2001

BLUE PLASMA

One stormy night in the late Eighties, I was watching TV in the living room and doing some ironing when a loud bang and flash came from the TV. A blue ball of something that seemed to be like plasma floated out of the front of the TV screen (which had gone off) and travelled about 3ft (90cm) across the room until it hit the hot plate of the iron. A loud bang came from the iron and the blue ball disappeared. Neither the TV nor the iron had any marks on them, but neither worked again.

Angie Mcquade, by email, 2010

LIGHTS OF COMFORT

Twelve years ago, tragedy struck our family: our 21-month-old son died in a house fire. We were absolutely devastated and beside ourselves with grief and guilt that we couldn't save him. It was horrendous. I can't begin to describe the pain and suffering we went through, and still do.

Two months later, with only three months left in my pregnancy, we moved away from the area with our two daughters and started a new life in a new house. This one, unlike the last, had a good feeling about it. I knew as soon as I walked in. I gave birth in October 1998 to our fourth child, our second son.

I found it difficult to sleep at night because of what had happened. Most nights I would just lie awake in bed until my eyes got so heavy I could no longer fight going to sleep. One night was the same as any other. My husband slept and I spent it wide-awake looking through the window and then glancing around the room. In the corner was our TV, which was switched off, but surrounding it were several balls of light in different sizes. They were flashing on and off like disco lights and I was fascinated and mesmerised. I didn't know what they could possibly be. I wasn't scared, just calm and relaxed. It lasted for five minutes before they went out one by one. I wanted to tell my husband the next day, but thought better of it in case he thought I'd gone round the twist.

The following night it happened again. I felt so at ease; they were so beautiful. I didn't want them to leave. I wanted to watch them all night, but after five minutes they went, leaving me with an inner peace. On the third consecutive night it happened again. This time my husband was awake. I watched, but didn't say a word to him. When it was over, he said to me: "Did you see that?"

"Did I see what?"

"The lights by the TV."

"You mean you've seen them too?" He nodded and smiled. I was thrilled because I thought maybe I had imagined it. It was the last time we saw them in that house.

We moved again several months later to the house that we now occupy. Two months after we moved in, I saw the lights for the last time on my landing. I wondered if it was our son, who had passed over, coming to let us know that he was all right. Maybe it was his way of trying to ease our grief – and for those few minutes it did.

Lisa Plowman, Pontypridd, Mid Glamorgan, 2010

Fortean Times would like to thank all those who have written to us, emailed, or posted on the 'It Happened to Me' forum at the *FT* website, to share their experiences over the past 37 years. A particular thank you goes to those whose stories appear in this volume:

Andy--, Gordon --, Kevin --, Portia --, Suzy --, TheQuixote, Seversm, Di Ablewhite, Jo Alder, Alan Lance Andersen, Pauline Barbieri, Richard Barden, Dean Ballinger, Ali Barnes, Michael Barwell, Matt Baylis, Martin Baynes, Malcolm Blacow, Sam Bradbury, Kate Brett, Greylyn Burk, John Burke, Paul Carey, Henry Chester, Jon Chidwick, John Coates, Danny Cogdon, Cez Connolly, Gavin Craig, AD, Christopher Davies, Jeremy Dennis, Elaine Dobson, Ryan Egesdahl, Martin Einon, Brian Ellwood, Hunt Emerson, Robert Euston, Hilary Evans, Rhodri Lyndon Evans, Patrick Foord, Bryan Fraser, Maureen Gaines, Paul Gallantry, Steve Gardiner, Sue Gardner, Jerry Glover, Izzet Göksu, Barry Harding, Anne Hardwick, Helen Harling, Amy Harrison, IR Harrison, Rachel Hayward, Tim Hill, Viv Hobbs, Louise Hodgson, Steve Hon, MJ, Norman James, Roni Jay, Eddy Jenkinson, Anna Kelvin, Bob Kingsley, Janusz Kozikowski, Lucy L, Jules Landau, Ian Lawes, Laura-Anne Leddie, Mr G Lester, Chris Lethbridge, Hilary Llewellyn-Williams, Dirck de Lint, Diana Lyons, Kevin Mahoney, Jim Mannix, Alexandria Martin, Henry da Massa, Angie Mcquade, Daniel McQueen, Steph Miller, Mr T Miller, Peter Millie, Alistair Moffatt, Francisco Morra-Cardoner, Jane Murray, Gillian Neuhauser, Pamela Nowell, Clive Parker, Don Parish, David Patrick, Laura-Esma Pearcey, Chris Peters, Shaun Petrie, Mike Philips, John Pickard, Dirk Pierce, Lisa Plowman, Mr R Pohl, Richard Porter, Victoria Price, Debbie Pryor, Tony Purcell, Carla R, Toby R, Brenda Ray, Paul Rebek, Simon Robbins, Jack Romano, Ronald Rosenblatt, Ian Sanders, Chante Sayers, Leo Scarpelli, Julia Morgan Scott, Ann Shenton, James Sherriff, Amanda-Jayne Sherwood, Nick Skerten, Steph Slater, Jacqueline L Spriggs, Hayley Stevens, Malcolm Stewart, Lois Stock, Niall Stone, Sam Stringer, Ruth Summersides, Scott Taylor, Tony Taylor, Pam Thornton, Dave Tiger, SW, Tim Weinberg, Roderick B Williams, Gloria Wilson, Pete Wilson, Daniel B Wood, Mary Worall, Marilyn Zavitz

Thank you to those who helped make the pictures in this volume happen: Capucine, Alix Fox, Gareth, David Newton, Jen Ogilvie, Pippa, Joe and Duke, Vicki Reeve, Ruby, Mike and Sian, Martin Sekera, Denise Stanborough.

FOR MORE REAL-LIFE STORIES OF THE UNEXPLAINED, SIGN UP TO THE *FORTEAN TIMES* MESSAGE BOARD AT WWW.FORTEANTIMES.COM/FORUM AND VISIT THE 'IT HAPPENED TO ME!' FORUM.

IF YOU HAVE YOUR OWN BIZARRE STORIES TO TELL AND WOULD LIKE TO SHARE THEM WITH US, THEN SEND YOUR LETTERS TO:
PO BOX 2409, LONDON NW5 4NP, UNITED KINGDOM,
OR EMAIL SIEVEKING@FORTEANTIMES.COM